MALAYALI DIASPORA

From Kerala to the Ends of the World

MALAYALI DIASPORA

From Kerala to the Ends of the World

Editors

Sam George & T. V. Thomas

SERIALS PUBLICATIONS
NEW DELHI (INDIA)

© Publisher

Edition: 2013

ISBN: 978-81-8387-582-0

Cover design by Karuna Jerome, By Faith Designz, Bangalore, India.

SERIALS PUBLICATIONS
4830/24, Prahlad Street, Ansari Road
Darya Ganj, New Delhi-110002 (India)
Phone : 23245225. Fax : 91-11-23272135
E-mail: serials@sify.com

Contents

Acknowledgements

This book is a testimony of the encouragement of several and the collaborative efforts of many.

Thank you to the global team of authors who volunteered to write the articles published in *Malayali Diaspora*.

We are grateful for kind endorsements given for this book.

We are deeply indebted to the following sponsors of this publishing project without whom this book would not have become a reality:

- Leena Easaw, Fair Lawn, New Jersey
- Joseph Mattackal, Long Island, New York
- Tom Philip, Eugene, Oregon
- Rajan Thomas, Floral Park, New York
- John Titus, Seattle, Washington
- Daniel Varghese, Manhasset Hills, New York

Our appreciation goes to S.K. Jha of Serials Publications in New Delhi and to Karuna Jerome of *by Faith designz* in Bangalore.

A big THANK YOU goes out to each of our family members for their sacrificial support to help us complete this project.

Sam George and **T. V. Thomas**
Editors, *Malayali Diaspora*

Introduction

SAM GEORGE

A few years ago, I was travelling through Kazakhstan in Central Asia. It is a former Soviet ruled state that gained its independence only in 1990. As I was walking through the streets of a large city there, I was pleasantly surprised to hear someone behind me talking in Malayalam. I turned around to ask, *"Malayaliano?"* (Are you a Malayali?). They were equally startled to find another Malayali in that lesser known part of the world. We went on to enquire about our *nadu* (hometown) and *veetuperu* (housename). Then I was reminded of similar serendipitous rendezvous with Malayalis in Brazil, Fiji Islands, South Africa and even on the Great Wall of China!

Malayalis are everywhere. They say even if one lands on moon, you will find a Malayali *chaikada* (teashop) there! They are scattered far widely than the popular destinations of Malaysia, Gulf, England and North America. I have personally known Malayalis who have lived in Argentina, Brunei, Chile, Indonesia, Laos, Somalia, Ukraine and Zambia. Though there is no known settlement of Malayali on the moon or elsewhere in the universe for that matter, Malayalis can be found in the furthest corners of the world that one may claim that 'the Sun never sets on the Malayalis'!

This interest in diasporic communities is deeply personal and long time in the making. I was born in the Andaman Islands and had a distinct privilege of travelling through much of the world. My dad left Kerala, looking for gainful employment soon after Indian independence. My maternal grandfather took his agricultural produce to other states. I have lived and worked in three continents. My wife's family is even more dispersed. Her grandfather travelled to the UK at the height of the Colonial Era and her mother sailed across the Atlantic Ocean to study in Kentucky (USA) before Malayali migration began in that direction. Within my own extended family, people live in all five continents and all major economic centers of the world, from Dubai to Dublin to Durban to Denver.

My early education was in Mechanical Engineering and Business Management from reputed institutions in India. I travelled extensively on work with an American company. Later I did some graduate studies on families and theology in leading schools in the US and continued my globe trekking. In all my travel, I became keenly aware of the dispersed Malayalis/Indians and with this growing interest, I ended up doing a PhD research on Indian diaspora. I am honored to undertake this book project and interact with a distinguished panel of professionals and scholars from around the world to enrich my own understanding of the adventurous temperament, survival mentality and the indomitable spirit of Malayalis.

Co-editor Dr. T. V. Thomas is a friend and mentor to me. I am so grateful that amidst our global wanderings, our paths intersected. A professor who painstakingly labored behind the contents of this book with detailed feedback and yet kept sight of the big picture with keen insights into the complex facet of global diasporas. Dr. Thomas and I are deeply indebted to all the contributors for countless hours they spend on reflecting and writing from their own distinct vantage points about the Malayali diasporic life. All of them have a Malayali heritage and are very accomplished in their respective fields in their chosen countries of domicile and beyond.

Malayali Dispersion

Malayalis are people of Indian origin from the state of Kerala in the southwestern corner of India. They speak Malayalam and are popularly called Malayali or Malayalee. They are also known as non-resident Keralites (NRK). Malayalis have a rich heritage of cultural and religious traditions mostly hailing from Hindu, Muslim or Christian backgrounds. They possess many distinctions and eccentricities. They also have long and convoluted history of dispersion across India and the world.

Diaspora is a Greek term used to describe dispersed people and finds its mention in the Bible. It literally means scattered and today it is widely used in academic circles and popular writings to refer to globally dispersed communities. Soon after the Indian independence, limited opportunities in Kerala fueled the migration of hundreds Keralites to the rest of India and outside of India. In the first half of the twentieth century, Malayalis went to the British colonies in Africa, Southeast Asia and Europe and in the later half they sought greener pastures in the West and the Middle East.

Migration has been the single-most vibrant aspect of development scene in Kerala in the last three decades. Migration has contributed more to poverty alleviation in Kerala than any other factor and has also driven the infrastructural needs for the sake of non-resident Keralites. The prosperity and economic growth of the state have a significant relation to the foreign currency remittance from Malayali diaspora. The total remittances by the emigrants have reached four times the Net State Domestic Product. The desire and cultural affinity of diasporic Malayalis to stay connected with Kerala make them as 'high contributors' to Kerala economy. They are a source of investment, know-how, ideas, expertise, contacts and charitable giving towards economic, social, religious and political activities. The primary reason for emigrating out of Kerala remains employment and marriage. The higher education and short-term computer jobs are growing reasons for young Malayalis to look abroad.

The diasporic life is not easy as it is often made out to be. Leaving kith and kin behind, going to strange places, adapting to people and customs of host nations, raising children in other cultures, uncertainties of future and others issues have taken a toll on global Malayali psyche. As Malayalis we are quick to recognize success stories of overseas Malayalis and ignore the grim reality of the painful struggle of expatriates for sheer survival. On their visits to Kerala they may show off wealth generated and talk highly of life abroad, but our sense of pride keeps us from sharing about harsh working conditions, turbulent family life, work related challenges, racism in host societies or brutality in the hand of your supervisors.

The decision to emigrate or remain behind is not made alone. It is often a family decision with much obligation from the emigrants towards those who stay behind. The emigrants often become economic saviors to the rest of the clan including welfare of aging parents, getting siblings educated and employed, dowry for sisters and building a home in their native land. The laws of migrations suggest push-pull factors determine flow of people, unfavorable push factors at home and promising pull factors from outside. The push factors included lack of employment opportunity for an educated populace and the pull factors include the oil economy of Gulf and nursing needs in the West. The global labor market and various economic theories of migration are helpful to understand human dispersion out of Kerala. The religious factors also played a critical role: Hindus showing resistance to move away from *punyabhoomi,* while Muslims gravitated toward the Middle East (closer to Mecca) and Christians migrated to the Western nations.

Centuries ago, traders from Kerala crisscrossed the sea and land with their goods and today Malayali businessmen seek opportunities across India and abroad. The graduates from medical and engineering colleges in Kerala are working in leading hospitals and companies worldwide. Malayali nurses are caring for the sick in hospitals around the globe, truly living out the vision of Florence Nightingale. Malayali professors teach in world renowned institutions in the fields of economics, surgery, psychology and robotics in English, German, Spanish and Mandarin. The call-centers and software parks in Kerala have clientele in all time zones. Malayali laborers have toiled hard in the desert heat in oil refineries and construction sites of the Middle East and sailors traversed the high seas from port to port. The foreign-born children of Malayalis have won major science and literary awards and many poor girls are trafficked out of Kerala with the lure of overseas employment. The preachers and missionaries are sent to minister to the needs of their scattered devotees, so much that Malayalis constitute a sizeable fifteen per cent of the world's Catholic priests and nuns!

Kerala became the first state in India to set up a separate department for the welfare of emigrants from the state, known as the Non-Resident Keralites Affairs (NORKA) and works closely with the Ministry of Overseas Indian Affairs of the Government of India. This department of the Kerala government receives grievances from the Malayali expatriates about job related problems, harassment by recruiting agents, repatriation of the stranded, providing assistance in bringing home the dead bodies of those deceased abroad and evacuation in emergency. They also facilitate banking, travel in and out of Kerala, educational and other needs of family members of overseas Malayalis.

Global Malayali Diaspora

The official demographic information in India or in host nations where Malayalis have settled is inadequate to access the size of the global Malayali population precisely. The best data comes from the research unit on International Migration at the Centre for Developmental Studies in Thiruvanthapuram, which bring out Kerala Migration report annually. NORKA and the annual gathering of NRKs also provide much needed research publications and networking opportunity for the globally dispersed Malayalis.

As of 2011, there are 2.28 million Malayali emigrants around the world[1], up from 2.19 million in 2008, excluding the children born to them in foreign lands. The emigrant population has steadily grown from 1.84 million in 2003 and 1.36 million in 1998. The number of Kerala emigrants who returned and living in Kerala in 2011 is estimated to be 1.15 million up from 1.16 million in 2008. Thus the total number of emigrants and returnees adds up to 3.43 million in 2011 up from 3.35 million in 2008. About 27.1 per cent of Kerala households are an emigrant or return emigrant in 2011, making Kerala as one of the largest emigrating regions of India.

The majority of the emigrants from Kerala in 2011 were Muslims (about 45 per cent) and Hindu emigrants were only 37.5 per cent in

2011, up from 29.5 per cent in1998. The Christian share shrank from 25.1 in 2003 to 17.9 by 2011. The largest number of emigrants originated from Malappuram district. Other major concentrations of emigration are Pathanamthitta and Thrissur districts. Nearly 90 per cent of the Kerala emigrants go to one of the Gulf countries. Within the Gulf region, the UAE retained its number one rank and Saudi Arabia moves to a second position amounting to nearly 40 per cent and 25 per cent respectively.

Table 1
Emigration from Kerala to Destination Countries 1998-2011

Country	2011	2008	2003	1998
UAE	883313	918122	670150	421959
Saudi Arabia	574739	503433	489988	510895
Oman	195300	167628	152865	139571
Kuwait	127782	129282	113967	68163
Bahrain	101556	101344	108507	74654
Qatar	148427	121613	98953	62969
Other West Asia	6696	NA	2047	NA
USA	68076	102440	98271	29862
Canada	9486	13695	4777	NA
UK	44640	38894	22520	NA
Other Europe	10602	9861	14331	NA
Africa	12834	12600	15696	NA
Singapore	11160	11504	14331	NA
Maldives	7254	7091	13649	NA
Malaysia	13392	12052	4777	NA
Other South East Asia	16182	8766	7507	NA
Australia/New Zealand	24552	21364	6142	NA
Other Countries	24552	13726	NA	53882
Total	2280543	2193415	1838478	1361955

Source: Adapted from Kerala Migration Report 2011. NA – Not available.

The emigrants from the state are younger and better educated, attributing to the brain drain phenomenon. The emigration has reduced Kerala's unemployment rate and the economic gains from the remittances are enormous, but at the loss of its human resources. At present, there is an acute shortage of qualified workers in many fields in the state. More than 30 per cent of persons with higher educational qualifications are now living abroad. Most Malayalis venturing out of the state and country are males. Females constituted only 14 per cent of the emigrants from Kerala, except for the age group 20-24 years in which females outnumbered males (51 per cent) on account of marriages. In 2007, the number of 'Gulf Wives' (married women living in Kerala whose husbands are emigrants living in other countries) was estimated to be about 1.2 million.

The total remittances from Malayali diaspora account for nearly one-third of Kerala's net state domestic product totaling to about USD 10 Billion (Rs 50,000 Crores). The Muslim households received 46.5 per cent, Hindus received 36.4 per cent and the Christian community received 17.1 per centof the total remittances in 2011. Remittances are 1.6 times the revenue receipt of the Kerala Government, 6.2 times what the state gets from the Centre as revenue transfer. It is more than twice the Government's annual expenditure. It is more than 60 per cent of the state's public debt. It is estimated that nearly 25 per cent of all remittances to India went to Kerala.

About the Book

This book is an exploration of Malayalis around the world, covering their historical, social, cultural, professional and religious life from a wide range of professionals in order to capture the insights and struggles as an overseas ethnic community. It includes sociologists, doctors, professors, a historian, a nurse, a psychologist, a theologian, a banker, a social worker and an accountant living in North America, Europe, Africa, Asia and Australia.

The book is divided into three major sections. The first section maps the global Malayali diaspora and it is not comprehensive in any manner but mere snapshots. We attempted to gather experience of Malayalis from different parts of the world. We begin this section with a brief history of migration out of Kerala by historian Dr. George Oommen. Other chapters in this section include an assessment of Malayalis in Malaysia by Dr. T.V. Thomas and Malayalis in Kenya by Dr. O.M. Panicker. Dr. Lina Samuel, who grew up in Canada of Malayali parents, shares her sociological research on Malayalis in Canada and Mr. Stanley John, who was born and raised in Kuwait and is now conducting his PhD research in the US, writes on labor migration to Kuwait. Dr. Mathew Thomas outlines formation of Kerala cultural associations in the United States noting its many valuable services to the dispersed community and problems.

The second section contains personal narratives of Malayali migrant journeys, starting with the serial migrant Dr. Ipe Mavunkal who have lived and worked in many countries, but the paper focuses on his time in Bostwana/South Africa. Mr. Roshan Varghese describe life of Malayalis in Australia. Prof. Prabhu Guptara takes us on his quest for the oldest living Malayali in the Continental Europe and in the final chapter of this section, medical doctor Dr. Roy Thomas looks at the thriving Malayali and Indian immigrants to America.

Finally, the third section of this book locates the life of the dispersed Malayalis from divergent vantage points. Dr. T.M. Thomas after a distinguished career as a professor, starting in Kerala and ending in a leading American university, reflects on the distinctive trait of Malayalis toward the noble profession of a teacher. Mrs. Sara Gabriel records the struggles of the early pioneering nurses to the United States and the formation of an Indian nurses association in North America. Sociologist Dr. Prema Kurien analyzes the religious life of Malayalis in the diaspora, particularly focusing on Hindus and Christians, and reputed cardiologist Dr. Enas Enas and his colleagues provide state of Malayali health in the diaspora. Then, psychologist Dr. Thomas Kulanjiyil analyses household relationships and domestic challenges facing the overseas Malayali families today, especially raising another generation in a foreign culture and a transnational household. I have a chapter on language proficiency of children of immigrants growing up in different parts of the world and explore the tension between ethnic identity and language competence. A social worker in New York, Mr. P. T. Thomas explains retirement options before Malayalis in the diaspora. Dr. Jesudas Athyal finishes the section on media-driven transnational linkages of diasporic life on account of print and virtual media. Dr. T.V. Thomas concludes the book with his reflections and some useful lessons from dispersed people of Kerala.

This is in no way an exhaustive analysis, but a primer on migrant studies pertaining to a particular Asian Indian people group. Our decision to undertake this project stems from the desire to 'tell the story' of Malayali immigrants around the world so that their aspiration, beliefs, talents, feelings and experiences are not forgotten. It hopes to inspire and connect people in the diaspora and their future generations to the rich heritage of culture and migratory history of people from the land popularly called "God's own country" to the ends of the world.

Note

1. See detailed report by K.C. Zachariah and S. Iridaya Rajan, *Kerala Migration Report 2011,* Centre for Development Studies, Thiruvananthapuram. Available online at website *www.cds.edu* (accessed Nov 25, 2012).

Part A

MIGRATION FROM KERALA

1

Re-imagining a Migratory Self:
A History of Malayali Migration

GEORGE OOMMEN

Introduction

The image of the itinerant Malayali is firmly planted in the Indian (and global) popular consciousness. Indeed, in 2011, there were an estimated 43.7 non-resident Malayalis to every 100 households, making Keralites one of the most migratory groups in Asia. Non-resident Keralites (NRK) numbered 3.43 million in 2011.[1] But little more than a century ago, Keralites showed few signs of this migratory instinct despite two millennia of trade and cultural relations with Europe and the Middle East. To an observer of the 19th century Malayali, the contemporary stereotype of the cold, calculated, venture-migrant "Mallu" would come as something of a surprise. This shift in Malayali attitudes towards migration is the result of a century's worth of complex social, economic and cultural changes.

The Migration-resistant Malayali

From the 3rd century BC onwards, the spice trade brought foreign peoples and cultures to Kerala's shores - Greeks, Romans, and Arabs.[2] Recent archaeological excavations confirm that Calicut (by the 13th century) and Cochin (by the 15th Century) had become undisputed centres of trade power. Vasco da Gama's arrival in 1498 commenced a period of intense trade with Portugal, Netherlands, Denmark and France. But despite these international comings and goings, Malayalis were uninterested in travel or migration. While enjoying the material benefits of these cosmopolitan interactions, they appeared keen to insulate themselves culturally until the mid-19th century.

Not only were Keralites resistant to crossing the seas to the West; they were equally unwilling to cross the Sahyadri Mountains to the East into the regions occupied by their Tamil and Kannada-speaking neighbors. Between 1834 and the 1910s, Tamil and Telugu-speaking populations eagerly migrated as indentured laborers to distant British, Dutch and French colonial territories. But colonials found few recruits amongst Keralites.[3] The 1911 Census of India described Malayalis as one of the least prone to migration.[4] But by the 1970s, a paradigmatic shift seems to have occurred and with Gulf migration boom, Keralites had become one of the most boundary-breaking communities in India, third only to Punjabis and Rajasthanis.[5] This transformation has its roots in the mid-19th century, sparked by trends in an unlikely section of Kerala society.

Transition to a Migratory Culture (1850-1910)

Dalits: The Pilgrim Parents of Migration

It was none other than the weak and the "wretched of the [Kerala] earth" who dared to make the first migratory forays into far-flung areas of Kerala. In Kerala's system of serfdom, Pulayas, Parayas and other Dalits were tied to a village (*"desam"*) and a landlord (*"tampuran"*) in perpetuity. Any attempts to leave a *desam* were punished severely. But in defiance of these rules, aided by Christian missionaries and the anti-slavery legislations enacted by Travancore State, these Dalits escaped, mostly to begin working for colonial plantations.[6] Many of these escapees were Christian converts, educated and armed with letters of introduction from missionaries to the plantation owners of the eastern and southern hills. These movements, primarily by able-bodied males and a few families marked the beginnings of Malayali migration in the mid-19th century.

The rapid growth of colonial plantations ushered in a host of economic and social shifts. By the middle of the 19th century, the

British colonial economy had reached its peak, and it dramatically restructured Kerala's agricultural sector. Coffee plantations, which started in the hilly areas east of Quilon in the 1830s, began to expand by the 1860s, with the chief planting areas being concentrated in the Peermade and Ashambu hills of Travancore, and later in Wyanad.[7] In 1878, the acquisition of land for coffee and tea plantation by Kannan Devan Hills Produce Company further expanded the plantation land area, and by 1945, it was a 100,000 acre holding. Colonial agents, missionaries, and local kings were all invested in this expansion. Lt. Gen. Cullen, the British Resident, introduced coffee plantations to the Ashambu Hills in South Travancore in the 1850s, and King Vishakam Thirunal and Dewan Madava Rao soon became owners of coffee estates as well. By the 1860s, Rev. J. Cox of the London Missionary Society (LMS), Rev. Caldwell of the Society for the Propagation of the Gospel and Rev. H. Baker of Church Missionary Society (CMS) also held coffee plantations. By the 1870s, the LMS missionary organization itself tried its hand at the coffee estate business.[8]

With the increased need for labour in Kerala's huge plantations, as well is in neighbouring Coorg and the Nilgiri hills, Kerala's old patron-client system proved difficult to sustain. Pulayas and Parayas began to respond to this demand, providing them access to a cash economy and better socio-economic status — distinct improvements over the subsistence-level existence they eked out under the *Thampuran* families. Wages also increased rapidly; a coolie's wage increased from one *anna* per day in the 1850s to four *annas* by the 1870s.[9] The coffee boom of 1890s only further increased the demand for labour and the readiness of Kerala's Dalits to migrate. Their initial numbers were relatively small, especially compared to Tamil migrants, but they signalled a significant shift in Kerala's attitudes and experience with migration. By the beginning of the 20th century, these numbers had climbed significantly. According to Menon, most of the emigrants from the Malabar region of Kerala were from the Dalit groups. Between 1900 and 1921, around 10,000 *Parayas* had emigrated from the Malabar area alone to these new plantations.[10] Kooiman estimates that 10% of the more than 1.5 million Indian emigrants who had moved to Ceylon's plantations by 1867 had originated in Travancore.[11] Thus, the plantation economy and the need for cheap labour set in motion an unprecedented internal migration process, signifying fundamental attitudinal shifts to migration by the mid-19th century.

Peasant Farmers' Internal Migration

The second group of pioneers of migration which were almost exclusively confined within Kerala's boundaries, were small and mid-size peasants. These entrepreneurial farmers took advantage of the growing demand for spices and consequent government support for agricultural forays into forest lands, further demonstrating the effects of colonial priorities on the local economy. In the 1870s, projects began to reclaim waste lands along the newly developed Kottayam-Peermade/Madura road, for example. These efforts created unparalleled change in the nature of land ownership in the region. In a radical departure from the perpetuation of land ownership within certain privileged castes and communities, Dewan Madava Rao of Travancore granted full private ownership rights to 200,000 acres of government land in 1865.[12] The Travancore government's monopoly on pepper ended in 1860, and the rise of pepper prices in the world market in 1880 brought more cash into the hands of farmers.[13] The matrilineal joint family system and *tharavad* property system changed rapidly from 1890s in Malabar, Travancore and Cochin, leading to the fragmentation of large land holdings, further aiding shifts in land ownership and migrations.[14] Buying lands and migration now became more of a way of life for some Syrian Christian peasants and other middle income farmers. The Syrian Christian community was already commercially savvy due to their involvement in spice trade, and by the 19th century, with the help of the colonial apparatus, they were also becoming cash savvy. Thousands of small farmers moved away to Peermade, Wynad, Malabar, Nilamboor, and Gudalloor, mainly to the eastern boundaries of Kerala's mountainous regions. This movement which began by the end of 19th century reached its peak by the 1930s.

These migrations signalled more than just economic shifts for peasant families. They often involved painful changes – the uncertainty of migrant life, the disruptions in traditional family structures, the challenges of deforestation, the uprooting of large sections of Kerala's society, and the weight of the disapprobation of the extended families they were leaving behind.[15] Ultimately, these changes ushered in widespread shifts in societal values around migration and displacement, but the pioneers' attitude at the time could only be portrayed as ambivalent, at best.

Individuated Migrations

Although in less significant numbers, the third group of 19th century migrants came from the lower-middle strata of Kerala society e.g. Shanars of South Travancore, Izhavas of North Travancore, Syrian Christians and a few higher castes, who were educated but ineligible for government jobs due to caste restrictions. They began to migrate to British-run plantations of Kerala, Tamil Nadu and Ceylon during the second half of 19th century as *kankanies*, clerks, managers, and bankers. Missionary education created a mutually beneficial system: it gave the migrants economic mobility, and it provided plantation owners with reliable sources of mid-level labour. The cash gains of these individuals were handsome considering the economic context of the time.

These highly entrepreneurial individual migrants were products of Kerala's unique educational context. Kerala had a strong pre-British tradition of literacy.[16] The British system of education, especially the missionary effort to create a constituency of literate converts, reinforced this tradition. Both the British government and missionaries during the middle of 19th century emphasised the commercial value of the English language. The CMS College Kottayam and the Nagercoil Seminary of LMS were only the first symbols of the English language's prestige as the language of the Raj and as a generator of high wages. By 1891, 14% of the male population of Travancore was literate in English and a 'widespread craving for higher English education' in the region was recognised.[17] Also from 1891 onwards, female children were encouraged to become literate. The number of students rose from about 8,500 in 1872 to 50,000 in 1890 in Travancore. However, government jobs only increased from 14,700 in 1875 to 20,000 in 1891. Furthermore, government jobs were available only to Brahmins and Nayars by caste rule and tradition, further adding to the frustration of these highly motivated individuals from the middle and lower social hierarchy.[18]

T. C. Poonen, the first Malayali to study in Britain and a product of CMS College Kottayam, lived in London from 1869 to 1872. He was called to the bar from the Inner Temple in 1872, but was refused a government job when he returned to Travancore and had to migrate to Cochin to find employment. His experience illustrates the rigidity of Travancore's system of entitlements and employment on the basis of caste. Government jobs were inaccessible to lower ranks, even those with foreign education with missionary connections.[19] Between 1875 and 1891, literacy among Ezhavas in Travancore had increased from 3.15% to 12.1%, and under the social reformer Dr. Palpu's leadership, they began to demand government jobs.[20] As a result of high literacy and knowledge of the English language, these groups increasingly sought jobs in cities and plantations outside Kerala, especially in Ceylon after 1847. Thus, individuals and families, both middle-income job-seekers and lower-income labourers moved to Ceylon, though a substantial majority subsequently returned to Kerala. The colonial cash economy provided an excellent alternative for the frustrated English-educated youth struggling against a system of caste-based entitlement and religious orthodoxy.[21] We will see later how these individual migrations proved to be a harbinger of a much larger and systematized migration to Ceylon, and subsequently to Malaya and Singapore. Although racial and caste hierarchies were still at work in these contexts, they also provided a space for inter-racial association, as well individual prestige and economic mobility.

Whether these audacious migratory forays helped galvanize the whole Malayali community around migration is a matter of some debate. But there is no doubt that, encouraged by the changes associated with the colonial political economy, the Malayali resistance towards relocation for the sake of socio-economic gains was beginning to erode. The modern desire for consumption and mobility was steadily overtaking the orthodoxies of class and caste rigidities, and as a result, the Malayali psyche began to embrace the risks (and the gains) of the migratory culture. The changes in land-ownership patterns, the decline of feudal peasant-landlord dependencies, and the breaking down of traditional joint-families, further accentuated this shift.

Expansions in Malayali Migration (1910 - 1960s)

The Malaya-Singapore Wave

By the turn of the 20th century, the substantial majority of Malayali migrants who had left to Ceylon in the late 1800s returned to Kerala, and their wealth and affluence were on display.[22] By 1910, the indentured labourer system ended in Malaya, and the 'new system of slavery' of colonial capital formation was coming into serious disrepute in other colonies as well. This opened up opportunities for Malayalis who were already migrating as a result of the local colonial economy and higher education levels. In the 19th century, Malayalis moving to Ceylon might have been perceived as exceptional, but by the 1920s and 1930s, South East Asia became a natural destination for entrepreneurial and educated Malayalis.

Simultaneously, Kerala was experiencing some profound socio-cultural shifts. The state and the missionary investment in literacy (especially English education) during the last decades of 19th century was beginning to bear fruit. In Travancore between 1901 and 1941, the population more than doubled, and the literacy rate rose to 47%, including among women. Among Syrian and Nayar men, it reached the high mark of 73%.[23] Hundreds of youngsters were contestants for upward mobility, affluence and commercial success. They were also freed from the obligations to manage the farming fields or the spice trade of Travancore and Malabar. Thanks to the near demise of the *Marumakkthayom* system of matrilineal Hindu families, young educated Nayars were either being unshackled from the encumbrances of huge landed properties or their lands were being divided and sold. Izhavas and other lower castes were at the threshold of liberation through social reform movements like Sree Narayana Dharma Paripalana Sangam. Syrian Christians were emerging as one of most commercially and educationally influential communities, especially benefiting from the redistribution of fast-fading Nayar *tharavadu* properties.[24] The ground was now perfectly laid for international migration by larger numbers of people seeking semi-skilled, middle-income jobs. Thus, it was mainly the Syrian Christians and Izhavas, as well as some Nayars, who were making the move to South East Asia.[25]

Migrants to the Malaya-Singapore belt came primarily from semi-elite families or from members of the disenfranchised lower-middle castes. In 1926, 10,572 people emigrated from Malabar to Malaya and the Straits Settlements.[26] Significant numbers of people also moved from central Travancore. Places like Thiruvella, Kumbanad, and Kozhencerry became pejoratively synonymous with the Malaya-Singapore "migration syndrome". They worked in the plantations and colonial offices mostly in semi-skilled white collar jobs: as clerks, supervisors, managers, accountants, and compounders. By the late 1930s, due to the Great Depression and World War II, the flow declined, and most migrants returned to Kerala with accumulated cash. The flow resumed after the war and picked up in the 1950s.

Locals had mixed views of the migrants who returned from South East Asia. Their affluence inspired narratives about the glories of migration, but it also led to envy and exclusion. The 'Malayan Cottages' and walled compounds that came up in Kerala villages, as well as the tales of parsimonious dealings with neighbours, only added to further alienation. The traditional elite orthodox Hindus and other families were only willing to afford migrants a limited elevation in their social position. Migration and homecoming became associated with a kind of "pseudo" prestige, but importantly, it was not viewed in an altogether bad light.

Indian Internal Migration

Around the same time as Malayali migration to Malaya and Singapore, another migration story began to develop: internal migration to India's urban centres. This trend acquired a massive scale with the post-independence industrial developments in mega cities like Calcutta, Bombay, Madras, and Bangalore.[27] As with previous migration movements, the three-quarters of a century's worth of exceptional educational and literacy among Malayalis meant that they were better prepared to exploit India's advancement to the industrial age.[28] While the first wave of migrants (between the 1950s and 1960s) acquired mostly office jobs as typists, secretaries and clerks, the second wave that commenced in the 1970s accessed semi-skilled and skilled jobs as nurses, technicians, railway workers, and military personnel.[29] For instance, Malayali migration to the cities of Tamil Nadu increased by 64 per cent between 1961 to 1971, with a nearly equal number of male and female migrants. While Nayars and Syrian Christians had dominated these migration waves during the 1930s and 1940s, the demographic character changed substantially after the 1950s to include communities such as Kerala's Muslims and Scheduled Castes.[30]

Thus, educated Malayalis became an integral part of the large-scale urbanization that accompanied India's industrialization, and it was through the medium of these migrants that Kerala's own urbanization occurred. One major consequence of this wave was the expansion of Kerala's middle class in the 20th century.[31] During the 1970s, there was a steady flow of Malayali migrants to India's city centres and semi-urban areas. Malayalis even migrated to the remotest regions of North-East India, mostly as teachers and some as construction contractors, and private secretaries of highly placed officers, a trend which continues even now, although at a much smaller scale. The educational level of these migrants is typically very high, although more unskilled and semi-literate groups have become part of the migrant population in recent years. According to the most recent study, 25.1 per cent of these migrants are college degree-holders (or higher). However, while only 7.5 per cent of Kerala's population is illiterate, 17.4 per cent of these internal migrants are illiterate.[32] It should be noted that, as per a 2007 survey, internal migrants tend to be somewhat better-educated than international migrants — 54.4 per cent of internal migrants hold secondary or higher levels of education, while only 44.1 per cent of international migrants had the same level of education.[33] The internal migration phenomenon has diminished somewhat in recent years, according to Kerala Migration Study of the Centre for Development Study. It observed that while this "out-migration" rate had increased by 61 per cent during 1998-2003, there was a 22 per cent decrease between 2003 and 2007.[34] Whether this is part of a larger, long-term trend in Malayali migration is yet to be determined, but it could be due to the massive rise in migration to the Arabian Gulf.

Mass Migrations (1970s – 2011)

Migration to the Arabian Gulf

The "Gulf Boom" represents one of the most complex chapters in Kerala's migration story. Since the 1970s, this boom has dominated the Malayali exodus. This movement to the Persian and Arabian regions started in the 1910s and increased significantly by the 1930s, often using old trade connection or the British colonial network to find jobs. But with the 1970s oil boom in the region, they began to move there in massive numbers, transforming both the face of Malayali migration as well as the socio-economic trajectory of their home state. Migration is now seen as a way of Kerala life, rather than as a divergence from the norm. Kerala's destiny was now intertwined with the fortunes of these Gulf Boom migrants.

The Gulf is the destination of the choice for 90 per cent of today's international migrants from Kerala (though it has reduced from 96 per cent in 1998). Furthermore, in 1998, Malayalis constituted 50 per cent of all Indian migrants to the region.[35] The United Arab Emirates (UAE) welcomed the largest proportion (42 per cent) of Malayali migrants in 2007, a spot held by Saudi Arabia until quite recently. At first, it was mostly nurses and technicians who moved to the Gulf. The 1970s boom in the oil and construction sectors steadily attracted more workers, both skilled and unskilled, until 1983 when oil prices crashed. Migration underwent a dramatic decline but picked up again between 1990 and 1995. However, about 100,000 Malayalis returned to Kerala in 1990 due to the first Gulf war.

The transformation of the UAE into a global financial capital in the 2000s added to the complexity of Malayali migration to the region. For instance, the movement of construction workers, masons, and carpenters to the Gulf created a real shortage of these workers in Kerala, and the state began to attract migrants from Tamil Nadu and elsewhere for its own construction jobs. Wage increases as a result of this shortage have meant that pay-rates in Kerala have almost reached parity with the Gulf. Additionally, due of the rising cost-of-living in Kerala and the desire for further prospects and affluence, more highly-skilled workers such as engineers, doctors and nurses are moving to the Gulf. Thus, the Gulf now attracts labourers from both ends of the economic spectrum – those who move to ensure their economic survival, and those who move to further their economic affluence.

This boom has transformed Kerala's economy. Because permanent residency for expatriates is a rarity in the Gulf region, Malayali migrants to the region maintain a constant attachment to Kerala – remitting money, moving back-and-forth, or by returning permanently. A study of the utilization of foreign remittances between 1983-86 demonstrated that nearly 57% of this money was spent on land purchases and house construction.[36] The fact that a large per centage of Kerala's domestic product is dependent on remittances from Gulf means that any volatility in migration directly affects its fortunes.[37] Thus, the welfare of migrants is now seen as a matter of state, not just a family affair. This is indeed a major shift in the history of migration and the attitude towards migration in Kerala.

But this boom is not without its costs. Migration often takes an enormous emotional toll on families, especially among women who are "left behind" in Kerala.[38] Furthermore, while the successes of middle-class migrants are often celebrated, especially in books and movies, the trials of lower-class labourers in the Gulf is often forgotten. But the recently-published Malayalam novel, *Aatujeevitam* by Benyamin, provides a vibrant portrayal of the dehumanizing experiences of these workers, who live far away from home, cut off from their families, and treated as modern-day slaves.[39] *Aatujeevitam* ("the goat's life") is a metaphor for the profound sense of loss of personhood and enslavement in the desolate Arabian Desert, reducing the protagonist's life to a sheep's existence. It describes the absolute despair of the thousands of migrant men and women (especially housemaids) who are caught in this illegal human trade. These experiences are neither accounted for nor lamented in Kerala, mostly due to sheer number of successful migrants who return.

The Non-Gulf Overseas Migration

Though dwarfed by the Gulf Boom, Malayali migration to other parts of the globe has a much longer history. The Colonial connections led many Malayalis to the United Kingdom and some African countries, especially in 1950s. While they moved to the UK via many old British colonies, Malayalis were recruited directly to Africa as teachers, surveyors etc. In recent decades, large groups of Malayalis have migrated to Australia and New Zealand. It was during the 1970s that the stream to the United States, Canada and other European countries picked up momentum. In the 1970s, there was a wave of nurses, doctors and academics and who migrated to the United States through their family networks. There has been a significant increase in migration of engineers, information technology professionals and nurses since the late 1990s, many moving to the United States from the Arabian Gulf.[40] Of all the overseas Malayali migrants, 5.6 per cent of them are currently in the United States, making it a distant second destination.[41]

Migration to non-Gulf countries has some distinct features. Non-Gulf migration tends to display a better balance of genders, unlike Gulf migration, which is dominated by men. Migrants to non-Gulf countries are also largely composed of highly-skilled labour. But most importantly, unlike their Gulf-based compatriots, Malayali migrants to the United States and elsewhere are somewhat more disconnected from their Kerala roots. Not only do they send less remittances home, they often find more welcoming immigration policies in places like the United States, and decide to stay.

Shifts and Impacts

The Kerala Migration Survey of 2011 identifies a number of communal shifts in migration patterns:

> "...the vast majority of the emigrants from Kerala in 2011 were Muslims (about 45 per cent), although their share in the total population was only about 26 per cent. ...On the other hand, the Hindu emigrants were only 37.5 per cent of the total, although their share in the total population is about 56 per cent. However, over the years, the Hindus have improved their share, from 29.5 per cent in 1998 to 37.5 per cent in 2011. The gain

among the Hindus was mostly at the expense of the Christians whose share shrank from 25.1 in 2003 to 17.9 by 2011."[42]

In order to explain these shifts, we need to take into account the role of ethno-religious value systems as well as the desire and opportunity for upward social mobility. As we noticed earlier, the Syrian Christian and Izhava communities' early investments in education, their limited access or attachment to traditionally-inherited landed property, and their push for upward mobility made them some of the most migratory peoples in Kerala. Hindus, especially the land-owning Nayar community, found migration to be a less useful means for upward mobility and income generation. The Muslim community had embraced the modern educational system only in the 1960s, and they joined the bandwagon of migration only in the post-Independence period, especially with the Gulf migration boom.[43] Muslims are now the most migratory community in Kerala. There also is a regional shift in migration from the south to the northern districts of Kerala, lending a true heterogeneity to the demography of migration. From a historical point of view, these recent shifts only demonstrate the ever-widening nature of Malayali migration, across religious, ethnic and regional boundaries.

But there is another side to this story, which exposes certain systemic exclusions from this widening migration. Despite the large number of Malayali migrants, substantial majority of the households in Kerala have no overseas or internal migrants. The Kerala Migration Survey of 2011 observes,

> "Not all households in Kerala had an emigrant [international] or return emigrant in 2011. Only about 18.2 per cent of the Kerala households had an [internal] emigrant in 2011 and only 27.1 per cent had a Non Resident Keralite. The vast majority of the households – nearly 82 per cent – did not have an emigrant member. Nearly three-fourths had neither an emigrant nor a return emigrant. A surprising aspect of this ratio is that although the number of emigrants increased by 24 per cent between 2003 and 2011, the proportion of households with at least one emigrant or one NRK remained fairly constant."[44]

This confinement of migration to only a minority is an indicator of widening inequalities that migration ushers in. Furthermore, recent studies observe that when it comes to migration, Dalits are the most marginalized, and they are victims of a culture of sustained exclusion.[45] Ironically, the pioneers of Kerala's migration history have no place in today's migration story.

It is generally established by researchers that migration is one of the major sources of socio-economic transformation in Kerala, especially at the rural level, where it has significantly improved people's purchasing power. In one village studied by Osella, 30 per cent of the village's economic resources were migration-based.[46] It was estimated that in 1983, 50 per cent of the state's domestic product came from foreign remittances. In 2011, household remittances amounted to Rs. 15,129 crores (over US$ 3 billion) and the total remittances an estimated Rs. 50,000 (Rs. 49,695) crores (over US$10 billion). But again, the 2011 survey warns us that only 17. 1 per cent of Kerala's households received any of the household remittance, meaning "that a very vast majority of the Kerala households are not direct beneficiaries of the vast amountthat comesto the state as worker's remittances".[47] The migration that fuelled Kerala's transformation into a foreign remittance economy has also changed its traditional approach to income generation.[48] The economic culture of dependenceon migrationis colossal. The returned or diasporic Malayali is always perceived as a source of remittances – by the family, the locality, and the state.

Consumerism and consumption are at the heart of the changes that migration has brought to Kerala. Buying land, building a better house, decorating the house with consumer goods for both convenience and prestige are thus part of the story of migration. It is not just ostentatious displays of wealth, but part of upward mobility. As Osella puts it, "consumption takes on a substantial status aspect."[49] Migration and globalization have combined to create a narrative about Kerala that places it firmly in the global market.[50]

Migration has also brought with it certain shifts in gender dynamics in Kerala. Migration, especially to the Gulf, has long been dominated by males. This has subsequently led to changes in the role of women in Kerala society, especially after the 1970s. From a position of passivity and dependence, women have now transitioned to actively pursuing economic independence, even crossing into the public sphere. Women are now actively seeking seats in *panchayats* and local government, even in Muslim-majority districts where political activity amongst women was a historic rarity. The migration of female professionals, especially nurses and engineers from Kerala into various parts of India and abroad have only added to Kerala's changing gender roles.[51] In many cases, females are the primary income creator in the household, but whether there is corresponding status change is open to question. Furthermore, migration is no longer a male-dominated phenomenon, as it was generally perceived. More than a third of Kerala's internal migrants have been females, according to the 2007 survey, although there are fewer women among international migrants. Adding further complexity to the gender equation, it was noted that there were considerable differences in the proportion of females among international migrants belonging to different religious groups. While the highest proportion of females were found among Christian emigrants, Muslims had the lowest.[52] Among the recent outflows of students to cities in India, the female student population is substantial. Although a random situation, the Kerala Migration Survey of 2011 found that all the survey sample of student migrants from Pathanamthitta district, one of the major centres of early migration in 20th century, were girls. This could indicate a new trend of more girls migrating from Kerala in the future.[53]

Until recently, migration was hailed as a source of economic sustenance for the family, but in recent years, it has been lamented as a contributor to the breakdown of traditional family institutions. While we may not be able to attribute this change solely to migration, the demise of the once-resilient joint and extended family in Kerala is certainly part of the shifts that migration has engendered. There seems also to be a shift in attitudes towards old age and obligations to ageing parents. The proportion of single parents or elderly parents living alone is on the rise in Kerala. In 2007, about three per cent of Kerala's households had only one member. The number of single-member households has increased by 37 per cent between 1998 and 2007.[54] While celebrating the great educational and economic achievements of its migrants, there is a growing unease in Kerala over the losses sustained by the older generation – they are now forced to fend for themselves as their children work and sometime permanently move abroad. Parents having been effectively abandoned by their children, a sense of alienation sets in. The filial guilt that comes with this struggle is deep.

Migration is also affecting the religious sphere in Kerala, especially as wealth becomes part of the dominant narrative about migrants. For Hindus, expensive vedic rituals, which were once inaccessible to many, are now done with extravagance. *Poojas* at home, beliefs connected to the location of houses, the removal of *Doksham* along with life-cycle rituals, and festivals are becoming expensive and expansive. Along with such religio-cultural resurgence, there is an unprecedented growth of "blessing-oriented religiosity" among many. In a way, the recent Christian forms of charismatic and Neo-Pentecostal religiosity are a form of consumption-oriented religion and are fostered by rich members of the migrant community.[55] Shreena Banu's research on the influence of Gulf migration on Muslims, while concluding that affluence does not reduce the hold of religious values, also affirms that migrants new-found wealth comes into play in the formation of revived religion: "Migrant's families flaunt their wealth for their religious rituals, donation for construction of religious institutions like mosques, *Madrassas* and religious-cultural organizations and charitable activities."[56] The same can be said for most religious communities. This trend, augmented by the redefining of religious identity and identity politics in India, is also entangled with the affluence and income that migration generates.[57]

Kerala society has experienced well over a century-and-a-half of migration, evolving from a migration-resistant people to embracing the migration culture. Over the last 50 years, the scale and culture of migration has undergone a radical transformation in terms of its sheer numbers, its preoccupations, and its impact. The changes – both gains and losses — that Kerala has endured in its pursuit of economic upward mobility through migration will have a continuing impact on Kerala and Malayalis in years to come.

Notes

1. That is, those who are 'usual members of a household' in Kerala, not counting the diasporas who are permanently settled outside the state. Zachariah and Rajan, 2011, 2.

2. George, 2002. 123-32.

3. Peach, 1994. 42.See Mangru, 1987. 95-106 for details.

4. Lewandowski, 1980, 3.

5. Lewandowski, 1980, 3.

6. See for details Oommen, 1996 and 2007.

7. Jeffrey,1976.89., Osella and Osella, 2000. 49.

8. Kooiman,1984. 200.

9. Jeffrey, 1976. 100.

10. Menon, 1994. 15.

11. See Kooiman, 1984. 195.

12. Jeffrey, 1976. 89.

13. Lewandowski, 1980. 36.

14. Lewandowski, 1980.31f.

15. See Parapuram'sand others' literary works on these. Also see the novel by Pottekadu, *Vishakanyaka* in 1980. See a very recent novel by James, *Purappadinte Pusthakum*, 2006.

16. Jeffrey, 1976. 75.

17. Lewandowski, 1980. 30.

18. Jeffrey, 1976. 106.

19. Jeffrey, 1976. 122.

20. Jeffrey, 1976. 147.

21. Kooiman, 1984. 196.

22. See Osella and Osella 2000, an excellent anthropological monograph on Kerala and case studies capturing the local narratives on migration and money. 3ff. See for mobility offered by the plantation economy, 1f.

23. Jeffrey, 1976. 261.

24. Jeffrey, 1976. 248ff.

25. Kurien, 2002. 107-108.

26. Menon, 1994. 15.

27. See an extensive analysis of the Malayali migration to Madras city, Liwandowski 1984.

28. Lieten, 2003. 137f. See also Osella and Osella, 2000. 76.

29. See for a recent web comment on this, Samuel, 2010.

30. See for details Liwandowski, 1984. 95-99.

31. Liwandowski, 1984. 77.

32. Zachariah and Rajan, 2011. 6.

33. Zachariah and Rajan, 2007. 27.

34. Zachariah and Rajan, 2007. 20.

35. Zachariah and Rajan, 2007.

36. Prakash, 1998), 3212.

37. See for detailsPrakash,1998. 3209-3213.

38. Gulati, 1995. 191-202.

39. See *Aatujeevitam* by Benyamin published by Green Books Private Limited in 2012 (originally published in 2008). This novel has been awarded the Kerala Sahitya Academy Award.

40. See Daniels, 1994.

41. Zachariah and Rajan, 2011. 13.

42. Zachariah and Rajan, 2011. 2.

43. Sharafudeen, 2003. 113.

44. Zachariah and Rajan, 2011. 2.

45. Kurien, 2002. 126.

46. Osella and Osella 2000. 55. See also Kurien, 2002. 69-71.

47. Zachariah and Rajan, 2011. 9

48. This could be viewed against the background of the Kerala Model of Development. See Tharamangalam, 1998.

49. Osella and Osella, 2000. 126.

50. See for some of the recent trends Lukose, (June 2005). 915-935.

51. See Gulati, 1994.,Ossella and Osella 2000. 78., Kurien, 2002. 82f, 127ff. Osella and Osella, March, 2000. See Percot and Rajan, 2007. 318-325 for migration of nurses.

52. Zachariah and Rajan, 2007. 23.

53. Zachariah and Rajan, 2011. 8.

54. Zachariah and Rajan, 2007.

55. Kurien, 2002. 114ff., Osella and Osella, 2000. 153f, 168.

56. Banu, 2006, 323.

57. Banu, 2006, 323. See also Osella and Osella, 2007, 25.

References

Banu, Shreena, C. P. "Influence of Gulf Migration on Identity Assertion Patterns: Denominational Contestations and the Emerging Public-Sphere among Muslims of Kerala", ed. Nadeem Hasnain, *Islam and Muslim Communities in South Asia.* New Delhi: Serials Publications, 2006.

Benyamin. *Aatujeevitam.* Trissur: Green Books Private Limited, 2012.

Daniels, Roger. "The Indian Diaspora in the United States", ed. Judith M. Brown and Rosemary Foot, *Migration: The Asian Experience.* Oxford: St. Martin's Press, 1994.

George, K. M. *The Malayalis: the People, their History and Culture.* Vol. I. New Delhi: Cosmo Publications, 2002.

Gulati, Leela. "Migration and Social Change in Kerala", *India International Centre Quarterly.* 22, 2/3 (1995).

Jeffrey, Robin *The Decline of Nayar Dominance; Society and Politics in Travancore, 1847-1908.* New York : Holmes and Meier Publishers Inc, 1976.

Kooiman, Dick. "The Gospel of Coffee; Mission, Education and Employment in Travancore (19th Century)", pp.185-214, ed. Dick Kooiman, Otto van den Muijzenberg and Peter van der Veer, *Conversion, Competition and Conflict: Essays on the Role of Religion in Asia.* Amsterdam: Free University Press, 1984.

Kurian, Raju. "Patterns of Emigration from Kerala", *Social Scientist.* 7, 6 (Jan., 1979).

Kurien, Prema A. *Kaleidoscopic Ethnicity: International Migration and the Reconstruction of Community Identities in India.* London: Rutgers University Press, 2002.

Lewandowski, Susan. *Migration and Ethnicity in Urban India: Kerala Migrants in the City of Madras, 1870-1980.* New Delhi: Manohar Publishers, 1980.

Lieten, G. K. *Politics and Human Development: Essays on India.* New Delhi: ManoharPublishers, 2003.

Lukose, Ritty, "Consuming Globalization: Youth and Gender in Kerala, India." *Journal of Social History.* 38. 4, (June 2005).

Mangru, Basdeo. *Benevolent Neutrality: Indian Govt Policy and Labour Migration to British Guiana 1854-188.* Hertford: Hansib Publication, 1987.

Menon, Dilip M. *Caste, Nationalism and Communism in South India: Malabar, 1900-1948.* Cambridge: Cambridge University Press, 1994.

Oommen, George. "Dalit Conversion and Social Protest in Travancore 1854–1890", *Bangalore Theological Forum.* XXVIII, 3 & 4, (1996).

Oommen, George. "Education, Self-perception, and Identity: The Experience of Pulaya Christians of Kerala (1860-1930)", ed. Krishna Kumar and J. Oesterheld, *Education and Social Change in South Asia.* New Delhi: Orient Longman, 2007.

Osella, Filppo, and Caroline Osella. *Social Mobility in Kerala: Modernity and Identity in Conflict.* London: Pluto Press, 2000.

Osella, Filippo and Caroline Osella. "Migration, Money and Masculinity in Kerala",*The Journal of the Royal Anthropological Institute.* 6, 1 (March, 2000).

Osella, Filippo and Caroline Osella. " "I am Gulf": The production of Cosmopolitanism among theKoyas of Kozhikode, Kerala", ed. Edward Simpson and Kai Kresse, *Struggling with History: Islam and Cosmopolitanism in the Western Indian Ocean.* London: Hurst, 2007.

Peach, Ceri. *"Three Phases of South Asian Emigration",*ed. Judith M. Brown and Rosemary Foot, *Migration: The Asian Experience.* Oxford: St. Martin's Press, 1994.

Percot, Marie and S. Irudaya Rajan. "Female Emigration from India: Case Study of Nurses", *Economic and Political Weekly.* 42. 4, (Jan. 27 - Feb. 2, 2007).

Prakash, B. A. "Gulf Migration and Its Economic Impact: The Kerala Experience", *Economic and Political Weekly.* 50. 33, Dec. 12-18, (1998).

Samuel, John. "Patterns and Consequences of Migration from Kerala: Preliminary Notes", Thursday, November 4, 2010. (From the blog cite, "Bodhigram").

Samuel, John. "Where is Kerala going?" *http://www.mathrubhumi.com/english/story.php?id=116880,* (accessed Nov 30, 2012).

Sharafudeen, S. *Muslims of Kerala; A Modern Approach.* Trivandrum: Kerala Historical Society, 2003.

Tharamangalam, Joseph. "The Perils of Social Development without Economic Growth: The Development Debacle of Kerala, India", *Bulletin of Concerned Asian Scholars.* 30. 1, (1998).

Vora, Neha. "Producing Diasporas and Globalization: Indian Middle-Class Migrants in Dubai", *Anthropological Quarterly.* 81. 2 (2008).

Williams, Raymond Brady. *Christian Pluralism in the United States: Indian Immigrant Experience.* Cambridge: Cambridge University Press, 1996.

Zachariah, K. C. and S. Irudaya Rajan. *Kerala Migration Survey 2007.* Thiruvananthapuram: Research Unit on International Migration, Centre for Development Studies, Department on Non-Resident Keralite Affairs, Government of Kerala, 2008.

Zachariah, K. C., and S. Irudaya Rajan. *Migration, Remittances and Inequality.* Thiruvananthapuram: Centre for Development Studies, 2011.

2

Malaysian Malayalis

T. V. THOMAS

Indian Influence in South East Asia

The popular notion is that Indians first came to Malaya (now Malaysia) during the British rule. The fact is that Indians came much earlier than the 1800s. In fact, India has more than 2000 years of cultural history and commercial relations with South East Asia.[1] One of the early Indian influences is the advent of Indian merchants and religious leaders from the second century BCE onwards resulting in the spread of Buddhism and Hinduism to Southeast Asia. Later cultural influences of India dates to 78 AD with the arrival of Aji Saka; he was a Brahmanical prince and scholar to Sumatra prior to travelling on to Bali, Borneo, Brunei, Vietnam, Cambodia, Thailand and Burma.[2] A clear evidence of this is the largest Hindu temple in the world is in Cambodia.[3] The Indian culture infiltrated the region through itinerant merchants and traders in the early centuries of the first millennium AD.[4]

The Sri Vijaya kingdom of India colonized Java and Sumatra before the fourth century AD and it rose to prominence towards the close of the seventh century AD. The locals adopted the religions, language, art and architecture of the Indians.[5] In 2005, the ancient civilization of Kota Gelanggi in Johor, Malaysia was discovered. This find was archeologically important because it pointed to one of the greatest empires in history.[6] The Hindu Chola King Rajaraja (985-1018 AD) and his son, Rajendra (1018-1035 AD) ruled from the Maldives through India, Sri Lanka and right down to South East Asia. The Chola power even threatened the Sri Vijaya Empire in Java and Sumatra.[7] It is clear from records that Parameswara, an Indian Hindu prince fled from Palembang in Sumatra and founded the Malacca Empire in the Malay Peninsula around 1400 AD.

More evidence of Indian influence in the region is through written text. For example, numerous words of Sanskrit or Tamil origin are found in the local languages. Some examples of this are from the national language of Malaysia, Bahasa Malaysia are: *bumi* (boomi), *kapal* (kappal), *kedai* (kadai), *menteri* (manthiri), *putra* (puthran) and *raja* (rajah).[8]

There was no massive wave of voluntary emigration from India in the early centuries. Instead a limited number of Indian princes, priests and traders settled all over the region and implanted their culture in South East Asia. Their long and deep imprint is still visible today.[9]

Indian Migration to Malaysia

From the late eighteenth to the twentieth century, there was a massive migratory flow from India to Malaya. This began when British control over the Malay Peninsula became an increasingly greater reality. An ambitious colonial economy flourished with the development of agricultural plantations, mining industries and the accompanying need for infrastructure development. The success of such an economy was largely dependent on cheap and easily managed labor.[10] To meet this ongoing need for laborers the British facilitated massive immigration from southern China and India. For example, during the 1880s about 140,000 Indians immigrated to Malaya[11]. From the founding of Penang in 1786 to Malayan independence in 1957, more than 4.2 million Indians arrived in the country. However, more than 3 million of them returned home upon completing their employment contracts. Therefore, the resident Indian population was only 820,000 in 1957.[12] Approximately 80 per cent of Indians who arrived in Malaya during the colonial era were labor migrants.[13] Majority were indentured laborers recruited by the *kangani* and *maistry* systems to work in plantations or as unskilled workers in government utilities. They were primarily South Indian in origin, poor, male and Hindu.[14] Women and children constituted less than 20 and 10 per cent respectively of this migratory flow.[15]

During this colonial period there were other streams of Indian migration to Malaya. The expanding resource-based economy in colonial Malaya attracted non-labor migration. The British recruited Ceylonese Tamils to serve in clerical jobs; educated Keralite Malayalis for administrative, clerical, technical, teaching and medical positions; Tamil-speaking Nattukottai Chettiars as merchants and financiers and Punjabi-speaking Sikhs for law enforcement.[16] It is not surprising that by 1939 approximately 700,000 Indians were residents in Malaya with the majority employed on plantations.[17] Therefore, the socio-economic profile of the Malaysian Indian did not change for decades.[18] The Indians in the labor force are still in a low-income bracket. Because of strict Malaysian immigration laws, the 1960s through 80s saw meagre migration from India except for wives joining their husbands.

From the late 1990s, the Information and Communication Technologies created a fresh wave of Indian migrants to Malaysia.[19] New legislation by the Malaysian government allowed companies to recruit young foreign software professionals to enter with temporary work visas. High tier Indian companies like TCS, Wipro, Infosys and HCL have successfully supplied hundreds of contract workers to develop the Malaysian Multimedia Super Corridor.[20] Of the 1.8 million people of South Asian origin in Malaysia in the year 2000, Tamils were 80 per cent, Sikhs were 7.7 per cent, Malayalis 4.7 per cent, Telugus 3.4 per cent, Sri Lankan Tamils 2.7 per cent, Pakistanis and Bangladeshis 1.1 per cent.[21] The Indo-Malaysian population had crossed 2 million constituting 7.3 per cent of the entire country by 2010.[22] The largest group is Tamils as much as three-fourth of all Indians in Malaysia. Together Tamils, Malayalis and Telugus represent 85 per cent of the Indians in Malaysia. Malayalis are predominantly located in Penang, Lower Perak, Kuala Lumpur and Selangor. According to the 2010 Census, Indians constitute 15.5 per cent of Malaysian professionals, including doctors (28.4%), lawyers (26.8%), dentists (21%), veterinary surgeons (28.5%), engineers (6.4%), accountants (5.8%), surveyors (3.0%) and architects (1.5%). Indians make up 38% of the Malaysian medical workforce.

Malayali Migration History

Older historical records identify Malayalam-speaking people from British Malabar and the princely states of Travancore and Cochin on the south west coast of India as 'Malabaris'.[23] Early evidence of Malabari presence in the Malay Peninsula can only be inferred from existing sources. Malabaris being a sea-faring and trading community would have been part of the South Indian trade system in South East Asia between the ninth and fourteenth centuries AD.[24] This is highly likely because Malabar was under the powerful Chola Empire.

The first concrete record of Malayalis setting foot on the Malay Peninsula is when the Portuguese Viceroy, Alfonso d' Albuquerque set sail from Cochin, India to Malacca, Malaya on May 2, 1511. He had 19 ships, 800 Portuguese and 600 Malabari fighting men with him.[25] The Portuguese successfully captured the port city in 40 days. It is possible some of the Malabari soldiers stayed back to help the Portuguese in building the infrastructure of the fortress port.

There is evidence of Malayalis on the island of Penang three years after British Captain Francis Light annexed the island and established a trading post there. A fire was reported on Malabar Street in 1789. There was obvious presence of Malabari migrants because a key street is named after them.[26] The existence of Kampong Kaka, Kampong Kolam and Kampong Malabar are further evidence of early Malabari influence in Penang. More evidence of a strong Malabari presence in Penang comes from the saga of one Narayana Pillai.[27] He was a Malabari from Calicut who had become an important merchant in Penang. Sir Stamford Raffles on his second visit to Singapore in 1891 brought Narayana Pillai and other Indians from Penang promising them better economic prospects on the island of Singapore. Pillai wrote to his friends in Penang to send him a few carpenters, brick-layers and cloth merchants. When they arrived Pillai established a construction business and a textile shop which soon made him a thriving merchant in Singapore.

Most Malabaris in Penang were Malayali Muslims. They were closely associated with the Tamil Muslims in Penang.[28] One can reasonably assume the size and influence of the Malabaris in Penang's first fifty years because Malayalam was one of the first languages taught in the Muslim school.[29] Two Malaysian cuisine favorites are "roti canai" and "teh tahrik", both Malabari concoctions!

The first super wave of Malayalis from Travancore, Cochin and Malabar arrived in Malaya and Singapore in the 1920s thanks to the British. The British colonial administration and the plantation owners needed personnel to manage the indentured laborers. The choice of Malayalis was inevitable. Lord Thomas Macaulay, a member of the Supreme Council of India under the British India Government, was quite successful in his work. In 1835, he used his Minute on Education to propel the English language into all Indian educational institutions. That produced a highly evolved system of education in Kerala which resulted in the most literate linguistic group in India. Therefore a regular flow of recruits emigrated from Kerala to be clerks, conductors and hospital assistants in the British-run plantations and industries.

Exact numbers of Malayalis who immigrated to Malaya are unknown because early records are unavailable. In 1921 they numbered about 17,000. That number doubled by 1931.[30] The Great Depression and the fall of rubber prices created a trickle-down migration in the late 1930s. Then the Japanese invasion of Malaya in 1941 halted all immigration from India for almost the entire duration of World War II.[31] By 1941 there were 44,339 Malayalis in Malaya.[32]

In the post-war years there was a substantial inflow of middle-class Malayalis. By 1957, the year of Malayan independence, Malayalis had emerged as the second largest Indian linguistic group in the country with a population of 72,971; still, they constituted only 7 per cent of the Indian population.[33] Among the Indian groups, Malayalis tend to have the strongest ties with their motherland. They stayed long, made their fortunes and returned to Kerala for retirement. This translated into having little or no interest in making a difference in the country which provided them gainful employment and considerable lifestyle advantages.

The end of the Second World War was when most Malayalis decided to actually settle down in the land to which they had come in search of employment. They decided that while their attachment to the motherland is important, they could survive without that umbilical cord and make Malaysia their home. Hence, communities of Malayalis began to get together and organize self-help and cultural organizations. This spawned the formation of several Malayali Associations or Kerala Samajams throughout the country.[34] Kerala Samajams were vital in keeping Malayali culture and tradition alive while learning about the cultures and traditions of their non-Malayali neighbors. Those associations helped inform and influence the second generation of Malayalis of their unique heritage and culture.. Kerala festivals like Onam, Vishu, or Christmas were celebrated by Malayali gatherings with food, music and the arts. A visit by a prominent Malayali actor, singer or writer would often draw a large crowd of Malayalis.[35]

Sensing the need for more contact and coordination between the Kerala Samajams, a Malaysia-wide entity was officially organized in 1972.[36] The All Malaysia Malayalee Association (AMMA) has its own constitution and is registered with the Malaysian government to emphasize education, welfare, culture and the well-being of the community.

When Malaya became independent in 1957, a small group of Malayalis uncertain of a secure future returned to India and a few even migrated to Australia, New Zealand and the UK. Then in 1975 when Malay was first introduced as the medium of instruction in schools,[37] there was a further exodus of Malayalis. However, the majority of Malayalis remained in Peninsular Malaysia, embracing the country as their permanent home and engaging in Malaysian society.

Recent emigration numbers from Kerala to Malaysia are quite impressive: 4,777 (2003), 12,052 (2008) and 13,392 (2011).[38] Many of them are Malayali IT professionals and who were part of a new wave of Indian immigrants since the late 1990s. Many of them would be classified as sojourners, as they will likely use Malaysia as a stepping stone for better opportunities in the USA, UK, New Zealand and Australia.[39]

Thriving Malayali Generations

The Malayali migrants between the early 1920s and the mid-1950s who continued in Malaya constitute the first modern generation of Malayalis. The first generation of Malayali Muslims were generally engaged commercially while the non-Muslim Malayalis took white-collar jobs. Both groups thrived in a middle-class lifestyle.

Realizing that advanced education was the passport to their children's progressive future, many Malayali parents sacrificed and saved to build a financial base for their tertiary level education. Every Malayali family seemingly desired at least one of their children to be a medical doctor or an engineer! Parents were willing to totally underwrite their children's higher education whether in Malaysia or overseas. Such concerted efforts have resulted in a wide array of highly skilled Malayali professionals – doctors, dentists, engineers, lawyers and educators. Similar patterns and practices also prevail among the third generation Malayalis in Malaysia and in neighboring Singapore.

In Malaysian Malayali culture, marriage is viewed as a noble institution and the ceremonial ritual in church, mosque or temple is a symbol of identity and status in the community. The expected and prevalent form of marriage among Malayalis is still the arranged marriage. Parents and older members of the extended familiar feel responsible for finding a suitable partner for their adult children. However, the prospective bride or groom has the freedom to meet each other and approve or disapprove of their parental choice. Though Malaysian society is multi-ethnic and multicultural, intercultural marriage among Malayalis is still relatively uncommon. Malayalis also greatly value close-knit families and kinship circles and no sacrifice seems too big to work towards family success. With advanced degrees, high salaries and two-incomes, many of the second and third generation Malayali families have grown in influence and affluence. Today, they form a substantial portion of the 20 per cent middle class of the Indian population.[40] Despite such admirable success, some Malayalis continue to explore migration prospects to Australia, New Zealand, Canada and the UK.

Malayali Contribution to Malaysia

Malayalis have contributed greatly to multiple facets of Malaysian life. Although there are many who made significant contribution to the welfare of the Indians in Malaysia and local communities and economy, it would be impossible to list all in this paper. However, some noteworthy individuals are listed here who are considered as prominent Malaysian Malayalis.[41] P.K. Nambiar, an advocate and solicitor from Penang with his brilliant legal reputation was the first appointed Indian member of the Straits Settlements Council in 1923. Nambiar's son, Dr. N.K. Menon was President of the Council of Indian Associations in 1932; he worked hard to alleviate problems of exploitation of Indian laborers in Malaya. N. Raghvan, son-in-law of P.K. Nambiar formed a pan Malaysian Indian organization, Central Indian Association of Malaysia whose goal was to improve the political, social and economic lives of Indians under the colonial government.

A. Balakrishnan, an insurance executive was one of the founding members of the Malaysian Indian Congress (MIC). He spearheaded the move of MIC joining the Malay-based United National Malay Organization (UNMO) and the Malayan Chinese Association (MCA) to form the national Alliance Party led by Tunku Abdul Rahman who brokered the Malayan independence from Britain. Tan Sri B.C. Sekhar, Director of the Rubber Research Institute (RRI) of Malaysia and recipient of the Magsaysay Award and Dr. P.O. Thomas, Consultant to the International Natural Rubber Organization (INRO) made remarkable contributions in the rubber industry. In the plantation industry, Mr. A.J. Menon, Mr. C.M. Menon, Dato V.V. Chellam, Mr. K.M. Samuel and Mr. M.V.D. Nair rose to key management positions in rubber companies.

Among those in the medical profession, Dr. K.L. Verghese, Dato Dr. K.A. Menon, Dato Dr. J.S. Eapen, Dato Dr. R.P. Pillay, and Dr. Jones Varughese, JMN, KMN, BSK were all nationally recognized. The Puthucheary brothers, James, George, Dominic and Francis were well-known advocates and solicitors. Tan Sri Justice V.C. George, Dato Justice Madhav Shankar and Dato Justice Varghese George have all made their mark in the legal field. Professor C.P. Ramachandran,

Professor K.K. Nair, Professor K.T. Joseph and Professor V. G. Kumaradas were Malayalis who excelled in academia. Mr. V. M. N. Menon was the first Indian cabinet minister in Malaya under the Membership system of the British and was later appointed a Commander of the British Empire, C.V. Devan Nair was Singapore's third President and Dato K. Pathmanaban was in the Malaysian cabinet. Tan Sri G.K. Rama Ayer had excelled in the civil service and was Secretary-General of the Ministry of General Planning and Social Economic Research. In the diplomatic camp, Mr. B. Rajaram and Ms. Lily Zachariah served as Malaysian ambassadors overseas. In the field of journalism, Mr. I.V.K. Nayar, Mr. Mohanan Menon, Mr. J.V. Morais, Mr. P.C. Shivadas, Mr. P.J. Joshua, Mr. N.G. Nair, Mr. M.G.G. Pillai and Mr. V.P. Abudallah had reached the apex of their careers.

How can anyone forget Dr. P.P. Narayanan and his lifelong pursuit of improving the lives of plantation workers through the National Union of Plantation Workers (NUPW). Mr. R.K. Pannickkar is another Malayali hero with his contribution to the blind, Mr. M.K. Menon is well known for his literary works and Mr. K.O. Mathai is known his promotion of Kerala cooking. In the promotion of Indian culture and arts, Mr. V.K. Shivadas and his wife, Vatsala, Mr. V. Aiyappan JP and his wife, Malayajadevi are well known. Mr. Bosco D'Cruz, Mr. William D'Cruz, Mr. N. Raghavan AMN, Mr. G.O. Kennet PJK, Mr. A.J. Stellus, and Mr. Rajan Nair kept the Malayali community entertained through their histrionics.

Conclusion

The first huge Malayali migration to Malaysia and Singapore in modern times began nearly a century ago. No other countries in the world can boast of such a large, well-established Malayali community that have prospered in one place for more than three generations! Over the decades the socio-economic, cultural and political environments have helped Malayali families thrive. Now, Malayalis are admired by fellow Malaysians for their positive impact and multiple achievements. Sadly, very little has been written about their journey and their important contributions to enrich Malaysian society and beyond. The ironic part is that the multicultural fabric of Malaysia has produced a unique breed of Malaysian Malayali who may not favourably survive in Kerala today.

Notes

1.   George Coedes, *The Indianized States of Southeast Asia* (Kuala Lumpur: University of Malaya Press, 1968), 14-15.

2.   Ong Kim Lee, (2005), "The Lost City of Kota Gelanggi. First Immigrants to Malaysia Archaeological Find" Unpublished paper, (Singapore, 2005), 1.

3.   Angkor Wat is a UNESCO World Heritage Site. See *http://whc.unesco.org/en/list/668* (accessed Dec 1, 2012).

4.   Rajesh Rai, "Positioning the Indian Diaspora: The South-east Asian Experience" in *Tracing an Indian Diaspora: Contexts, Memories, Representations,* Parvati Raghuram *et al.* (New Delhi: Sage Publications India, 2008), 31.

5.   B. D. Arora, "Indians in Indonesia" in *Indians in South Asia*, ed. J. Bahadur Singh, (New Delhi: Sterling Publisher, 1982), 195.

6.   Lee, 2.

7.   K. Laxmi Narayan, "A Brief History of Indian Emigration during Ancient and Medieval Period" in *Indian Diaspora: Trends and Issues*, ed. Ajaya K. Sahoo and K. Laxmi Narayan, (New Delhi: Serials Publications, 2008), 3.

8.   For more on this, see T.Wignesan, "The Extent of the Influence of Tamil on the Malay Language: A Comparative Study" Paper given at the VIIIth World Tamil Studies Congress, held in the Tamil University in Tanjavur, India, on December 1994. Also T.Wignesan, *Sporadic Striving amid Echoed Voices, Mirrored Images & Stereotypic Posturing in Malaysian-Singaporean Literatures,* (Allahabad: Cyberwit.net, 2008).

9.   K. Laxmi Narayan, 3.

10.   Carl Vadivella Belle, "Forgotten Malaysians? Indians and Malaysian Society" in *Tracing An Indian Diaspora: Contexts, Memories Representations*, ed. Parvati Raghuram *et al.* (New Delhi: Sage Publications India, 2008), 52.

11.   Thomas Sowell, *Migrations and Cultures* (New York: BasicBooks, 1996), 344.

12.   Kernial Singh Sandhu, *Indians in Malaya: Some Aspects of Their Immigration and Settlement (1786-1957).* (Cambridge: Cambridge University Press, 1969), 152, 182 and 309.

13.   Rajesh Rai, 34.

14.   Carl Vadivella Belle, 54.

15.   Kerniel Singh Sandhu, 107.

16.   Sinnappah Arasaratnam, *Indians in Malaysia and Singapore* (Kuala Lumpur: Oxford University Press, 1970), 67.

17. Carl Vadivella Belle, 56.

18. Rabindra J. Daniel, *Indian Christians in Peninsular Malaysia,* (Kuala Lumpur: Tamil Annual Conference, 1992), 53.

19. Eric Leclerc, "Circulation of Indian IT Professionals to Hyderabad and Beyond" in *The Indian Diaspora: Historical and Contemporary Context* ed. Laxmi Narayan Kadekar et al. (Jaipur: Rawat Publications, 2009), 202.

20. Eric Leclerc, (n.d.) "Reconnection of the Old and New Indian Diaspora in Malaysia" Unpublished paper, 5.

21. Tridib Chakraborti, "Minority Underclassed: Negating a Sociological Truism in Malaysia" in *Indian Diaspora in Asian and Pacific Regions: Culture, People, Interactions* ed. Lipi Ghosh and Ramakrishna Chatterjee (Jaipur: Rawat Publications, 2004), 196.

22. See Malaysian government official website for details of ethnic make up of 2010 census - *www.statistics.gov.my/portal/index.php?option=com_content&view= article&id=1215&lang=en* (accessed Dec 1, 2012).

23. Suresh Narayanan, *From Malabaris to Malaysians: The Untold Story of Malayalees in Penang.* Unpublished paper Universiti Sains Malaysia, n.d. 1. The term 'Malabari' is virtually unknown and unused in Kerala, but refers to people living in the Malabar Coast.

24. Suresh Narayanan, 1.

25. *Ibid*, 1.

26. *Ibid*, 2.

27. *Ibid*, 4.

28. *Ibid*, 3. Terms like *"kaka"* and *"mappila"* refer to Malayali Muslims and are still in use in Kerala.

29. *Ibid*, 3.

30. *Ibid*, 3.

31. Rajeskhar Basu, "Seach for Pastures: Tamil Migration to Malayan Plantations in the 19th and 20th Centuries" in *Indian Diaspora in Asian and Pacific Regions: Culture, People, Interactions* ed. Lipi Ghosh and Ramakrishna Chatterjee, (Jaipur: Rawat Publications, 2004), 180. In 1926, 10,572 Malayalis migrated from Malabar to Malaya and Straits Settlements. In 1931, the number had dropped to 2,807 because of the depression of the rubber trade. See Dilip M.Menon *Caste, Nationalism and Communism in South India. Malabar 1900-1948* (Cambridge: Cambridge University Press, 1994), 15.

32. Read about the amazing experiences of ten Malayalis pioneers in T.K. Nainan's compilation, *Shining Beacons: Life-Stories From Pre-War Years* (Batu Pahat, Johor: Advanco Digital Shop, 2010).

33. Sinnappah Arasaratnam, 33-45.

34. "History of Malaysian Malayalees" on All Malaysia Malayalee Association (AMMA) website, *http://amma.org.my/* (accessed Dec 1, 2012).

35. AMMA website, *http://amma.org.my/* (accessed Dec 1, 2012).

36. AMMA website, *http://amma.org.my/* (accessed Dec 1, 2012).

37. Koshy Philip, email message to author, December 5, 2012.

38. K.C. Zachariah and S. Iridaya Rajan, *"Kerala Migration Report 2011"* (Thiruvananthapuram: Centre for Development Studies, 2011).

39. Eric Leclerc, "Reconnection of the Old and New Indian Diaspora in Malaysia," 6.

40. *Ibid*, 3.

41. Drawn largely from "Lest We Forget: Malayalees of Malaya/Malaysia" Unpublished paper, Kuala Lumpur, n.d.

References

Arasaratnam, Sinnappah (1970), *Indians in Malaysia and Singapore*. Kuala Lumpur: Oxford University Press.

Arora, B. D. (1982), "Indians in Indonesia" in *Indians in South Asia*. ed J. Bahadur Singh. New Delhi: Sterling Publisher.

Basu, Rajsekhar (2004), "Search for Pastures: Tamil Migration to Malayan Plantations in the 19th and Early 20th Centuries" in *Indian Diaspora in Asian and Pacific Regions: Culture, People, Interactions*. Edited by Lipi Ghosh and Ramakrishna Chatterjee. Jaipur: Rawat Publications.

Belle, Carl Vadivella (2008), "Positioning the Indian Diaspora: The South-east Asian Experience." In *Tracing An Indian Diaspora: Contexts, Memories, Representations*. Edited by Parvati Raghuram, Ajaya Kumar Sahoo, Brij Maharaj and Dave Sangha. New Delhi: Sage Publications India.

Coedes, George (1968), *The Indianized State of Southeast Asia*. Kuala Lumpur: University of Malaya Press.

Daniel, J. Rabindra (1992), *Indian Christians in Peninsular Malaysia* Kuala Lumpur: Tamil Annual Conference.

Ghosh, Lipi and Ramkrishna Chatterjee. eds. (2004), *Indian Diaspora in Asian and Pacific Regions: Culture, People, Interactions*. Jaipur: Rawat Publications.

Kadekar, Laxmi Narayan, Ajaya Kumar Sahoo and Gauri Battacharya. Eds. (2009), *The Indian Diaspora: Historical and Contemporary Context*. Jaipur: Rawat Publications.

Leclerc, Eric. (2009), "Circulation of Indian IT Professionals to Hyderabad and Beyond." In *The Indian Diaspora: Historical and Contemporary Context*. Edited by Laxmi Narayan Kadekar, Ajaya Kumar Sahoo and Gauri Battacharya. Jaipur: Rawat Publications.

——. n.d. "Reconnection of the Old and New Indian Diaspora in Malayasia." Unpublished paper, 5.

Lee, Ong Kim (2005), "The Lost City of Kota Gelanggi: First Immigrants to Malaysia Archeological Find." Unpublished paper. Singapore.

Menon, Dilip M. (1994), *Caste, Nationalism and Communism in South India: Malabar 1900-1948.* Cambridge: Cambridge University Press.

Nainan, T. K. (2010), *Shining Beacons: Life-Stories From Pre-War Years.* Batu Pahat, Johor: Advanco Digital Print Shop.

Narayanan, Suresh. n.d. "From Malabaris to Malaysians: The Untold Story of Malayalees in Penang". Universiti Sains Malaysia. Unpublished paper. *http://www.penangstory.net.my/indian-content-papersuresh.html* (accessed December 1, 2012).

Raghuram, Parvati, Ajaya Kumar Sahoo, Brij Maharaj and Dave Sangha. eds. (2008), *Tracing an Indian Diaspora: Contexts, Memories, Representations.* Delhi: Sage Publications India.

Rai, Rajesh (2008), "Positioning the Indian Diaspora: The South-east Asian Experience" in *Tracing an Indian Diaspora: Contexts, Memories, Representatives.* Edited by Parvati Raghuram, Ajaya Kumar Sahoo and Dave Sangha. Delhi: Sage Publications India.

Sahoo, Ajaya Kumar and K. Laxmi Narayan. eds. (2008), *Indian Diaspora: Trends and Issues.* New Delhi: Serials Publications.

Sandhu, Kernial Singh (1969), *Indians in Malaya: Some Aspects of Their Immigration and Settlement. (1786-1957).* Cambridge: Cambridge University Press.

Sowell, Thomas (1996), *Migrations and Cultures.* New York: BasicBooks.

Zachariah, K. C. and Iridaya Rajan (2011), *Kerala Migration Report 2011.* Thiruvananthapuram: Centre for Development Studies.

Lest We Forget: Malayalees of Malaya/Malaysia. Unpublished paper. n.d. Kuala Lumpur.

3

Malayalis in Kenya

O. M. PANICKER[1]

The Indian Diaspora in Africa

Indians have had a long and significant presence on the continent of Africa. Indians and those of Indian origin in Africa today number over 1.5 million with the largest populations in South Africa (1,218,000), Kenya (75,000), and Tanzania (54,700).[2] Africa is significant in modern Indian history because Mahatma Gandhi worked in South Africa prior to his return to India to lead its struggle for independence from British colonial rule[3]. The African city of Durban, South Africa has the largest concentration of Indians outside of India.[4] The connections between India and Africa are historic. Indian traders are known to have traveled to East Africa two thousand years ago for trade in ivory, textiles, and pottery.[5] This important link was further enhanced and strengthened with the expansion of the British Empire and its colonial administration.[6]

The Malayali Migration to Africa

Malayalis first moved to Africa as early as the 1930s[7], but substantial numbers arrived in the late 1960s and 70s. Countries like Kenya, Nigeria, Tanzania and Uganda were the early recipients. Only much later did Malayalis enter South Africa, Zambia, Lesotho, Swaziland

and Botswana. Most Malayalis came to Africa as professionals – accountants, doctors, engineers and teachers. Only a small number were engaged in commerce. Malayalis' most significant presence was in the educational systems of English-speaking Africa, particularly in mathematics and the sciences. In the peak period, Nigeria had 20,000 Malayali teachers![8] The Malayali population in Africa has significantly declined in recent times. From 2003 and 2007 the number has reduced by 63 per cent.[9]

The Kenyan Scene

The Indian diaspora in Kenya began with ancient trade ties and grew rapidly in the nineteenth century with the conscription of laborers from India to work on the Kenya-Uganda railway line. Most of these laborers came from Punjab and Gujarat. A significant number of them established businesses and came to play an important role in the Kenyan economy although decades later many left for other countries,[10] due to insecurity in Kenya and new opportunities elsewhere. Indians comprise 0.36% of the total population and are for the most part citizens of Kenya.[11]

In the early 1930s, the first Malayali migrants arrived in Kenya.[12] The Kerala Association of Kenya which was established over 70 years ago still remains an active community association.[13] Malayalis who moved to Kenya were employed in the civil service, the railways, the medical field and in education. However, due to an increase of insecurity in Kenya many Malayalis migrated to other African countries or to the West leaving behind a very small population. In 2003, the estimated number of Malayalis in Kenya was just 400.[14]

Our Life in Kenya

My journey to Africa was preceded by that of my cousin. He and his wife had moved to Kenya in the 1970s as high school teachers. After college graduation he was unable to find employment in Kerala. He opened a tuition center for students, and that proved to be a difficult challenge to sustain because of huge competition and a meager income. An advertisement in the newspapers prompted him to explore employment in Kenya. The offer to be a teacher seemed reasonable and so he and his wife moved to Kenya and settled in Kitale, a small town in the western part of the country.

My family was no stranger to immigration. After the Second World War, my father moved first to Singapore and then to Malaysia where he worked as an accountant with a British palm oil company. That is the reason I was born in Singapore and spent the first fifteen years of my life in that part of the world. In 1969, I moved to India to pursue further education. When I completed my college education, I received an invitation from my cousin to join him in Kenya, assuring me of likely employment as a high school teacher. Experiencing little success in finding a teaching position in Kerala, I traveled to Nairobi in 1981 not knowing what to expect. Kenya was not as economically developed as it is today but Nairobi, the capital city was clean and beautiful. The people I met were kind and respectful. Though economically poor their smiles were bright and warm— there was just something this culture.

The first Kenyans I knew personally were part of a Christian church to which my cousin invited me. The Kenyan Christians welcomed me with a warmth and love I had not experienced before. I began working as a teacher with a monthly salary of about US $25. This meager salary was disappointing at first! The school was located in a remote village and I had no car. Each day after traveling by *matatu* (taxi), I would walk for about five kilometers on a lonely, dusty road to arrive at school. Although the school had offered me a little room for my accommodation, I chose to live in town with my cousin because there was no running water, electricity, or toilet facility within the building. The students were too poor to pay their fees and therefore the teachers did not receive salaries on time. I remember once receiving only a small portion of my salary after six months with no pay. Despite the low pay, I loved the students and worked hard. The school did not have a science laboratory and I was the first to transform a classroom into a laboratory with equipment. Not only did I teach science but I was intimately involved with the life of the school. I worked with students, for example, to help grow flower gardens on the school grounds.

The year after my arrival in Kenya, I returned to India to get married. My wife joined me in Kenya also as a high school teacher.

We were blessed with three children although the first did not survive childbirth, partly because of the inadequacy of medical facilities. I continued to teach for ten more years while also being involved in church activities. In 1992, I sensed the call of God to give myself fully to church work and so I resigned from my teaching position. I founded a small non-governmental organization (NGO) and have continued leading and growing that entity which now has a staff of about 30. In recent years, we have been engaged in many church and humanitarian activities including medical day camps that have treated thousands of people and relief work among victims of the 2007 election violence.

Social and Cultural Realities

Indians and other South Asians in Kenya are referred to as "Asians." In local parlance, the term used is *Muhindi*, meaning "people from India" or "people who speak Hindi". This term is sometimes used pejoratively for it can have the connotation of ridicule similar to the term "negro" in the American context. Having lived in Kenya for over 30 years, I have noted the existence of animosity towards the Indian community. Sadly this hostility is based on the historical reality that some African workers had been mistreated or exploited by Indian employers. However, there is also a nationalistic sentiment fueled by a jealousy that sets Kenyans against Indians, whereby Kenyans feel that Indians are taking away their jobs and profiting from their resources. The results of such inherent hatred can at times be fatal. During times of political violence Indians are often the target of frustration and anger. While it is true that some Indians have mistreated Africans, Indians have also contributed significantly to the Kenyan economy creating thousands of jobs for the locals.

Many local Kenyans are also unhappy that Indians stick within their own communities and do not mingle in the broader society. This was largely true of the older generation but Indians of the younger generation exercise an open attitude and have many African friends. Most of my personal friends come from various Kenyan tribal groups. The teacher community of which I was a part, generally had the advantage of developing good relationships with many African communities and were therefore well received and respected.

Despite the challenges of life in Kenya, we were not a miserable group of people. The Malayali community enjoyed times together; our kids would play together and we would watch Malayalam movies together. (It was expected that those visiting Kerala would bring back the most recent movies for the community to enjoy.) We would gather for *Onam* and celebrate it as in Kerala because we would eat on banana leaves. *Diwali* was celebrated annually with our North Indian friends. Christmas was one more occasion that would bring the Malayalis together. On school holidays, Malayali families would visit each other's homes and also plan picnics and outings. Among the holiday attractions in Kenya were the Maasai Mara Game Reserve, Lake Victoria, and the port city of Mombasa. Of all the regions of Kenya, Mombasa reminds us most of Kerala with its coconut, mango, and cashew trees.

The greatest social disadvantage was the separation of our children from Kerala. We were unable to provide our memorable experiences of a Kerala environment for our children who were Kenyan-born. They have had very limited exposure to Indian culture, Kerala, the family and its kinship network. Most of our children do not speak Malayalam though they may understand it. However, there are exceptional cases where parents enforced the learning and speaking of Malayalam at home. Kenyan-born Malayali children are typically well accustomed to African and Western cultures.

Religious Expressions

As immigrants from India we never forget our religious roots. Hindus, Sikhs, Muslims, Christians, and others have established places of worship in Kenya. The beautiful Hindu and Sikh temples in Kenya were built by artisans especially recruited from India. While various Christian denominations exist in Kenya, none of the historical Kerala denominations such as the Syrian Orthodox and Mar Thoma churches are established here. Malayalis from these traditions participate in either the Catholic or Anglican churches. The Protestant Keralite would often join a multicultural church or sometimes an African church. When we first arrived we were members of an African church but now we worship in a multicultural church. Our religious differences have not prevented us from seeing each other as one Malayali community. Therefore, our gatherings included people from different religious backgrounds.

Economic Situation

Malayalis in Kenya have been employed in a spectrum of professions. Some are accountants, doctors, engineers, and teachers, while others are employed by large corporations or manufacturing firms. Malayali engineers work in factories, such as the Pan African Paper Mills in the western town of Webuye. A handful of Malayalis have worked as managers of privates schools, factories and the farms and plantations of rich Kenyans. One Malayali managed a section of the busy port of Mombasa. Most Malayalis live in the larger cities of Kenya – Nairobi, Mombasa, Nakuru, Kisumu and Eldoret.

There is a wide range of income levels among Malayalis. Those working in private companies earn a substantially good salary along with other benefits, such as housing allowances and paid flights to India every two to three years. With low salaries the Malayali teacher community was probably the least affluent. However, teachers worked very hard and earned the respect of the Kenyan communities and leaders. Many of the Malayali teachers lived in villages with no access to electricity, water, medical care and transportation; some families would share housing because they could not afford it on their own. While visiting one Malayali in a rural area, we noticed that he only had two stools in his living room. Life was never easy for them and some families could only visit Kerala once in only eight to fifteen years.

During our visits to Kerala it was painful to realize the modesty of our financial situation compared to those in Kerala. The array of uninhabited palatial mansions of non-resident Malayalis in Kerala always amazed us. Most of our families and friends in Kerala were financially rich and independent. We, on the other hand,would borrow money to buy our tickets to visit Kerala.

Among the challenges facing Malayalis were rampant corruption, unaffordable housing, and obtaining legal status for which bribes were often demanded by government officials. Not many Malayalis in the 1970s and 1980s could make foreign remittances to Kerala for personal savings or to meet family needs. The laws in Kenya were strict and allowed for only a very limited amount of funds to be sent annually. Additionally, when dealing with the Kenyan banks one was faced with bureaucratic red tape and lots of paper work. They required notarized letters from families in Kerala for approval of remittances. Therefore, it would take days before the banks would issue the check for onward transmission to India. Many Malayalis had come to Kenya with the hope of financial prosperity but they had to struggle to survive. In the early 1990s many Malayali teachers left for greener pastures in Lesotho, Swaziland, South Africa, and Botswana.

Political Environment

The political situation in Kenya was relatively stable in comparison to other countries in Africa. The President from 1978 to 2002 was Daniel Arap Moi[15]. A few doctors and headmasters were closely associated with him. President Moi knew my wife and me because we had taught in one of the good national schools of which he was the Board Chairman. Some of the local chiefs, district and provincial officers and members of the Kenyan parliament were also close friends of a number of Keralites.

Despite relative stability, the political environment in Kenya was difficult for foreigners. The military coup of 1982 was devastating. Many Indian families were robbed and several Indian businesses were vandalized. Indian girls and women were raped and there were heartbreaking stories of families committing suicide as a result. Elections in Kenya are held every five years and usually were times of insecurity due to tribal clashes and violence. Affluent Indians would temporarily leave the country and return after the elections were over. Those Indians who remained maintained a low profile as they were an easy scapegoat for those looking to release their frustration. In 2008, post-election violence led to the death of many Kenyans and the destruction of homes and businesses. Most Indians had to go into some form of hiding. However, I was grateful to have a close network of Kenyan friends around me to ensure protection for me and my family.

Conclusion

Africa has been home for thousands of Malayalis for decades and they were scattered in many countries. While each country is different, many of the experiences described here are shared by most Malayalis living in other countries on the continent. Since the late 1980s the Malayali population has significantly decreased in Africa. Severe challenges of personal insecurity and financial instability caused many to leave. Some gravitated to southern African countries while many migrated to the US, UK, Canada, Australia and New Zealand where new opportunities were available. However, for those of us who have continued to live there, Africa remains a part of us and our families. We have learned to become more resourceful when faced with trying difficulties. We have been touched by the warmth of the African community through whom we have both understood and experienced the meaning of brotherly love.

Notes

1. The author's son, Kevin M. Panicker contributed to this chapter. He presently works with World Relief in Baltimore, Maryland, USA.

2. *Population of Non-Resident Indians: Country Wise*, (The Ministry of Overseas Indian Affairs, 2012).

3. "South Africa", The Ministry of Overseas Indian Affairs *http://moia.gov.in/pdf/South%20Africa.pdf* (accessed October 29 2012).

4. Anahita Mukherji, "Durban Largest 'Indian' City Outside India", *The Times of India http://articles.timesofindia.indiatimes.com/2011-07-23/mumbai/29807173_1_durban-south-africa-uk* (accessed October 29 2012).

5. Gijsbert Oonk, "'We Lost Our Gift of Expression': Loss of the Mother Tongue among Indians in East Africa, 1880-2000," in *Global Indian Diasporas: Trajectories of Migration and Theory*, ed. Gijsbert Oonk, Iias Publication Series (Amsterdam University Press, 2008), 69.

6. *Ibid.*, 70.

7. K. V. Joseph, *Migration and Economic Development of Kerala* (New Delhi: Mittal Publications, 1988), 41.

8. K. C. Zachariah, E.T. Mathew, and S. Irudaya Rajan, *Dynamics of Migration in Kerala: Dimensions, Differentials, and Consequences* (New Delhi: Orient Longman, 2003), 58-60.

9.   K. C. Zachariah and S. Irudaya Rajan, *Kerala Migration Survey 2007*, 48.

10. "Kenya", India Ministry of Overseas Affairs *http://moia.gov.in/pdf/Kenya.pdf* (accessed October 29 2012).

11. *Ibid*

12. Zachariah, Mathew, and Rajan, *Dynamics of Migration in Kerala: Dimensions, Differentials, and Consequences*, 2.

13. KAK, Kerala Association of Kenya *www.kak-nairobi.com* (accessed October 29 2012).

14. Zachariah, Mathew, and Rajan, *Dynamics of Migration in Kerala: Dimensions, Differentials, and Consequences*, 59.

15. "Daniel Toroitich Arap Moi: Profile", State House of Kenya.

References

State House of Kenya, "DaMoi, Daniel Toroitich Arap: Profile", *http://www.statehousekenya.go.ke/presidents/moi/profile.htm* (accessed November 1, 2012).

Joseph, K. V. *Migration and Economic Development of Kerala.* New Delhi: Mittal Publications, 1988.

KAK, Kerala Association of Kenya *www.kak-nairobi.com* (accessed October 29 2012).

"Kenya", India Ministry of Overseas Affairs *http://moia.gov.in/pdf/Kenya.pdf* (accessed October 29, 2012).

Mukherji, Anahita, "Durban Largest 'Indian' City Outside India", *The Times of India http://articles.timesofindia.indiatimes.com/2011-07-23/mumbai/29807173_1_durban-south-africa-uk* (accessed October 29, 2012).

Oonk, Gijsbert. "'We Lost Our Gift of Expression': Loss of the Mother Tongue among Indians in East Africa, 1880-2000." In *Global Indian Diasporas: Trajectories of Migration and Theory*, edited by GijsbertOonk, 1: Amsterdam University Press, 2008.

Population of Non-Resident Indians: Country Wise. The Ministry of Overseas Indian Affairs, 2012.

"South Africa", The Ministry of Overseas Indian Affairs *http://moia.gov.in/pdf/South%20Africa.pdf* (accessed October 29, 2012).

Zachariah, K. C., and S Irudaya Rajan.*Kerala Migration Survey 2007.* Thiruvananthapuram: Centre for Development Studies, 2008.

Zachariah, K. C., E. T. Mathew, and S. Irudaya Rajan.*Dynamics of Migration in Kerala: Dimensions, Differentials, and Consequences.* New Delhi: Orient Longman, 2003.

4

Malayali Diaspora in the Gulf:
Temporary Economic Migration

STANLEY JOHN

Introduction

Emigrants from Kerala to the Gulf countries outnumber emigrants from all the other states of India combined. Nine out of every ten emigrants from Kerala travel to the countries of the Arabian Gulf.[1] The sheer volume of emigrants from Kerala traveling to the Gulf states and its proportion to the overall Indian emigration to the region makes the Malayali diaspora in the Gulf, arguably, the most significant facet of the overall phenomenon of emigration from India in the last half century. This paper argues that the phenomenon of temporary economic migration produces a complex and diverse diasporic community that emigrate because of a set of multifarious but interrelated factors and agents that function in a global economy. To illustrate the phenomenon of Malayali migration to the Arabian Gulf, the paper will appropriatethe particular case of emigration from Kerala to Kuwait.

After laying the context for emigration from Kerala to Kuwait, first, I will show that migration to the Gulf falls specifically under the phenomenon of temporary economic migration and hence distinct from other migratory systems. Next, the Malayali diaspora, albeit sharing the same geographical origin, is far from being homogenous.

We will consider the complex identities of individuals and communities along three aspects: social markers, economic factors, and religious affiliations. Finally, the reasons for why people move are not reducible to individual decision, opportunity, or economics. Appropriating the synthetic theory of migration proposed by Douglas Massey, professor of Sociology at Princeton University, the paper will demonstrate the multifarious but interrelated factors that provide the impetus for economic migration to Kuwait.

Migration from Kerala to Kuwait

Migration to Kuwait and the other countries of the Arabian Gulf is a recent phenomenon prompted by the discovery of oil in the Arabian Gulf region in the middle of the twentieth century. With the revenue from the petroleum exports, the desert regions of the Gulf were transformed into rapidly industrializing nations. The expanding economy required a greater number of workers that the citizenry of the region could provide. The Arabian Gulf countries turned to their neighboring Arab countries of the Middle East and North Africa (MENA) as well as the countries of South Asia for their labor population. The dependence on migrant labor has continued unabated since the 1950's. Migrant workers now account for the majority of the population in nearly all of the Gulf countries.[2]

The representation of South Asians in the labor force of the Arabian Gulf countries increased steadily in the decades following the first Gulf-war of 1990. Arabs from other Middle Eastern countries, South Asians, and Southeast Asians composed the majority of the labor force in Kuwait before the Gulf-war (Kapiszewski 2006, 6). However, after the Gulf-war, there was a significant rise in the percentage of South Asians in the labor force to compensate for the expulsion of Palestinians for their support of the Iraqi regime during the invasion of Kuwait. Thus migration from India to Kuwait grew steadily throughout the 1990s and into the first decade of the twenty-first century.

Out of the 20-25 million emigrants from India, 19% reside in the oil-rich Gulf countries (Khadria 2006, 5). Some accounts estimate more than 3.5 million Indians in the Gulf. The *Report of the High Level*

Committee on the Indian Diaspora recognizes that more than half of these migrants to the Gulf originate from Kerala (ICWA 2011). More than 90% of all emigrants from Kerala travel to the Arabian Gulf countries. Out of 2,193,412 emigrants from Kerala in 2008, 1,941,422 traveled to the Gulf. The United Arab Emirates (47.29%) and Saudi Arabia (25.93%) received nearly 75% of all emigrants from Kerala. The remaining migrants went to Oman (8.63%), Kuwait (6.66%), Qatar (6.26%), and Bahrain (5.22%) (Zachariah and Rajan 2010).

Nature of Migration

Global migration differs greatly from region to region. Each regionhas unique systems, policies, and legislation for migration.[3] Thus, it becomes imperative that we identify the particular region and the nature of migration in that region. In this paper, we are primarily interested in migration to the Persian Gulf characterized by an immigration system governed by the *Kafala* sponsorship system, an immigration mechanism that links residency in the country directly to the employment contract with the particular employer who is the *kafeel*, or sponsor. Any attempt at conceptualization migration to the Arabian Gulf must take seriously the transient nature of employment and the skill-level of the migrants, which are the two key features of temporary economic migration to the Gulf.

Several attempts are made to conceptualize the diverse types of migrants that traverse the globe. Stephen Castles, sociologist from the University of Sydney identifies several types of migration. There are highly-skilled and low-skilled labor migration, forced migration, family reunion, and few others such as astronaut phenomenon, return migration, retirement migration, and even posthumous migration (Castles 2002, 1143-1168). Similarly, Ted Lewellen in *The Anthropology of Globalization* identifies nine types of migrants: internal migrants, international migrants, immigrants, transnational immigrant, diaspora, refugees, step-migration, migratory chain, and circular migration (Lewellen 2002, 130). The benefit of both these models lie in their ability to incorporate a broad range of migrants in a simple heuristic model. However, both these models are inadequate to capture the transient or temporary nature of economic migration embodied by the Malayali diaspora in Kuwait.

Migration to the Arabian Gulf is characterized by its transience rarely transferring into a permanent resident status as assumed by the term 'immigrant.' Labor migrants in the Gulf are not immigrants neither are they visitors. They encompass both short-term as well as long-term migrants. They represent a highly complex group of people from skilled to non-skilled labor, single migrants to migrants with families, limited labor contracts to extendable contracts, and their tenure in the Gulf is brought to an end either on their own volition, personal or familial commitments, or an unanticipated emergency. These factors affect the duration of a migrant's residence and tenure in Kuwait. K. C. Zachariah and Irudaya Rajan, professors at the Center of Development Studies in Thiruvananthapuram, Kerala, observes that among the migrants from Kerala the average length of tenure in the Gulf is seven years (Zachariah and Rajan, 2011, 25).

The migrant's tenure in the country is limited to the duration of the employment contract, which when concluded, requires the migrant's departure from the country or renewal of the contract or forces them to seek a new employer. In cases where the employer provides fair wages and favorable work environment, the migrant can expect a positive experience and seek a renewal of the contract. In cases where the employment experience is unfavorable, the migrant can secure a 'release' from their sponsor and seek a better employment opportunity with another sponsor. Most low-skilled workers come on a contract of two to three years, which is sometimes renewed upon extension of the contract. Others, who are highly skilled, are known to stay in the country even up to the second and third generation, although in a temporary status.

The migrant's experience in the diaspora is shaped by his or her skill level, which then informs the length of their tenure and prescribes their employment circumstances. Thus, migrants have two divergent experiences based on whether they are low skilled workers or high-skilled workers. The vast majority of the non-skilled labor force travel to the Gulf States to work in labor-intensive fields of construction, domestic work, or in the service industry. In most cases, these expatriates are unable to bring their families with them and travel to their home country for the duration of two years. The discrimination by the dominant society combined with the constant threat of deportation affirms the marginal position of these workers in the society (Longva 1996, Gardner 2010, HRW 2010).

The circumstances are far less dismal for the highly skilled migrant workers than for the low-skilled workers. The duration of their employment and length of stay is significantly longer, even extending up to several generations, albeit in a temporary status. These are engineers, health care professionals, educators, and executives who are typically able to meet the minimum salary requirement to bring their families with them to the diaspora. The duration of their stay varies. These migrants occupy the middle and upper classes of the Indian community in the Gulf.

Composition of Migrants

The diaspora context is far from homogenous. The Malayali diaspora in Kuwait comprise diverse groups of people albeit from the same geographical origin. In this section, we will take a closer look at the Malayali diaspora in the Gulf to ascertain the complexity embodied in the migrant context along three aspects: social markers, economic markers, and religious composition.[4]

Social Markers

More than 85% of the migrants are between the ages of 20-40 years. In fact, nearly 60% of all emigrants are between the ages of 20-29 years (Zachariah and Rajan 2012, 5). Also of importance is the gendered nature of the migratory phenomenon. More than 85% of all migrants from Kerala are male (Zachariah and Rajan 2012, 6). While female emigration plays a significant role in the overall global phenomenon, Kerala emigration is primarily a male prerogative.

In regard to their marital status, 56% of the migrants to the Gulf are unmarried. While 61% (903,308) of the males were unmarried in 2004, the numbers were inverse for the women with nearly 75% (169,732) being married (Zachariah and Rajan 2004). Being that Gulf migration from Kerala is predominately a male endeavor and many of the migrants are married, a large number of female spouses remain in Kerala. There are a significant number of spouses who did not join the male emigrants in the diaspora resulting in a phenomenon termed "Gulf wives." Zachariah estimates that nearly 105,000 wives live apart from their husbands during their Gulf employment (Zachariah, 2004). The psychological morbidity arising from the physical separation of the spouses and the children from their parents is the high price of emigration exacted both in the homeland and in the diaspora.

Economic Markers

Prior to their employment in the Gulf nearly fifty percent of emigrants from Kerala worked as drivers, salesmen, agricultural laborers, construction workers, electricians, nurses, and motor vehicle mechanics (Zachariah and Rajan 2012, 7). While 50% of the male emigrants received primary-level education and another 30% completed their secondary education, only 15%of them possess a college degree (Zachariah and Rajan 2004, 11). In contrast, among female emigrants, an overwhelming 45% obtained college degrees. The majority of emigrants from Kerala are likely to secure jobs in low-skilled or semiskilled professions, although a sizable minority find work in occupations requiring highly skilled workers.

Remittances are an important facet of the emigrant lifestyle; in fact, it is arguably the main reason the migrant workers travel to the Gulf. The total remittance to Kerala in 2011 was $9 billion (Rs. 50,000 crores) and contributes to 31.23% of the net state domestic product (NSDP), while remittance nationally stood at $63.7 billion representing 4.2% of the GDP (Zachariah and Rajan 2012, 9).

Remittances vary considerably among the regions and among the religions. Muslims sent the highest amount, $4.14 billion (Rs. 23,089 crores), from the Gulf; Hindus sent $3.2 billion (Rs. 18,089 crores); and Christians remitted $1.53 billion (Rs. 8508 crores). Because of the sheer volume of emigrants, it comes as no surprise that the Malappuram district received the highest remittance with a total of $1.6 billion (Rs. 9,040 crores), followed by Ernakulam with $1.1 billion (Rs. 6,127 crores), and Thiruvananthapuram with $0.8 billion (Rs. 4,740 crores) (Zachariah and Rajan 2012, 27).

Religious Composition

Muslims outnumber the other religious groups in the Gulf emigration from Kerala. According to the 2011 Census, out of a population of 33.3 million, 56% of the State were Hindus, 26.5% were Muslims, and 16.6% were Christians. However, among the emigrants from Kerala43.7% are Muslims, 31.2% Hindus, and 25.1% are Christians (Zachariah and Rajan 2012, 15). The largest proportion, about 45%, of emigrants from Kerala to the Gulf are Muslim.

The three religious groups are concentrated in different geographical regions of the State. While Hindus are distributed throughout the State, Muslims are concentrated in the northern districts and the majority of the Christians are located in the central districts. Hindus constitute a majority in every district except Malappuram. Malappuram has the largest Muslim population, followed by Kannur, Kozhikode, and Wayanad, all located in northern Kerala. The central districts from Pathanamthitta, Kottayam, Idukki, Ernakulam and Thrissur have over 70% of the Christian population of the State, while the northern districts from Kasargode to Palakkad have only 14% of the Christian population. The top three emigrant sending districts in 2008 were Malappuram with 15.25%, Thiruvananthapuram with 14.06%, and Thrissur with 12.95% (Table 15). These three districts alone account for more than 40% of the total emigrants. (Zachariah and Rajan, 2010).

A demographic analysis informs us regarding the composition of the diasporic community. The data above demonstrates that the Malayali diaspora in the Gulf captures the diversity and complexity embodied in the diaspora. First, with regards to social markers, the majority of emigrants are between the ages of 20-39, nearly 85% of emigrants are male, many of the emigrants are single, and a significant number travel to the diaspora without their spouses. In economic terms, 70-80% of emigrants are likely to work in either low-skilled or semi-skilled labor since they do not possess the educational qualifications to work in a highly skilled occupation. Finally, nearly half of all emigrants from Kerala are Muslims and originate from the northern part of the state.

Theorizing Migration: Massey's Synthetic Theory

Migration is a vast enterprise touching every facet of society with implications for a wide spectrum of interest groups such as policy makers, economic advisors, and religious leaders. It is crucial that agencies and individuals are informed of the reasons for why people migrate. Too often the discussion has been limited to economic motivations and individual choice. In this section, we will consider the multifarious but interrelated factors that provide the impulse for migration.

Several attempts have been made to understand why people migrate. One of the earliest of these theories, neoclassical theory, articulated the economic motivation highlighting individual choice and decision (Castles and Miller 2003, 22). The primary factor in the choice to move is the wage differential, in other words, people move because of the possibility to earn a higher income. New-Economics theory recognized that the primary motivation is not only higher wages or individual choice, but a mode of insuring one's household against the highly oscillating and volatile economy (Massey 2008, 21). Labor segmentation theory contends that local citizenry in post-industrial capitalist economies will prefer to be employed in the primary sector known for job security and high remuneration instead of the secondary sector where the wages are lower and less stable (Massey 2003, 15). This creates a structural demand for immigrant labor in the secondary sector. While the neoclassical and new economics theories considers individuals and their social networks highlighting their motivating factors, world systems theory looks at the role of the state in facilitating or restricting migration (Castles and Miller 2003, 26). Social capital theory asserts that once a migration system is in motion, the system will self-perpetuate as a result of the growth and elaboration of migrant networks (Massey 2003, 16).

Recognizing that these theories are not mutually exclusive, the International Union for the Scientific Study of Populations commissioned a multi-disciplinary study to survey existing migration theories garnered from the strengths of the major theories in the field (Massey 2003). Douglas Massey, professor of sociology at

Princeton University, proposes five critical questions that form that backbone of the synthetic theory:

1. What are the structural processes in developing nations that produce emigrants?

2. What are the structural forces in developed nations that create a demand for their services?

3. What are the motivations of people who respond to these macro-level forces by moving internationally?

4. What social and economic structures arise in the course of international migration and globalization to support and sustain international movement, and how do they feed back on the migratory process?

5. How do national governments respond to the resulting flows of people and how effective are their policies likely to be?

I will now appropriate Massey's synthetic theory to understand why people move from Kerala to Gulf and how it is illustrated in the Kuwait context. The synthetic theory considers both the labor-sending country as well as the labor-receiving country. There are many factors that are at play in the migrant-sending country that create the atmosphere for migration. For the highly skilled migrants, unemployment or lack of suitable employment propels them to seek opportunities in other countries. Khadria observes, "The failure of India's industrialization program to absorb the increasing numbers of qualified personnel from educational institutes coupled with the shrinking employment space in the science agencies led to a serious problem of supply and demand," which increased the rate of emigration of highly skilled workers (2006, 23). Another reason to migrate involves the social ills inhibiting advancement in the sending country, such as caste system, corruption, bribe, gender disparity, and nepotism. While educational qualification and work-skill can prove to be assets for employment, the location of the individual in the social and cultural system determines the opportunities to which they have access. Among the unskilled labor migrants, not just poverty but generational poverty and debts propel them to seek employment abroad.

There are also structural forces at work in migrant-recipient countries that create demand for migrant labor. One of the most significant factors in the case of migration to Kuwait is the severe polarity of employment in the public sector and private sector. On the one hand, 86% of the citizenry is employed in the public sector, while 95% of the non-Kuwaitis work in the private sector. Furthermore, the majority of Kuwaitis work in two occupational sectors: professional and technical, and clerical. More than 70% of Non-Kuwaitis areemployed in the production and labor sector, and the services sector. Thus, there is severe labor segmentation with popular identification of jobs with certain ethnicities. For example, the domestic workers are overwhelmingly from Indonesia, Philippines, India, Sri Lanka, Nepal, and Ethiopia. This ethnic and gendered employment distinction facilitates the dependence on migrant labor to fulfill those roles. A second reason is the low population of the citizenry and significantly low labor force participation. Citizens make up only 16% of the total labor force in Kuwait. These factors, combined with low literacy rates and educational levels and a high degree of non-labor income, fosters dependency on migrant workers.

A third aspect of the synthetic theory considers the motivations for people moving internationally. The most significant reason is the wage differential and presumed job security, especially if one travels on a labor contract. For their work in India, a male manual laborer receives Rs. 100- Rs.175 ($2-$3) per day working from 14-16 hours. Women receive nearly half of this amount in wages for the same duration of work. Furthermore, many of them work as day laborers, i.e. there is no guarantee of work for the next day. Thus, they are all the more eager to accept when presented with an employment contract that provides food, accommodation, and a monthly salary of Rs. 9,638- Rs.11,565 ($180-$215). However, upon arrival in the desert, some of them find themselves in deplorable conditions and recognize that life in the Gulf is not as glamorous as they had dreamed. Others, especially the medium skilled and highly skilled workers, are able to find work with significantly higher wages and far fewer persons vying for the same job. The prospect of saving money for a house, to provide for their children, or to pay debts is the motivating factor in accepting a job abroad.

The fourth aspect of the synthetic theory considers the social and economic structures that are formed in the context of international migration and globalization to support and sustain the migratory process. The *Kafala*, or sponsorship, system of migration management links a migrant worker with a local citizen. The citizenry of the Gulf states may obtain business licenses that permit importing a certain number of migrant workers who are given work visas for this purpose. Instead of starting a business, they may sell these visas in a high-demand market. Nasra Shah, professor at Kuwait University, observes that in the UAE, it is estimated that nearly 27% of the total work force arrived in the country through such fictitious companies (2008, 9). A visa to work in the UAE for an Indian national costs approximately Rs. 1,10,682 ($2,042) while for an Iranian national the cost is Rs. 2,21,365 ($4,084). Visa-trading is a continuous source of income for the local sponsor since the demand for these visas is so high and migrant workers are willing to pay exorbitant prices to secure such a visa. It is difficult to implement policies that will curb this trend without a fundamental revision of the immigration and labor policy.

Finally, the theory considers the measures the government employs to respond to the flow of people. Kuwait employs an active strategy to restrict the arrival of and dependence upon migrant workers and to enhance employment opportunities for the local citizenry. Restrictive policies include direct and indirect taxes on migrant workers. Although there is no taxation in Kuwait, the government implemented fees for primary care and hospital visits. Increased housing rent raises the cost of living, making it unaffordable for the middle class populations. The country also offers periods of amnesty where illegal residents may leave the country without punishment. The government has installed stricter regulations for visa issuance such as work permits, sponsorship permits, and quota regulation. Also, the government has banned 16 jobs from foreign worker employment and has reserved them for the nationals. These jobs include computer programming, computer operation and data entry, secretarial, typing, and clerical jobs, cashiers, and car drivers (Shah 2008, 11). The other set of policies favor and facilitate employment opportunities for the nationals. The government has taken proactive steps in creating jobs and providing vocational training for nationals. Recognizing the heavy concentration of nationals in the public sector, the government offers benefits to those employed in the private sector. In some countries of the Gulf, the government will pay up to half of the salary of the national if the company hires them. The companies are given cash benefits for hiring nationals and are penalized through fees for hiring expatriates. This dual nature of restriction of expatriate labor while enhancing nationals in the labor force is the strategy adopted by the government. The severe labor segmentation as previously discussed makes one skeptical regarding the implementation of the labor policies since Kuwaitis and non-Kuwaitis are concentrated in highly gendered and ethnically defined sectors of employment. Furthermore, the significantly low population among the citizenry and the rapid industrialization and expansion of the economy necessitates dependence on foreign nationals (Shah 2008, 13-14).

Migration does not occur in the abstraction of global realities or in mere individual decisions, rather it is initiated, propelled, and fueled by the global economy. Globalization and capitalism transform what were previously peasant or agricultural societies, creating disruption in the social and economic fabric of everyday lives. Massey claims that the global economy brings about widespread displacement of people "from customary livelihoods, creating a mobile population of people who are actively searching for new ways of achieving economic security and advancement" (2003, 11).

Conclusion

Migration to the Gulf countries is often romanticized in the homeland. The economic gains displayed by the emigrants upon their return to the homeland foster an imagery of the Gulf States as an utopia of economic success. Peering behind the curtains of economic success and failures, the paper takes the readers backstage bringing to the forefront the complex realities embodied by the migrant and the migrant context. This chapter informs the readers of the phenomenon of temporary economic migration highlighting the varying tenure and skills of the migrants, the diversity embodied amongst the Malayali diaspora in the Gulf, and identifies the multi-faceted factors and agents that facilitate economic migration to the Gulf.

The Malayali diaspora in the Arabian Gulf region occupies an important facet of the global phenomenon of migration. They inhabit a migratory system characterized by its transient and economic nature and comprised of individuals from diverse social, economic, and religious backgrounds who move to the diaspora propelled by the global economy. The vulnerabilities and opportunities faced by many of the Malayali migrants in the Gulf countries in the context of temporary economic migration warrants further reflection and advocacy. Religious leaders must be informed of the diversity embodied amongst the diaspora to adequately serve the spiritual needs of the migrants. Policy makers must be informed of the critical role played by the Malayali diaspora in the economies of the host countries, home country, and in the global economy.

Notes

1. The Arabian Gulf and the Gulf countries are used interchangeably in this paper referring to the United Arab Emirates (UAE), Saudi Arabia, Oman, Kuwait, Qatar and Bahrain.

2. The two exceptions to the case are Saudi Arabia and Oman with expatriates accounting for 31.7% and 29.5% respectively. Although nationals outnumber expatriates in the overall population in Saudi Arabia, the country receives the highest number of expatriates, of 8.9 Million, than any other country in the GCC.

3. Massey identifies five types of migratory systems: North American, European, Persian Gulf (Arabian Gulf), Asia-Pacific, and the Southern Cone of South America (Massey 2007, 7).

4. The paper will utilize data on overall Malayali emigrants to the Gulf as reflective of the data for Kuwait

References

Castles, Stephen (2002), "Migration and Community Formation under Conditions of Globalization" in *International Migration Review*. Vol. 36: 4 (Winter 2002): 1143-1168.

Castles, Stephen. and Mark J. Miller. (2003), *The Age of Migration: International Population Movements in the Modern World.* 3rd Edition. New York: The Guilford press.

Gardner, Andrew M. (2010), *City of Strangers: Gulf Migration and the Indian Community in Bahrain.* Ithaca: Cornell University Press.

Human Rights Watch. (2010), *Walls At Every Turn: Abuse of Migrant Domestic Workers through Kuwait's Sponsorship System.* New York: Human Rights Watch.

ICWA. (2011), *Report of the High Level Committee on the Indian Diaspora.* Indian Council of World Affairs.Electronic Media. *<http://indiandiaspora.nic.in/contents.htm>* Accessed December 1, 2011.

Kapiszewski, Andrzej. (2006), "Arab Versus Asian Migrant Workers in the GCC Countries." Paper prepared for *United Nations Expert Group Meeting on International Migration and Development in the Arab Region.* 15-17 May. Beirut, Lebanon.

Khadria, Binod. (2006), "India: Skilled Migration to Developed Countries, Labour Migration to the Gulf" in *Migracion Y Desarrollo.* Zacatecas, Mexico: International Network on Migration and Development.

Lewellen, Ted. (2002), *The Anthropology of Globalization: Cultural Anthropology Enters the 21st Century.* Westport, CT: Bergin and Garvey.

Longva, Anh. (1997), *Walls Built on Sand: Migration, Exclusion and Society in Kuwait.* Boulder, CO: Westview Press.

Massey, Douglas S. (2003), "Patterns and Processes of International Migration in the 21st Century." Paper presented at *Conference on African Migration in Comparative Perspective.* June 4-7, 2003. Johannesburg, South Africa.

Massey, Douglas S. (2008), *World in Motion: Understanding International Migration at the End of the Millenium.* Oxford: Oxford University Press.

Public Authority for Civil Information.*Statistical Overview* (2011), Central Statistical Bureau, Edition 34. 2011. State of Kuwait.

Shah, Nasra. (2008), "Irregular Migration and Some Negative Consequences For Development: Asia-GCC Context" Global Forum on Migration and Development. Manila, Philippines.

Shah, Nasra M. (2008), "Recent Labor Immigration policies in the oil-Rich Gulf: How Effective Are They Likely To Be?" ILO Asian Regional Programme on Governance of Labour Migration. Bangkok: ILO. (Working Paper; no 3).

Zachariah, K. C. and Rajan, S Irudaya. (2004), "Gulf Emigration of Women in Kerala" in *Samyukta: A Journal of Women's Studies.* Eds. Jayasree, G.S. *et al.* Thiruvananthapuram.

Zachariah, K. C. and Rajan, S Irudaya. (2010), "Migration Monitoring Study, 2008 Emigration and Remittance in the Context of Surge in Oil Prices" Working Paper 424. Thiruvananthapuram: Center for Development Studies.

Zachariah, K. C. and Rajan, S Irudaya. (2011), "From Kerala to Kerala Via the Gulf: Emigration Experiences of Return Emigrants" Working Paper 443. Thiruvananthapuram: Center for Development Studies.

Zachariah, K. C. and Rajan, S. Irudaya. (2012), "Migration, Remittances and Inequality" paper presented at Center for Development Studies. Thiruvananthapuram. January 13, 2012.

5

Malayali Diaspora in Canada

Lina Samuel

Introduction

Indians have been coming to Canada since the early 1900s. Studies have examined the history of South Asian migration in Canada[1], and the experience of women in the South Asian diaspora.[2] However, there has been minimal research on the Keralite diaspora[3], or the Syrian Orthodox Community of Kerala.[4] Much of the Malayali diaspora in Canada dates from the initial waves of immigrants who entered Canada in the 1960s and 1970s, including a number of single women. The experiences of women in particular stand in contrast to what is traditionally written and assumed about Indian female immigrants.This chapter provides a general overview of the Malayali Diaspora in Canada. It examines the history of migration of those from Kerala and the evolution of Canadian migration policy under which this occurred, and documents the current size and geography of the diaspora. Furthermore, it provides some qualitative discussion of how the process of migration has affected the identities and subjectivities of those in the diaspora among different cohorts, and documents some of their migration narratives.

History of South Asian Migration to Canada

Male immigrants have been coming from India to Canada since 1904. The first South Asians to land in Canada were the Sikhs who arrived in British Columbia. Their arrival coincided with an already rising animosity toward Chinese and Japanese immigration. South Asians thus were identified as part of the larger "Asian Menace".[5] The federal government responded by imposing a $500 head tax and began to restrict an already rigid immigration policy. In 1907 South Asians were disenfranchised in the province of British Columbia.[6] The provincial disenfranchisement led to federal disenfranchisement and denial of economic rights in terms of labour contracts and access to improved employment opportunities.[7] In 1908 the "Continuous Passage" act stipulated that immigrants may be prohibited from landing in Canada unless they came from the country of their birth or citizenship by a continuous journey.[8] This legislation was directed specifically at South Asians as it was impossible for them to meet this condition. By 1909 the government banned the immigration of South Asians, including the wives and children of those who had already arrived, a ban that lasted until 1947. The Immigration Act of 1910 explicitly used racial terminology for the first time and restricted British Indian immigration by name, terminology that remained until legislative reform in 1967.[9]

The ban on South Asian immigration was relaxed after the end of the Second World War. In 1967, new immigration guidelines and regulations were implemented by the federal government that disregarded race, ethnicity and nationality in the selection of immigrants, replacing them with a new "merit points" system in which prospective applicants were given points for possessing various skills needed in the Canadian labor market. South Asians were thus able to respond in large numbers to Canada's need for professionals after 1967.[10] Although immigration was opened up, Women during this immigration period were still typically classified as "dependents" even in cases where the wife held better qualifications than the husband. Besides the stigma of dependency, this status had several legal implications such as accessibility to government sponsored services such as subsidized language training programs.[11]

After the removal of explicit racist immigration regulations against non-traditional, non-white, sources countries, the focus has been on filling labor force needs in the Canadian economy. Applicants entering into the labor force from 1974 onwards (excluding immediate family members) had to enter into an occupation for which there was demand in Canada.[12] The new points system allowed for the re-assigning of different numbers of points as the demand for different skills in Canada's labor market changed. New regulations introduced in 1978 also focused on "designated occupations" and sought to orient flows of new immigrants to "designated areas" to both meet necessary skill shortages, but as well to encourage immigrants to settle away from the major metropolitan areas.[13] South Asians hence dispersed throughout the country, encouraged to fulfill Canadian labor force needs in the more peripheral regions. Family reunification policies at the same time led to greater number of female immigrant applicants into Canada.[14] Female immigrants in some years outnumbered male applicants, as evidenced by data collected by Citizenship and Immigration Canada in 1999, 2000, and 2001.[15]

The Canadian immigration system was tweaked further at the end of the 1980s under the Conservative federal government. A new category of business-entrepreneurial class migrants was instituted, allowing those with a high net worth who also agree to invest a sizable amount in a new business (and willing to employ at least one Canadian citizen or permanent resident for at least one year) to gain entry outside of the points system.[16] A number of wealthy Indians have taken advantage of this new category from the late 1980s up to the present. Also, Canada changed its policy from varying the intake of immigrants depending on labor force demand and the rate of unemployment, to a permanently high rate of intake. This meant that the flows of immigrants were not reduced in the face of the recession that Canada experienced in the early 1990s, and many immigrants at that time had difficulty finding work. This is a problem that remains to this day, with subsequent cohorts of immigrants from about 1991 onward less likely to attain the incomes or levels of homeownership of earlier waves.[17] Approximately 60% of immigrants entering Canada in the 1980s and 1990s can be classified as "economic immigrants" – those who immigrate on the basis of specific qualifications and skills, or via the new investor-class category - while around 30% entered under the family reunification program (many of whom are sponsored by relatives), and the remainder, about 10% (though very few from India), entered as refugees.[18]

Malayali Immigration to Canada

The Malayali diaspora in Canada originated in the post war period. While a number of early migrants arrived between the early 1950s and 1967, the vast majority immigrated after changes to the immigration act in 1967. With a disproportionately educated workforce, those from Kerala were better able to take advantage of Canada's new points-based immigration system, and many entered Canada with professional qualifications. Nurses in particular were in high demand, gaining many single women, as well as families, entry on the basis of points assigned to these skills. The first wave of migrants dates to approximately 1968 through to the early 1980s. Migration remained somewhat flat through the 1980s, but increased again in the late 1980s and 1990s with changes to Canada's immigration policies and the new business-class category. Immigration rates increased further in the late 1990s and early 2000s.

Table 1 document the immigration status of those whose mother tongue is Malayalam, as recorded in the 2006 and 2011 Census of Canada. It should be noted that not all of those in the Malayali diaspora report Malayalam as their mother tongue, and this is particularly true for those who were born or raised in Canada, who tend to claim English as their mother tongue. Thus, these numbers do not reflect the full extent of the Malayali diaspora, but do help delineate changes in the flow of migrants. They roughly suggest a doubling in the rate of Malayali immigration in each decade, from flows of less than 1,500 per decade before 1991, to a flow of over 3,000 in the 1990s, to almost 4,000 in just the first half of the 2000s. This remains, however, small in relation to the total flows of migrants from India (129,140 people born in India migrated to Canada between 2001 and 2006 – note that the 2011 census does not contain information on immigration, so 2006 is the most recent data available).

Table 1
Immigration Years for Malayalam Speaking Individuals into Canada

	Malayalam Mother Tongue (#, 2006)	Malayalam Mother Tongue (#, 2011)
Total Malayalam Mother Tongue	11,925	16,080
Non-immigrants (born in Canada)	1,195	NA
Immigrants (foreign born)	10,280	NA
Immigrated Before 1991	3,295	NA
Immigrated 1991 to 2000	3,040	NA
Immigrated 2001 to 2006	3,945	NA
Non-permanent residents	445	NA

Source: Census of Canada, 2006, topic-based tabulation 97-555-xcb2006008, and Census of Canada, 2011, topic-based tabulation 98-314-X2011041. Note: The 2011 Census of Canada does not contain information on immigration, so the most recent immigration data are from 2006.

The Extent of the Malayali Diaspora in Canada

Estimating the size of the Malayali diaspora in Canada is made difficult by the way that data is collected and categorized, and there is no mandatory registry for those identifying as from Kerala. One way to estimate the extent of the diaspora is to use the data contained in the Canadian census on those who report Malayalam as their mother tongue[19], or alternatively, being able to speak Malayalam as a first or second language (only in the 2006 census). Of course, these produce a very conservative estimate, as they do not include the children of Malayalam speakers who do not report also speaking the language. But this indicator can be used to gauge the relative concentration of the diaspora across the country. A total of 14,100 reported being able to speak Malayalam as a first or second language in the 2006 census. This represents 1.46 per cent of the 962,665 in Canada whose ethnic identity originates in India in 2006 (and 3.2 per cent of the 443,685 who were born in India, although many Malayalam speakers were not born in India). A total of 16,080 reported Malayalam as their mother tongue in 2011, approximately 1.54 per cent of the 1,047,235 whose mother tongue is classified as either a Dravidian or Indo-Aryan language.

The Malayali diaspora in Canada is very urban, and heavily concentrated in the Toronto census metropolitan area (Table 2).

Remarkably, over half (52 per cent, more than 8,000 people) of all those whose mother tongue is Malayalam in Canada live in the Toronto region, with the next three largest metropolitan areas (Edmonton, then Vancouver, and Calgary) housing between 1,100 and 1,350 people each (each with 7 to 8 per cent of all those whose first language is Malayalam). A number of other metropolitan areas contain between 95 and 535 Malayalam speakers (0.7 per cent to about 3.5 per cent of the total). The remainder of Malayalis, approximately one tenth of the diaspora,are spread thinly across the country. Of course, as noted above the total numbers of Malayalis will be larger than reported in Table 2, as there will be some who do not report speaking Malayalam, but they cannot be tracked in the census[20].

Table 2
Metropolitan Areas Containing the Largest Populations of Malayalam Speakers

CMA	Total Population 2011 (#)	Malayalam Mother Tongue 2011 (#)	Malayalam Mother Tongue 2011 (% Share)
Toronto	5,541,880	8,400	52.2
Edmonton	1,146,600	1,350	8.4
Vancouver	2,292,120	1,245	7.7
Calgary	1,205,175	1,115	6.9
Hamilton	712,575	535	3.3
Ottawa - Gatineau	1,222,760	450	2.8
Montréal	3,785,915	290	1.8
Kitchener-Waterloo	472,095	295	1.8
Winnipeg	721,120	290	1.8
London	469,005	280	1.7
Windsor	316,515	145	0.9
St. Catharines	386,525	115	0.7
All other places	14,848,890	1,570	9.8
All Canada	33,121,175	16,080	100%

Source: Census of Canada 2011

Three-Cohort Study of the Malayali Diaspora in the Toronto Region

A study of the Syrian Orthodox Malayali diaspora community in the Greater Toronto Area conducted by this author in the mid-

2000s sheds light on the migration experience in Canada. The research details some of the decisions around migration for early first generation female nursing migrants, as well as newer migrants who have chosen to emigrate to Canada since the early 1990s. While the earlier cohort came directly from India in the 1960s and early 1970s, the newer immigrant cohort arrived in Canada between the years 1993-2005 and came directly from India, as well as from Malaysia, Persian Gulf, South Africa and the United States. Their immigration narratives, motivations, and experiences around settlement, vary substantially from the immigrants who arrived in the 1960s and 1970s.

The study examines at a micro level the decisions around which these early immigrants left their homeland and examines experiences they had with settling in new environments and raising families. Within the context of raising children these early immigrant families faced new hurdles which challenged their strongly held traditional values and beliefs. Women in particular were forced to redefine and reconstruct their identity as they confronted children who did not subscribe to the same set of cultural values and traditions. The narratives from these first generation respondents point to the difficulty in constructing migrant identities particularly in a society where they are still seen as an immigrant/outsider.[21] The larger study also explores the lives of second generation children who face specific challenges in the construction of their identity.[22] These children, who attempt to balance the expectations of their parents, as well as the demands from the dominant society, are placed in a very particular position as they must find a way of negotiating the cultural traditions and religious obligations of their parents.[23]

Methodology

In the formal survey a purposive sample of 64 individuals, 50 women and 14 men, between the ages of 20-71 was conducted, with a combination of purposive sampling and snowball sampling techniques employed, while additional informal semi-structured interviews with priests and leaders of community organizations provided further context and narratives (Table 3).

Table 3
Malayali Three Cohort Study Details

	Year of Arrival	Arriving From:	Number of respondents
1st Cohort (1st Gen.)	1965-1977	Kerala, India	17
2nd Cohort (2nd Gen.)	NA	children of parents arriving from Kerala	26
3rd Cohort (1st Gen.)	1993-2005	India, Malaysia, Persian Gulf Countries, South Africa	21

Source: Samuel, *Forthcoming March 2013.*

First Generation Cohort

The stories of the first generation migrants spoke to a number of themes: the pursuit of higher education, liberation from traditional structures, freedom from parents, and the need to help with the finances of the household they had left behind. Many of this cohort included women who entered Canada as professionals. Many of these women left home around the age of 17 or 18, entered nursing schools which were out of state, and then left for abroad, despite resistance by family members who wanted them to remain home and marry. Because their nursing qualifications were recognized these women were able to not only find work, and although they had to write their registration exams to work in Ontario, many women took additional courses during their career to advance their professional skills. When asked about their work experience as a nurse, all respondents reflected positively.

After securing employment in Canada, a number went back home to marry and there was the added issue of husbands whose educational qualifications were not recognized and thus they were unable to find appropriate employment. Often husbands had to re-train at a local college or university or take up employment in manual labour. However the family structures remained resilient, and for the most part this cohort integrated well into Canadian society (in terms of finding employment, raising children, and accumulating wealth). Many retirees continue their linkages to their homeland though frequent trips back to Kerala, India.

Second Generation Immigrant Cohort

The second-generation of the early immigrant cohort, typically the children of the first migrants, experienced uneven success in their life in Canada. Most were able to attain university education, and were able to attain professional employment. However, tension arose between the younger generation brought up in Canada and largely assimilated into Canadian culture, and their immigrant parents and the community they had formed, particularly when it came to household rules, marriage and dating. The strong collectivist culture in the Syrian Orthodox community and the emphasis on loyalty to family places specific limitations on second generation youth, which result in conflict and strain, for both parents and children. Thus, second generation youth faced many struggles in making a place and space for themselves in Canadian society. Their attempts to forge their own path were often met with resistance by parents attempting to maintain some aspects of tradition. These tensions are revealed in their stories of growing up in immigrant families. The narrative from Tammy, a medical professional and second generation respondent, is indicative of the kinds of challenges faced by this cohort:

> As the oldest of my sisters and my cousins, I had to break my parents into everything. Every major event in my life has been stressful and difficult from my high school graduation to my engagement and wedding to the birth of my children. Even though I was born here, it was hard fitting in between my parents and the culture of Canada. Both my parents and I had, and continue to have, many battles. As the oldest in my family and I guess the circle of our family and friends, I was the one that did everything first. I was the one that fought all the battles for my sisters and the one that broke barriers. It was and still is exhausting.

Such stories are reflected and confirmed in research[24], who shows that daughters in particular have felt pressure as the "keeper" of culture and tradition. The research on adolescent females[25], reveal similar findings as they conclude that the degree of control on the child depends on the level of parents' conservatism and fear of the host community.

Newer Immigrant Cohort

More contemporary Malayali migrants have arrived in Canada from diverse regions such as South Africa, the Middle East and Malaysia. They are coming for similar reasons as did earlier cohorts - employment opportunities, career advancement, and better education for their children. Some of these newer immigrants are also migrating to escape insecure regions plagued with rising civil unrest and crime. This newer cohort was able to capitalize on established migratory paths taken by earlier cohorts, and in turn could often rely on existing family or community members to greet them in Canada.

However, a number of these migrants first worked in other overseas nations, particularly in the Arabian Gulf region. Many who come from the Middle East interpreted their sojourn there as a temporary pit stop on their way to other countries like the United States, Australia, New Zealand and Canada. They had gone with their family to the Gulf to make money. As Peter, the father of a family who had remained in the Middle East for 15 years before emigrating, stated quite adamantly, "…the Gulf States are the best place to make money. So we made good money working there, we had decent jobs, comfortable life and at the same time we were able to put aside a lot of savings…When we started out I thought we would stay for maybe 5 years, make some money and then move on, but 5 years went by so fast, before we knew it, it was gone." Peter stated that one of the primary reasons for moving was his career. Because of the "Reservation Policy", which preferences native born Arabs, there is a "ceiling" to his career and a constant threat to his employment as an engineer in Kuwait. Another motivating factor was the inability to own property and a feeling of exclusion due to limited educational opportunities (which are restricted to native born Arabs), particularly for their children:

> […] even if you live there for forty or fifty years…even if you live there until you retire, it will be company provided accommodation, nothing of your own and then you leave and go once for all and then you spend the best years of your life working for somebody and living in somebody's accommodation…you have nothing to call your own, you can't grow roots anywhere. Whereas here [in Canada] you have that ability, once you have

immigrated here[…] whether you work or don't work, or you do business or whatever it might be, it is a land of free opportunities. You can build, you can buy a house, do whatever you want, it is all up to you. You kind of shape your destiny here. […]

This narrative is more reflective of contemporary migrants. For this family and for many others, moving to Canada in general, and Toronto in particular, was doubly appealing because of the well-established Malayali community. Migrants were able to establish contacts and find community groups with which to make necessary relationships. Many of these new immigrants are coming with their families and setting up life in quite a different set of circumstances. The earlier nursing immigrants, for instance, came alone, often with no prior contacts, and established themselves with little community support, though they had professional support from the hospitals and nursing staff. These early immigrants, once they married and started establishing community churches and associations, then encouraged others to migrate. For new comers, these established organizations play a factor in choosing where to migrate. Malayali community associations also help to maintain linkages with Kerala, as well as with those in the many regions from which immigrants into the Malayali diaspora originate. Members of more recent cohorts also have been able to avail themselves of greater mobility in travelling back to Kerala for visits, and a number lead transnational live, maintaining linkages and in some cases businesses in two places at once.

Conclusion

Malayali immigration to Canada has produced a small, but vibrant and geographically concentrated diaspora. Migrants constitute what Mishra[26] refers to as the diaspora of the border, families who keep in touch with India through family networks and marriage. These individuals, particularly the first generation respondents, often construct a particular image of the "homeland". This image, based on past memories, is central to their image and identification as Malayalis. The second generation respondents, however, just as often distanced themselves from this vision of homeland stating it was more their parents' homeland. However, the region still held importance for them since they are deeply affected by the cultural values which their parents attempted to maintain. For the newer cohort, their identification as Malayalis is strong and their affiliation with the community and religious institutions are central to the construction of self.

Notes

1. Buchignani, Indra and Srivastava, 1984.

2. Ghosh, 1979, 1981; Naidoo, 1980, 1985a, 1985b, 1987; Dhruvarajan, 1991, 1992, 1996; Ralston, 1991, 1996; Handa, 2003.

3. Samuel 2010a, 2010b.

4. The Syrian Community claims the origin of Christianity in Kerala stems from Saint Thomas the apostle who landed in north Kerala in 52 AD (Alexander Mar Thoma Metropolitan, 1985).

5. Buchignani, 1980: 122.

6. Buchignani *et al.* 1985: 21.

7. Ralston, 1996: 23.

8. Bhatti, 1980: 43.

9. Ralston, 1996: 26.

10. Das Gupta, 1986, 68.

11. Ghosh, 1983, 91; Boyd, 1986, 45.

12. Department of Immigration, Annual Report 1973-1974, xi.

13. Hawkins, 1989, 77.

14. Ralston, 1996: 35-36.

15. Citizenship and Immigration Canada, 2002.

16. Canadian Citizenship and Immigration, 2010.

17. Mok, 2009; Walks, 2011.

18. cited in Momirov and Kilbride, 2005: 99.

19. 2006 and 2011 Canada census.

20. The figures presented for the "Can speak Malayalam" category are not quite representative of the population as my own research shows. Of the 26 second generation respondents only one respondent said they spoke the language (she returned to Kerala to complete her high school studies), the remaining respondents did not speak the language, and understood it only minimally. None of these second generation respondents were fluent in

reading or writing the language. There has been a very sharp loss of language skills in this community with the second generation and this loss must be taken into account when attempting to categorize individuals based on language.

21. Samuel, Lina 2010a.

22. Samuel, Lina 2010b.

23. Samuel, Lina 2013 forthcoming.

24. Talbani and Hasanali 2000, Handa, 2003.

25. Talbani and Hasanali, 2000: 625.

26. Mishra 1996: 422.

References

Alexander Mar Thoma Metropolitan. (1985), *The Mar Thoma Church Heritage and Mission*. Houston: T & C Copy and Printing.

Bhatti, F. M. (1980), A Comparative Study of British and Canadian Experience with South Asian Immigration. In Victor K. Ujimoto and Gordon Hirabayashi (Eds.), *Visible Minorities and Multiculturalism: Asians in Canada* (pp. 43-61). Toronto, ON: Butterworth and Co.

Boyd, Monica. (1986), Immigrant Women in Canada. In Rita James Simon and Caroline B. Brettell (Eds.), *International Migration* (pp. 45-61). New Jersey: Rowman and Allanheld.

Buchignani, Norman L. (1980), Accommodation, Adaptation, and Policy: Dimensions of the South Asian experiences in Canada. In Victor K. Ujimoto and Gordon Hirabayashi (Eds.), *Visible minorities and multiculturalism: Asians in Canada* (pp. 121- 150). Toronto: Butterworth and Co. Ltd.

Buchignani, Norman, D. M. Indra and Ram Srivastava. (1985), *Continuous Journey: A Social History of South Asians in Canada*. Torono, ON: McClelland and Stewart.

Canada. Department of Immigration. (1973-1974), *Annual report*.

Canada. (2002), Department of Citizenship and Immigration Canada. *Annual Report*.

Canada. (2006), Census of Canada.

Canada. (2011), Census of Canada.

Canada. (2010), Canadian Citizenship and Immigration Report *Coming to Canada as a http://www.cic.gc.ca/english/resources/publications/busimm.asp* (accessed Dec 1, 2012).

Das Gupta, Tania. (1986), Looking under the Mosaic: South Asian Immigrant women. *Women and Ethinicity: Bulletin of the Multicultural History Society of Ontario*, 8(2), 67-69.

Dhruvarajan, Vanaja. (1991), Women of Colour in Canada: Diversity of Experiences. In Sandra Kirby *et al.* (Eds.), *Women Changing Academe. The Proceedings of the 1990 Canadian Women's Studies Association Conference* (pp. 3-12). Winnipeg: Sororal Publishing.

Dhruvarajan, Vanaja. (1992), Conjugal Power among First Generation Hindu Asian Indians in Canada. *International Journal of Sociology of the Family*, 22: 1-34.

Dhruvarajan, Vanaja. (1996), Hindu Indo-Canadian families. In MarionLynn (Ed.), *Voices: Essays on Canadian families*(pp. 301-327). Scarborough, ON: Nelson Canada.

Ghosh, Ratna. (1979), Women and the Politics of Culture: South Asian Women in Montreal. *Resources for Feminist Research*, 8 (3), 21-22.

Ghosh, Ratna. (1981), Minority within a Minority—on being South Asian and Female in Canada. In *Women in the Family and Economy: An International and Comparative Survey* (pp. 413-426). London, England: Greenwood Press.

Ghosh, Ratna. (1983), Sarees and the Maple Lead: Indian Women in Canada. In George Kurian and Ram P. Srivastava (eds.), *Overseas Indians: A Study in Adaptation* (pp. 90-99). Delhi: Vikas Publishing House.

Handa, Amita. (1996), *Of Silk Saris and Mini-skirts: South Asian girls walk the Tightrope of Culture.* Toronto: Women's Press.

Hawkins, F. (1989), *Critical Years in Immigration: Canada and Australia compared.* Kingston and Montreal: McGill-Queens University Press.

Mishra, Vijay. (1996), The Diasporic Imaginary: Theorizing the Indian Diaspora. *Textual Practice*, 10 (3), 421-447.

Mok, Diana (2009), Cohort Effects, Incomes, and Homeownership Status among Four Cohorts of Canadian Immigrants. *The Professional Geographer.* 61 (4): 527-546.

Momirov, Jilianne and Kenise Murphy Kilbride. (2005), Family Lives of Native Peoples, Immigrants, and Visible Minorities. In Nancy Mandell and AnnDuffy (Eds.), *Canadian families: Diversity, conflict and change 3ʳᵈ Ed* (pp. 87-113) Toronto: Thompson and Nelson.

Naidoo, Josephine C. (1980), East Indian Women in the Canadian Context: A Study in Social Psychology. In Victor K. Ujimoto and Gordon Hirabayashi (Eds.), *Visible Minorities and Multiculturalism: Asians in Canada* (Pp. 193-219). Toronto, ON: Butterworth and Co. Ltd.

Naidoo, Josephine C. (1985a), Contemporary South Asian Women in the Canadian Mosaic. *International Journal of Women's Studies*, 8 (4), 338-50.

Naidoo, Josephine C. (1985b), A Cultural Perspective on the Adjustment of South Asian Women in Canada. In I. R. Lacqunes and Y. H. Poortinga

(Eds.), *From a Different Perspective: Studies of Behaviour Across Cultures* (pp. 76-92). Lisse, The Netherlands: Swets and Zeitlinger.

Naidoo, Josephine C. (1987), Women of South Asian Origins: Status of Research, Problems, Future Issues. In Milton Israel (Ed.), *The south Asian diaspora in Canada: Six essays* (pp. 37-58) Toronto: The Multicultural History Society of Ontario.

Ralston, Helen. (1991), Race, Class, Gender and the Work Experience of South Asian Immigrant Women in Atlantic Canada.*Canadian Ethnic Studies*, XXIII (2), 129-139.

Ralston, Helen. (1996), *The Lived Experience of South Asian Immigrant Womenin Atlantic Canada*. Lewiston: The Edwin Mellen Press.

Samuel, Lina. (2010a), South Asian Transnationalism in Canada: Effects on Family Life. In Bonnie C. Hallman (Ed.), *Family Geographies: the Spatiality of Families and Family Life*. Oxford: Oxford University Press.

Samuel, Lina. (2010b), Mating, Dating and Marriage: Intergenerational Cultural Retention and the Construction of Diasporic Identities among South Asian Immigrants in Canada. *Journal of Intercultural Studies*, 31 (1): 95-110.

Samuel, Lina. (forthcoming 2013), South Asian Women in the Diaspora: Reflections on Arranged Marriage and Dowry among the Syrian Orthodox Community in Canada. *South Asian Diaspora* 5 (1): TBA

Talbani, Aziz and ParveenHasanali. (2000), Adolescent Females between Tradition and Modernity: Gender Role Socialization in South Asian Immigrant Culture." *Journal of Adolescence* 23: 615-627.

Walks, Alan. (2011), Economic Restructuring and Trajectories of Socio-spatial Polarization in the Twenty-First Century Canadian City, in Bourne, Larry S. Bourne, Tom Hutton, Richard G. Shearmur, and Jim Simmons (Eds.) *Canadian Urban Regions: Trajectories of Growth and Change*. Toronto: Oxford University Press. 125-160.

6

Associations Formed by the Malayali Diaspora in North America

MATHEW T. THOMAS

Introduction

This is a historical perspective of the evolution and growth of major associations formed in North America by people of Kerala origin[1]. The information presented has been collected and compiled from knowledgeable individuals[2] and reliable websites. This overview is far from being exhaustive.

Waves of Immigration

There is no reliable documentation of when exactly the immigration of people from Kerala to the United States of America started. We know of Malayalis who came to the USA in the 1940s and 1950s, primarily for seeking higher education. The passage of the Immigration and Nationality Act of 1965 facilitated an influx of Malayali immigrants to the United States in the late 1960s, 1970s, and 1980s. Most early Malayali immigrants came to America because of the country's need for people with specialized skills especially health care professionals that included doctors and nurses. Others who found the USA a place of opportunity included students, teachers, and clergy. After these initial immigrants established themselves, they began filing the necessary papers for the immigration of their relatives and friends.

Thereby USA witnessed a second wave of immigration of Keralites in the 1980's when the relatives of the initial batch of immigrants started arriving. While the immigration of relatives continues to date, in the 1990s there was a third wave of influx of Malayali professionals working in the information technology (IT) field who were drawn to the U.S. on H-1B visas to address the potential threat of the Y2K issue. The year 2000 came and went without the materialization of any predicted disasters. Some of the H-1B visa holders returned to India, while many remained in the USA. The majority of those who immigrated to the USA in the last five decades have remained in the country and thrived, and so have their children.

Malayali Associations

As the new Kerala immigrants trickled in during the early years, they would randomly meet at grocery stores, gas stations, or at places of work and eventually develop lasting friendships with one another. However, they lacked a sense of an ethnic community in which they could socialize and rely on for mutual support. As their friendships evolved and strengthened, they decided to form Malayali Associations that were primarily intended to satisfy their nostalgia and help them gather together and celebrate common traditions and festivals like Onam and Christmas and foster a culture that was built around their common language - Malayalam. The religious and caste-based diversity that separated Malayalis for years, back in Kerala, was not an issue anymore. They were one, and formed bonds that encouraged their children to grow together in love and harmony. As they became economically stable many Malayalis gained the opportunity to train their children in dance forms such as *Mohiniyattam, Bharathanatyam, Kuchipudi*, etc., and/or to learn *Carnatic* and/or western music. Hence, the Malayali Associations also became a forum for the Malayali parents and children to display their talents and gain recognition. The festive occasions also were opportunities to dress in traditional attire and eat traditional food.

Many of the original Malayali Associations in the United States were formed in the late 1970s and early 1980s. Their objectives were to bring the community together, to offer a forum for celebrating common festivals, to provide opportunities for displaying the talents and skills of the members, to help one another in time of need and for finding jobs, finding homes, acquiring insurance policies, licenses, etc. These Associations also became a forum for some people to display their potential to consume alcoholic beverages, that were a rarity and quite unaffordable in Kerala, and at times display their lack of manners by showing off their drunkenness at public events. The Malayali Associations also became an avenue for people to promote their businesses, such as insurance under-writing, real estate sales, grocery sales, etc. These Associations also provided an opportunity for people to assume positions of leadership and cater to the needs of the community.

The urge to gain positions of leadership within Malayali Associations often led to frictions amongst the members and eventually caused the formation of newer organizations. As a result there are many Malayali Associations in some cities and regions of North America.

Umbrella Associations

As the number of the Malayali Associations in the United States began to multiply, with major cities in the US having at least one Malayali Association, some visionaries imagined bringing all Malayali Associations in North America under one umbrella organization. A preliminary meeting was held in Washington D.C, in 1982 which was chaired by the then Indian Ambassador to United States, Mr. K. R. Narayanan, who later became the President of India. This meeting initiated the formation of the *Federation of Kerala Association of North America* (FOKANA). FOKANA was formed on July 4, 1983, in New York to unite all Kerala or Malayali organizations on the American continent, and the first Kerala Convention was held in New York City. FOKANA was conceived to be a secular, objective, non-political, not-partisan, and not-for-profit organization that was intended to promote cultural, economic, educational, and social matters applicable to the Keralites in North America and Kerala. The objectives of FOKANA as listed on its website are[3]:

(1) to represent the interests of Kerala community in North America;

(2) to preserve and popularize Kerala culture and heritage;

(3) to promote the cultural, educational and social life of Keralites and their descendants in North America;

(4) to foster friendship and understanding between the Keralites and others;

(5) to organize and co-ordinate activities for the purpose of contributing to Kerala's development; and

(6) To raise, solicit and receive funds, charities and donations to carry out the above and other worthy humanitarian causes.

Over time, dissention within FOKANA led to the creation of another umbrella organization called the *Federation of Malayalee Associations of Americas* (FOMAA), in 2006. On its web site[4] FOMAA claims to represent more than 110,000 Malayalis in the United States and Canada. Forty-nine non-profit organizations from different parts of North America, all led by highly dedicated community activists and professionals are reportedly members of FOMAA. FOMAA believes that while maintaining the cultural heritage of Kerala and India, it is their duty to participate in and contribute to the mainstream of our adopted countries. FOMAA's objectives as listed on its website are:

(1) To organize conventions of Malayalees;

(2) To educate the youth of Kerala origin and provide them a social forum to experience and appreciate the richness of Kerala/Indian culture;

(3) To take a leading role in promoting Malayalam language and Kerala culture in North America;

(4) To organize and coordinate activities that will promote medical, social, and economic development of Kerala/India;

(5) To foster understanding and friendship among various Indian organizations, especially Malayalee organizations, and coordinate activities of common interest;

(6) To represent the interest of the Kerala community in North America and serve as its voice; and

(7) To raise funds to carry out the above-mentioned and other worthy humanitarian charitable causes.

Another umbrella organization for Keralites that exists in the USA is the *World Malayalee Council*[5] (WMC), which was formed on July 3, 1995 in New Jersey. The main objective of this organization is to provide a non-political forum to bring together the widely scattered community of people of Malayali or Kerala origin and strengthen the common bonds of culture, tradition and way of life. WMC reportedly works towards an international brotherhood of Malayalis or people of Kerala origin to bolster their cultural, artistic and social uniqueness and give resilience and understanding towards other cultures with which they have to co-exist and interact. WMC has a three-tier organizational structure, (i) a Global Council, (ii) six Regional Councils (America, Europe, Africa, Middle East, India, Far East, and Australia) and (iii) local units called Provincial Councils. Membership in WMC is in through the Provincial Councils. Each province is the body that serves the local Malayali community. WMC also has International Forums.

The umbrella Malayali organizations listed above are also either members of Indian-American umbrella organizations with a broader agenda or at least are participants in the activities of such entities. Some of these larger umbrella organizations are the *Federation of India-American Associations*[6] (FIA), the *National Federation of Indian-American Associations*[7] (NFIA), and the *National Council of Asian Indian Associations*[8] (NCAIA). Each of these organizations has their loyal supporters and organizes events on behalf of the Indian community. Representatives of these organizations also maintain close connections with representatives of the Government of India who work at the Indian Embassy and Consulates and serve as liaisons to establish better ties between the governments of India and the United States of America. However, these umbrella organizations have not helped propel any individual or cause to a local, regional or national status, perhaps because of their lack of unity towards any cause and also perhaps due to a natural sense of selfishness that loathes the advancement of another member of the community.

Religious Organizations

Religion is a core value of life in Kerala and is readily reflected in the life of Malayalis in North America. With the increase in immigration from all regions of Kerala one can notice the variety of religious expressions.

The 1970s and 1980s witnessed the birth of many Christian congregations, churches and denominations of Keralite origin. In the late 1980s and 1990s we have seen the emergence of many Ecumenical Councils of Kerala Christians. The Malayali Churches and Ecumenical Councils have generated their own religious and social activities and programs that have removed many once-active members of the Malayali Associations to just focus more on the activities of their respective church affiliations. This trend has caused a considerable reduction of involvement of members of the Christian community in wider causes pertaining to the Malayalis in their community. It is interesting to note that in recent times the Christmas programs run by the Malayali Associations are mostly coordinated and attended by the non-Christian Malayali community.

The organization that provides a platform for all Malayali Hindus in North America to get together without any social divisions of caste or creed is the Kerala Hindus of North America[9] (KHNA). Though formed only in 2001, it now claims to have grown to a family of several thousand members.

The Malayali Muslim community that immigrated to the USA is relatively small. While they do play an active role in some of the Malayali Associations, they too are drawn closer to their own religious institutions and activities, thereby dedicating only a very small amount of time and involvement in the broader activities of the Malayali Associations.

Over the years, Malayalis have witnessed the birth of other Malayali organizations that cater to the needs of specific communities. For instance, in the Washington D.C. area we have the *Nair Society of Greater Washington in the Commonwealth of Virginia*[10] from April 24, 2004. This organization conducts *Satsangs*, articulated in the form of *Bhajans* in the homes of members, and offers charitable aid to those in need in Kerala. Another organization that is quite active in many parts of the USA and especially in the Washington D.C. region is the *Sree Narayana Mission Center* (SNMC), which celebrates Guru Dev Jayanthi annually along with Onam celebrations and engages in many charitable activities. There are inevitably many other such Malayali organizations that have evolved over time, and while they each have a role to play in bringing people with a common ideology together, they along with the many other religious organizations play a role in keeping the Kerala community segregated and prevent it from mustering strength to unite and speak with one voice.

Professional Networks

The Malayalis have also generated many professional networks but only a few can be listed here. The *All Kerala Medical Graduates[11]* (AKMG) is one of the most prominent among them. AKMG membership is open not only to physicians and dentists who are alumni of medical and dental schools of Kerala, but also to any physician or dentist of Malayali heritage practicing in the United States or Canada. It is noteworthy that a large segment of active AKMG participants hail from medical and dental institutions outside Kerala including those from the United States, Canada and the United Kingdom.

The *National Association of Indian Nurses of America[12]* (NAINA) is a not-for-profit organization in the United States of America. NAINA's primary goal is to unite all Indian nurses and nursing students of Indian origin and heritage as a professional body under one umbrella at the National level. NAINA serves as the official voice for Indian nurses in America and abroad, and focuses on addressing professional nursing issues and concerns.

The *Malayalee Engineers Association in North America[13]* (MEANA) is a non-profit, non-political organization. Reportedly, MEANA was formally established in 1992 with the help of a few Malayali engineers in the Chicago area, and its primary objective is to provide an off-line and on-line meeting place for *"Malayali Engineers"* in the USA, and hopes to enhance the growth of a network of engineers with diverse engineering backgrounds.

The Future

The vision of the various Malayali Associations, organizations and networks is similar. All of them wish to see their organizations and networks grow. They wish to do something good for the community here in the USA and to those in need in Kerala or in India. Above all, they provide a forum to bring their families and children together. They desire to see their children uphold the traditions and culture that have been brought into the USA by their parents. As long as immigration to the USA continues, such traditions and culture will be fostered by the immigrant community. However, with time, and the gradual melting of the cultures and values of the Malayali community into everything that is brewing within the American melting pot, there is bound to be lesser amounts of the second and third generation immigrants as active participants in the above mentioned Malayali Associations, and in some of the religious, and professional organizations. A majority of the children of the early Malayali immigrants are currently not associating with these established organizations. Very few of them play an active role in the Kerala Associations in the USA. They seem perfectly fine to blend into the American fabric without any significant identity that would separate them from being called Americans. The few who associate are truly those who love and cherish their Malayali heritage and traditions and wish to pass the culture and values to their own children.

Notes

1. The words "Keralites" (denoting people of Kerala origin) and "Malayali, Malayalis, Malayalee, or Malayalees" (denoting the people who speak Malayalam - the language of Kerala) are used interchangeably.

2. Dr. Parthasarathy Pillai (Prominent Indian-American and Malayali community leader) and Mrs. Nancy Thomas (Past Vice-President of the Kerala Cultural Society of Metropolitan Washington) of Maryland.

3. *www.fokanaonline.com* (accessed Nov 30, 2012).

4. *http://fomaa.org* (accessed Nov 30, 2012).

5. *http://worldmalayalee.org/* (accessed Nov 30, 2012).

6. *http://www.fiaonline.org/* (accessed Nov 30, 2012).

7. *http://www.nfia.net/* (accessed Nov 30, 2012).

8. *http://www.ncaia.org/* (accessed Nov 30, 2012).

9. *http://www.khnayouth.org/namaha/index.php/en/* (accessed Nov 30, 2012).

10. *http://www.nsgw.info/about-us/* (accessed Nov 30, 2012).

11. *http://www.akmg.org/* (accessed Nov 30, 2012).

12. *http://www.nainausa.com/* (accessed Nov 30, 2012).

13. *http://www.meanausa.org/* (accessed Nov 30, 2012).

Part B
PERSONAL NARRATIVES OF KERALA MIGRANTS

7

Migratory Malayali Expatriates of Africa

IPE MAVUNKAL

"Is it truly Africa?" Minu's mother asked us with disbelief brimming over her face as we drove her home from the Sir Sereste Khama International airport in Gaborone, Botswana. She was visiting us for the first time in 2002 and I could identify with her confusion. As a small boy in India, I had always visualized Africa as a place very different from anywhere else. When we were taught in elementary school about Africa, the "Dark Continent", my visualisation of Africa was rather primitive, with dark-skinned people, dirt roads, wild animals, and so on. That picture slowly started changing when a considerable number of people from Kerala began moving to Africa in the 1970s in search of lucrative jobs. Some of my family friends employed inAfrican countries returned homewith swelling bank accounts. I started viewing Africa slightly differently. I still cherished the idea that the people who lived there were primitive, but I realised that one could find opportunities towork, (mainly in the form of teaching jobs) and make big bucks.

The change happened so gradually it was practically subconscious. An interest in Africa and African people germinated while I doing my doctoral studies in Mumbai. My primary source of information in those days was disseminated in articles I read in *Newsweek* magazine, which was freely available in the library. I was moved by the sufferings of people who were affected by famine in places like Ethiopia. The pictures I saw were very disturbing, and I felt an urge to travel to Africa in the future. I had no idea how that would happen, but I knew that I wanted to assist in some measure to help the people of Africa. My first trip to Africa in 1997 did not fetch me the job that was promised, and it took a little longer before my dreams to live in Africa became a pleasant reality.

When I boarded South African Airways in 1998 from Mumbai for Africa, I knew that it was the beginning of a new chapter that would be dramatically different from the life I had lived up until then. The consecutive two years that my family and I spent in Cape Town, as I did post-doctoral research at the University of Cape Town, made it to the list of highlights of my entire life. The true Africa impressed me greatly, but those rich experiences are outside the scope of this chapter. I fondly treasure the memories from Cape Town and South Africa, so much so that I always refer to Cape Town as my second home.

It was while we were in South Africa that I tried my fortune in finding a job in Botswana. It materialized in a rather dramatic way and I left for Gaborone, the capital of Botswana to take up a teaching position as a lecturer at the University of Botswana. My family joined me couple of months later to embark on the second leg of our African adventure. In Botswana I met a number of Malayalis in Botswana who had migrated from other African countries and were prospering there.

One of the first Malayalis I met in Gaborone was a very successful businessman by the name of Rajan. He had come and introduced himself to me after the first church service I attended in Botswana. He came along with his family to visit me at the hotel where I was staying, and invited me for supper to his home. While there, I learned about Rajan's journey to Bostswana. Rajan's story was an amazing tale of success His first trip to Africa was when he was a young boy. He went with his family to Tanzania in the 1960s where his dad was teaching. When his dad chose to move to Zambia like many other Malayalis, he went back to India for further studies. Upon graduation, he returned to Zambia to take up a job as an accountant. In Zambia he had very successful stints with a couple of companies, and then he moved to Botswana where he saw fresh opportunities for advancement. Hestarted his first business in the restaurant industry. Rajan's remarkable knack for sensing the needs and opportunities around him caused him to switch to other business arenas that made him extremely successful. His admirable vision, confident leadership and hard work directed him to diversify his business investments. Since then his whole family has moved to New Zealand for his children's higher education, but Rajan maintains his business base in Botswana and continues to be a shining example for aspiring business people.

'Babychayan', as he was affectionately known by Malayalis,invited me to his home for supper the very first week I landed in Botswana. The dinner table was literally overflowing with all kinds of dishes from Kerela. It was beyond my comprehension that Babychayan's wife would find enough time to prepare so many dishes after her teaching responsibilities at the university. I quickly learned that dinner meetings at Malayali homes were a culinary delight, as the women subtly competed with each other to display their skills with mouth-watering Malayali delicacies.

Babychayan first traveled to Tanzania in 1960 when it was still a British colony. While he was working in North India, a relative working in Tanzania got Babychayan a job as an accountant. The many years he spent in Tanzania etched an unforgettable journey in his life which he narrated with amusing charm. During that period he saw Tanzania transitioning from British rule to independence. He married and had children. In his career heplayed key roles to elevate several companies to expand to great profitability. By the late 1970s, the political climate in the region was changing and the value of the shilling started spiralling down. These and other inevitable changes caused many expatriates to contemplate alternate options for jobs or careers in Southern African nations. Some decided to migrate to Western nations like the UK, US, Canada, Australia and New Zealand. A close relative and friend in Botswana was instrumental in Babychayan scouting thatland for better opportunities. He found a job in the only university in Botswana. So in 1983 he moved with his family to spend the next 21 years in the comforts of Botswana.

When I first met 'Thampu Sir', (as he was known among Malayalis) he had already retired, but his wife Annie was still teaching High School. Their youngest son was still with them, but their two older childrenhad already left the nest for greener pastures in the West. I have heard many fascinating stories from my Malayali friends in Africa but this particular one Thampu Sir shared stands out as an incident in a comedy. In 1965, Thampu Sir was posted in a place called Goba, the then administrative capital of Bale province in Ethiopia. The place was accessible only by airplane. It was a propeller-driven DC Dakota aircraft that was used to transport people. And everything else! Wooden benches were placed on one side of the fuselage for passengers to sit with the opposite side 'reserved' for other things including live animals. What an interesting plane journey it would have been! In-flight entertainment included 'live' music from goats, chickens, etc. As the plane descended to land, one could only see a grass patch instead of the landing strip. The plane WOULD NOT land when it first came down. This strategy was to ensure that the sound from the aircraft would scarea way the animals that are grazing in the grass patch. Then the plane came in for a landing a second time when the landing strip was finally cleared.

Thampu Sir was teaching in Calcutta when he made the move to Africa through an Ethiopian recruiting agencyin 1965. He was transported by a chartered flight to Ethiopia via Yemen. The Indo-Pak War was still going on. To the relief of all on board, the tense journey eventually ended in Ethiopia safely and without incident. Many Malayalis made their way to seize job opportunities in Ethiopia in the 1960s and 1970s. Similar migration of Malayalis to other countries in northern, western and eastern Africa occurred in this period of time.

Situations changed in many of the African countries where Malayali migrant populations were enjoying the fruit of the land. Several destabilizing factors including the Ugandan war in the late 1970s, contributed to all the expatriates including Malayalis scurrying to find greener and safer pastures in Africa. A large number of Malayalis who went to Ethiopia, Nigeria, Tanzania, Kenya and Uganda in the 1960s, 70s and 80s, started moving further south as conditions in those countries became less favorable. They went job hunting in

South Africa and Zambia (which was called Northern Rhodesia before independence).

South Africa was an attractive prospect, although the apartheid policy prevented foreign workers from direct entry into that country. Information about indirect routes to enter South Africa for employment circulated through the grapevine. This provided an impetus for many to seek visas to enter countries like Lesotho and Swaziland and attempt entry into South Africa. South Africans needing service personnel in non-White communities and regions welcomed the job-seekers who showed up at the border crossings. Many Malayalis took advantage of this pathway and became gainfully employed in South Africa. Some who could not make it to South Africa ended up staying back in Lesotho or Swaziland. Many Malayalis found ways to reach Botswana from those countries.

Malayalis who moved to Zambia enjoyed a time of unparalleled luxury in the comforts of the newly formed African democracy. Their lives were filled with stories peppered with unimaginable financial benefits and hair raising adventures. Certain things are too good to last forever. Zambia went through a terrible economic slump when the world copper prices plunged. The friendly atmosphere prevailing in the neighboring Botswana was a natural attraction for the next leg of migration for those in Zambia. Many teachers, including Thampu Sir, made their way to Botswana while others traveled the known routes to reach South Africa.

Both Thampu Sir and Annie are now retired and are enjoying a quiet life in the suburbs of Kottayam, Kerala with occasional visits to their children abroad. Their youngest son who is still in Botswana is contemplating a move to the US. Both his siblings are happily settled in the US, as is the case of many other Malayali children who grew up in Botswana.

Malayalis who landed in Botswana found it easy to adapt to their new surroundings. In general, life in Botswana was quite simple and manageable. The friendliness of the people coupled with gracious responses from government authorities made life even more enjoyable in this land-locked country. The political stability of the country, promises of a steady income with a prospect for their children to seek higher education in the West,was a wonderful bargain. There was a great incentive to put down roots in Botswana. Malayalis who sought permanent residence permits received them without any bureaucratic hassle. Others even acquired Botswana citizenship. I have seen numerous Europeans and some Americans taking a Motswana bride from the country that proudly presented the Miss Universe of 1999 but I know of no Malayali who has married one.

Private schools were the schools of choice for the majority of Malayali families, although free education was available for all in the government schools. Botswana followed the Cambridge schooling system, and Malayali children are known for their academic excellence. The private schools were primarily in the capital city of Gaborone, and therefore Malayalis working in other areas had no other choice but to send their children to the local government schools. The trend for Malayali parents sending their children for higher education back to India slowly diminished and the colleges and universities in the United States became the preferred destination. Africans in general prefer colleges and universities in the UK for their higher education, and Botswana was no exception. However, Indians favored US over UK for their children's undergraduate or graduate studies. Many probably did this with the hope of retiring in the American dream they had instilled in their children. Babychayan's children were the early trend-setters. They left the nest for the US to secure highly valued American degrees. They completed their education on time, secured good jobs and are well settled with their families. Happily retired, Babychayan and his wife share times with their children and grandchildren in the US. Occasionally old friends like us visit him and we sit over a cup of tea to reminisce the wonderful memories from a time well spent in Gaborone.

Botswana was quiet and very peaceful. It was interesting for us who came from India to note that even the President of the country was accessible to the common man. Thampu Sir's wife, Annie fondly remembers the then President Masire visiting their school. His Excellency (as they were addressed) chatted with each staff member individually. Everybody was surprised when he went straight to meet the kitchen staff before even meeting with the headmaster of that school. One could meet the President in shopping malls and other public places without a security guard accompanying him.

The majority of the Malayalis I met in Botswana had at least one stopover in another African country before landing in the virgin land of Botswana. The severe unstable political and economic environments of many African countries prompted these Malaylis to test their fortunes in Botswana. Many who landed in Botswana through mutual contacts or direct recruitment from India soon realized the beauty of a laid-back life with good returns. A friendly group of people and a government with practically no corruption added to the ease of an enjoyable life in Botswana. In all of my travels, I have never come across an airport friendlier than the small Sir Sereste Khama International airport in Gaborone. The police carried no guns and the police stations entertained people with respect and ill-treated no one.

Botswana's prosperity primarily stemmed from the discovery of diamonds soon after the British left in 1966. Botswana produces 30 percent of all the diamonds mined in the world. The founding president, Sir Seretse Khama, was a man of great vision. His judicious use of national resources saw this land-locked country making enviable progress. Botswana's beef industry enjoys ready markets in Europe because of the high quality of its meat. Though diamonds and beef are the major revenue earners for Botswana, very few Malayalis were employed in these industries. Neither were Malayalis with business inclinations tapping into the great potential of the thriving tourism industry. South Africans and Europeans dominated that sector. However, Malayalis were primarily engaged in meeting some of the very basic needs of that country. Education was one big needy sector, and Malayali teachers contributed immensely to it. A vast majority of the expatriates teaching in secondary schools were Malayalis. They were able to invest their lives in educating the emerging generation who needed to be prepared to take up responsibilities in nation building. Though the people of Botswana may recognize Malayalis only as Indians they fondly acknowledge the great role Indians played in the government's initiative to invest in their younger generation.

Some of the teachers who had entrepreneurial inclinations wasted no time in merely teaching in secondary or higher secondary schools. Fruits of a capitalistic system became too tempting for many others who witnessed attractive changes in the lifestyles of some of their Malayali colleagues in business. Those who moved to the greener pastures of business started to bring their relatives and friends from their homeland. Fascinating stories abound through the grapevine. Those who were successful in their business endeavors continued to expand their business territories. It is interesting to note that I didn't come across a single Malayali who had invested back in Kerala (or India) to advance their business. Some of them were happy to expand only within Botswana but others crossed the border to make ripples in the South African economy. Still some others were bold enough to venture into the markets of other African countries. Although most of them invariably built houses back in Kerala, the majority of them invested in properties in places where they thought it could bring better returns. Thus it is not uncommon to find Malayalis who were very successful in investing in Dubai or in the US.

Localization is an inevitable result in any country where the services of expatriates are employed. As more and more nationals started graduating with honours and degrees, existing expatriate teachers had to make way for the qualified local citizens. Interestingly, non-renewal of teaching contracts did not diminish the number of Malayalis existing in Botswana but the opposite. In the earlier days most Malayalis worked for government and parastatal organizations. Currently the larger share of Malayalis living in Botswana is associated with some kind of business enterprise. The largest grocery chain in Botswana is owned by a Malayali who employs lots of Malayalis!

I fondly look back at the time I spent in Gaborone, Botswana. From the myriad of stories heard from other Malayalis, I assume that most of the African countries provided a wonderful life in all aspects at some point in time. However, deterioration of those conditions prompted migration from one place to another and to many that migration culminated in Botswana. Although I have only outlined three people, the stories of other Malayalis have remarkable parallels. I saw a very small percentage of Malayalis who came directly from

India to Botswana. Barring some exceptions, the younger generation who grew up or studied in Botswana were not influenced by the charm of the backwaters or coconut trees or any other attraction to relocate back to Kerala. Most of them joined the migratory flock headed to Western countries to nest and to raise the next generation as they themselves somehow lost their ancestral identity.

I truly miss Botswana and long to go back there someday just to sit under the shade of a *marula* tree to enjoy its pleasant smell saturating the atmosphere and to suck the juice out of the flesh surrounding the seed.

8

New Horizons for Malayalis in Australia

ROSHAN VARUGHESE

Introduction

Malayalis have taken up residence in every part of the globe and Australia is no exception. It has been more than three decades since the first Malayalis arrived in Australia. It was a time when foreigners in were in limited numbers in Australia. As with every other developed country, Malayalis have faced oppression whether it is in the form of racism, repression or ridicule. Due to the long drawl in the Australian accent, sometimes words did not seem to be what they were to migrant Malayalis. I recall a Malayali telling me that when he met an Australian back in 1975, he was asked, "Have you come here to *day*?" Unfortunately, the question was understood as "Have you come here to *die*?" For which the immediate response of the Malayali was a firm "No". Since then Australia has developed into a community with a rich multicultural heritage which has learnt to accommodate the interests of migrants from different nations. In addition, Australia still remains as one of the countries with the best balance of work and lifestyle which continues to attract migrants from the Asia Pacific region.

Waves of Immigration

The main motive for Malayali migration is the hope of pursuing better employment and lifestyle opportunities. This is the primary reason behind the brain drain from Kerala to the rest of the world. Malayalis have had to look for good opportunities which were not available in their own country. Malayalis have been able to acclimatize to new environments with relative ease. Among Indians, Malayalis have always known to be hardworking with a desire to invest their savings for a better future. This explains why Kerala receives the highest influx of non-resident foreign remittances compared to the rest of India.

The first wave of Malayalis to arrive in Australia was nurses. That profession was and still is in great demand. Most of the Malayali nurses work in hospitals of the government health care system. A significant number of these nurses have, together with their husbands, been able to successfully establish quality care facilities for the aged. The majority of these facilities are located in the south eastern region of Victoria. In the late 1980s and early 1990s, there was a second wave of migration when a substantial number of Malayalis arrived in Australia from Africa due to the unstable or volatile political and economic conditions in multiple countries of that continent. Malayalis from Africa have established small retail businesses in Australia while the remainder have continued with their occupations in teaching and administration.

The most recent influx of new Malayalis arriving in Australia is international students. They have seized the opportunity to come and study at institutions of higher learning in Australia with the hope of eventually gaining employment upon graduation and putting down roots here. The reality is that the majority of them are unable to obtain employment and therefore need to move on to Singapore, the Middle East or return to India. These students could benefit from early moral support and sound guidance from the local Malayalis to ensure they are enrolled in the right programs of study that will give them a hopeful future in Australia.

The Malayali presence in Australia is significantly on the rose. Analysis of the demographics of the Australian population reveals that both the Indian and the Malayali numbers have more than tripled in the last two decades.

Demographic of Malayalis in Australia

	Total Population	%	Indo Australian Population	%	Malayali Population (Approx)	%
1990	17086200	100%	80130	0.47%	16026	0.094%
2001	18769249	100%	95452	0.51%	19090	0.10%
2010	22342400	100%	295362	1.32%	59072	0.26%

Source: Australian Bureau of Statistics 2011.

Cultural Expressions

There are currently Malayali associations formed in every state of Australia. The Malayalee Association of Victoria was formed in 1976 when there were only 30 Malayali families in the whole state. Prior to 1976, the existing groups of families would meet in each other's houses on weekends and enjoy a day together. They would also spend school holidays in the camping sites of Yarrawonga close to the border of New South Wales. This community feeling has been a great help in instilling cultural values and traditions of Kerala in the second generation Australian Malayalis.

Malayalis born in a different country other than India often seem to struggle in accepting their heritage roots. The clash of cultures – Australian culture and Malayali culture coupled with peer pressure, puts the second generation in a great deal of stress and tension. However, from my personal experience and observation, it is evident that the second generation Malayalis who have been brought up and exposed to Keralite culture and tradition seem to have a better understanding of their parents' generation and are able to process issues with them. This emerging generation can be categorized as a new and improved version of the Malayalis who originally migrated to Australia. Having already grasped the Australian accent and way of life, the younger generationhas made great strides in their personal careers. While some choose to succeed their parents in the family business, others choose to be professionals in their field and may move to settle far away from their nest.

During festivals like Onam and Christmas, families and the youth come together and participate in various programs and enjoy delicious

Kerala-style food prepared and served to guests. There is a great deal of involvement by different family members to ensure the success of these events. In a Malayali Christian congregation the youth play a great part in the church's operations. Whether it is delivering sermons, singing or mastering the audio-visual processes of the church, the youth willingly participate thus ensuring that the church is growing with the new generation. Today the Malayalee Association in Victoria boasts of more than 500 families and are still growing. It brings Malayali families together to ensure that youth are able to experience their heritage, culture and traditions.

If anyone is ever invited to a Malayali's house for a meal, it is not an opportunity to miss. Malayalis are famous for their cuisine as well as the level of spiciness. I have on many occasions been invited to an authentic Malayali feast and have relished the dishes. Be it *idli* and *sambar* for breakfast or rice and beef curry for lunch, the mix of spices coupled with the aroma it generates is a treat for the senses. Be prepared to be assaulted by the level of spiciness of some dishes. I was left teary eyed and with a watery nose on many instances after consuming a plate of spicy meats. Tomato chutney, *appam* and egg curry, *wadda*, and *inju theyeyal* are some of the favourite dishes I have come across. The Malayali youth born here have fondly nicknamed some of the dishes to their fancy.

There are numerous Indian grocers located throughout Australia that cater to the Kerala cuisine of spices and condiments required to prepare their tasteful dishes. These grocers are family businesses run by Malayalis that supply our community. Even my Australian neighbour purchases food items from these grocers. Malayalis also tweak their dishes to include other cuisines. The second generation Australian Malayalis enjoy Italian and modern Australian cuisine with a hint of spice to tickle the taste buds and add some flavour to an otherwise ordinary dish. Even the traditional Australian barbeque has been modified with some flavor and zing which has found its place in the hearts of some local Australians.

Remarkable Success

Australia being one of the youngest countries in the world has numerous investment opportunities and foreigners have taken an avid interest in reaping the benefits of a growing economy. Moreover, small and medium enterprises constitute more than 70 percent of the local economy. Malayalis have their fair share in this whether it is in real estate, development, healthcare services or retail industries. I have come across numerous Malayalis who are reaping the rewards for all the sweat and labor they have exerted over the years. One such example is Mr. Chacko Samuel (Sam) who is based in one of the premier suburbs in Victoria. Sam has been in the Aged Care industry since 1988. Prior to this, he had accumulated extensive experience working in the various small and medium enterprises in Melbourne. Originally from India, Sam and his wife Kunjumol through teamwork have built up a successful business over more than two decades and currently employ over 60 staff members, many of whom are Malayalis. Sam has been blessed with great business acumen and has utilized it to create a successful and effective business portfolio. Sam is currently exploring the potential for growth and expansion of Aged Care in other areas of Melbourne.

Similar stories can be said about other notable Malayalis in Victoria, many of whom have their core business in Aged Care. Still other Malayalis have their roots in real estate with plenty of opportunities in Australia to develop existing land and build numerous townhouses or apartments.

However, we need to acknowledge that success is not purely measured by monetary worth. There are many other successful Malayalis who have put their stamp on Australian history. Mathai Varghese, a mathematician affiliated with the Australian Research Council and University of Adelaide was elected to the Australian Academy of Science. Peter Varghese, a politician is currently the Australian High Commissioner to India. George Varughese from Sydney was one of the first Malayalis to arrive in Australia almost 50 years ago.[1] He helped establish the Malayalee Association in Sydney. He is currently involved with the World Malayalee Council and has also been appointed as an Ambassador of Peace by the Universal Peace Federation.[2]

We hear stories of how immigrants come to a new country and facehardships in order to start a new beginning. It is not an easy task and it takes great determination to continue to move forward. I often hear the story of how the older Malayalis first came to Australia with a mere eight dollars. The first generation Malayalis toiled night and day, and saved and sacrificed many of the finer luxuries in life in order to ensure that their children would get a good education and gainful employment. Most Malayali youth have attended some of the most prestigious private schools in Australia. Although most second generation Malayalis do not complete a post graduate degree, many of them earn an undergraduate degree in order to pursue the career of their choice. The older first generation vicariously expect the younger generation to accomplish the goals in life which they were unable to fulfil. However, this push is what is required in order to ensure that the younger generation attains a secure future. It has been suggested that if one saves the price of a cup of coffee a day, in a few years' time, a person would have sufficient money for a down payment on a house! The younger folk pursue their interests in travel and adventure and choose to spend their vacations overseas exploring cultures and traditions of other nations. They developed a keen interest in understanding the lifestyle and values practiced in other countries.

Conclusion

Australia is a great and constantly evolving country. Malayalis need to do their part to ensure that Australia continues to grow. It can be said with confidence that the world is a better place because of the hardwork, dedication and skills of the Malayali diaspora community. We need to take great pride in how we make a positive contribution to the economy of the country. We are expected to make sacrifices in order to ensure that our future is secure in this country. We will always acknowledge the rich heritage of India and take the steps to ensure that our community in Kerala is always safe and secure.

It is truly a great feeling to be able to meet a Malayali when shopping, or dining, or simply out for a stroll in Australia. We can only imagine how it would have been thirty years ago when we were significantly smaller in number and unaware of the whereabouts of another Malayali. We need to be grateful that technology in communication has helped make our world grow smaller and closer.

Australia is a great land down under and is open to see many more of our community migrate here.

Notes

1. For more of the story, see *www.migrationheritage.nsw.gov.au/exhibition/belongings/varughesegeorge/ (accessed Nov 30, 2012).*

2. Ramsey, Alan. 2005."All for the Sum Total of Nothing" in Sydney Morning Herald. February 19.

9

The Oldest Malayali in Continental Europe: *The Story of a Quest*

Prabhu Guptara

Introduction

In researching the subject of Malayalis in Continental Europe, I discovered there was a total absence of any written material on the subject. Contacts made with community organizations, mass media and social media equally yielded nothing. Through enquiries in my personal network, I located Jacob Matthan, the oldest living Malayali in continental Europe.[1] Jacob lives in Finland, one of the most northerly European countries. He resides in Oulu, the largest city in northern Finland and the sixth largest city in the country with a population of 146,000. Conducting multiple interviews with Jacob and through extensive research on the Internet I have been able to craft this chapter.

The Early Years

Jacob descends from a distinguished family. His paternal grandfather who came to be known as 'Mysore Matthan' graduated from Madras Christian College in Tambaram, Madras. He had an illustrious career in the Mysore Civil Service, and rose to be First Member of the Council of His Highness, the Maharaja of Mysore, and was awarded the title Dewan Bahadur. During his long career, he was responsible for the establishment of several industries in the state and served as Chairman of a number of corporations.

Jacob's maternal grandfather was K.C. Mammen Mappillai, who had only one daughter who eventually became Jacob's mother. Her eight brothers were K.M. Cherian, K.M. Oommen, K.M. Varghese Mappillai, K.M. Eapen, K.M. Chacko, K.M. Philip, (former President of the World YMCA), K.M. Mathew and K.M. Mammen Mappillai. The industrial empire they built includes MRF, Malayala Manorama, several plantation companies and many other industrial enterprises, K.C. Mammen Mappillai and Mysore Matthan studied together at Tambaram. He had wanted to join his two friends, Mysore Matthan and Chandy (another distinguished Malayali) in the Mysore Administration but K.M. Varughese Mappillai, who founded Malayala Manorama, requested his nephew to return to Kerala to help him run the newspaper. It was the friendship of Mysore Matthan and K. C. Mammen Mappillai which led to the marriage of Jacob's father and mother.

The story of Jacob Matthan's European connection starts with his being sent by his parents to study in the UK in 1963 after receiving his Bachelor's degree at St. Stephen's College in New Delhi. Why was he sent to the UK for further studies? It was partly because his father and others in his family had studied at Cambridge and London, and partly because, in those days, the UK was the destination of choice for further studies by Indians. As a result, there were lots of Malayalis in England in the 1960s. Many migrated on to the USA or Canada; others married Britishers and were absorbed into the mainstream of British life. The question of how many Malayalis married non-Indians has never been researched. However, a large number kept their Malayali identity, which is why there are so many Malayali organizations in the UK today.

During the course of his studies in England, Jacob shared an apartment with four other Indians in London. One of the Indians had a girlfriend from Finland. This lady's friend, Annikki, and Annikki's sister came to London for a visit in December 1963. When Jacob set eyes on Annikki, it was love at first sight and Jacob says "this has not changed in 49 years!"

Immediately after completing the Graduateship of the Plastics Institute of England (Grad PI) in 1966, Jacob joined the Rubber and Plastics Research Association of Great Britain (RAPRA), the government research body. Later Jacob was awarded the Associateship, APRI. When the Plastics and Rubber Institutes merged in 1978, this led to the award of the Fellowship, FPRI, making Jacob the youngest Fellow ever at the age of 35. That Institute later merged with the Ceramics and Metals Institutes to become the Institute of Materials, thus making Jacob a Fellow of the Institute of Materials (FIM).

Meanwhile, news of Jacob's feelings for Annikki had set off a reaction in his conservative Malayali family.[2] On the other hand, Annikki's family had no opposition to their marriage whatsoever. Her elder brother and one of her younger sisters attended the wedding in January 1967 in Shrewsbury, Shropshire, in England. Jacob recalls what transpired, "I was blessed to enter a loving family headed by a devout Christian. However, the day we got married, the situation on my side of the family changed as my mother declared to all, "what God has put together, let no man put asunder" which meant that Annikki was welcomed into the family as a daughter.

Jacob and Annikki's two older children, Susanna Mariam and Jaakko (Jacob), were born in England, in 1967 and 1968 respectively. Jacob worked at RAPRA until 1969, when he decided to return to India, and settle in Madras, where Jacob and Annikki's two younger children, Joanna and Mikael were born. The plan for his return to India was to form the first professional consultancy in India with his brother who had by this time obtained his Ph.D. in Polymer Science from England. Polymer Consultancy Services eventually created many other service organizations around that base. Jacob's first customer was MRF Tyres and, immediately following that all the other subsidiary and ancillary companies. Jacob then ventured outside that "family base" and initially began working with companies such as Carborundum Universal, and then with a whole host of major multinational companies. However, his main goal and task focused on bringing fresh ideas and new industrial projects to India and to raise the information base within India through his continuing links with RAPRA. Jacob began publishing RAPRA Abstracts in India which significantly increased his profile and firmly established the consultancy as the leading organization in the "polymers knowledge base" in India. In his assessment, "no major project in the fields of rubber and plastics including the Indian Petrochemical Corporation was without our stamp". He was also given the responsibility of running the Malaysian Rubber Bureau as another Malayali friend from his RAPRA days in England, Tan Sri B. C. Sekhar, originally from Trichur, was Chairman of the Malaysian Rubber Research and Development Board.

Move to Finland

Jacob's first visit to Finland was en route to India in 1969. The family travelled by ship taking the long route via the Cape. He vividly remembers his trip, "as we drove from Helsinki to Oulu, a drive of 600 km, with the midnight sun, I was astonished by the beauty of the country, of never ending green forests and blue lakes from south to north. That beauty has remained unchanged for the last 43 years, despite efforts by some Finnish industrialists to pollute the country!"

Jacob's second visit in 1975 turned out to be four or five months longer than intended. In India, Prime Minister Indira Gandhi had declared a National Emergency, as a result of which Jacob and his family were stuck in Finland because of some misunderstandings regarding Annikki's status in India. In their third visit in 1979, Jacob gained a clearer understanding of how the Finns operated and how Finnish society functioned.

With Annikki's parents getting older and India becoming increasingly more and more corrupt, Jacob with his family decided to move from India to settle in Finland in 1984. Jacob recalls how difficult it was to live and operate in India, "I was disillusioned with how India was turning out. You had to live within the system, and many of us couldn't do that – we couldn't live with spending the whole day greasing the system". Though Jacob moved with his family to Finland he continued to hold on to his Indian passport.[3]

When they arrived in Finland in 1984, Annikki found that their two younger children, being Indian nationals would not be entitled, for a minimum of two years, to all the benefits afforded to Finnish and European children. So she applied for Finnish citizenship for them. Within days of the children being granted Finnish passports, the Indian Embassy in Helsinki demanded that Jacob return the children's Indian passports as it was thought that they were not entitled to dual citizenship.

Instead of returning the passports to the Indian Embassy, Jacob sent the passports by Registered Mail directly to the President of India saying that although his wife wanted their children to have Finnish citizenship, Jacob wanted them to retain their Indian citizenship as well. Jacob had also sent a copy of his appeal letter to the Indian Prime Minister. The Prime Minister's Office replied immediately saying that the children could not have dual citizenship. Meanwhile, the President of India had forwarded Jacob's letter of appeal to the Ministry of Law. After careful investigation of the facts, the Ministry of Law informed Jacob that the children could have dual citizenship until the age of 18.

A copy of Jacob's letter to the President was forwarded to the Indian Ambassador in Finland who quickly responded to Jacob with an apology for the Embassy's over hastiness. The children were granted dual citizenship which meant they could enjoy Finnish benefits and yet travel to India without any problems using their Indian passports. However, Jacob received an official admonishment for sending Indian passports internationally by postal mail! As a result of all this, the Ambassador who was a Malayali became a life-long friend and together they facilitated a cooperative arrangement between the University of Oulu and the Indian Institute of Science, Bangalore.

The Career Season

Upon moving to Finland, Jacob joined the University of Oulu as Researcher and Scientific Editor in the Microelectronics Laboratory. Within three years, he became the Laboratory Manager and soon after, the Chief Engineer. Jacob worked as the Scientific Editor not only for the Microelectronics Laboratory but also for the entire Electrical Engineering Department, the Physics Department and the Biology Department. To cope with the volume of work that ensued, Annikki and Jacob established the company *Findians OY* in 1992 to handle this work as well as similar work from the Finnish State Research Centre, Nokia Mobile, Nokia Networks and other major Finnish multinationals.

As a parallel operation, Jacob started to introduce India to Finnish organizations and vice versa while promoting Finnish technology to India. He established Findians Briefings as a monthly printed in-house newsletter with a circulation of 110. Then the newsletter went online and the circulation soared to 6,000 after only a half a dozen issues. As the associated website became more and more popular, Findians Briefings was converted into a fortnightly web letter in 1994, and had a worldwide readership of around 80,000 by the end of 1999. With such a large base on the internet, *Findians OY* became the first major Associate of Amazon for both Amazon US and Amazon UK, picking up a 15 per cent commission on all book sales linked by his website to Amazon. Jacob credits his professional and business success to his broad educational experience in India and England in Mathematics, Physics and Chemistry, coupled with the entrepreneurial heritage of his family.

Jacob and Annikki were social activists and they began addressing two critical issues in Finnish society: corruption and xenophobia. They used the internet domain *Findians.com* to expose acts of corruption among judges, police, bureaucrats, lawyers, social workers, and politicians. Their main correspondent was publicly persecuted for her column "Finnish ?? Oligarchy = Democracy ??" The Finns are experts in creating an image and the media exposure kept blowing up that image. As a result, the attack on Findians continued.

Jacob still has a few hundred active web sites, and runs several blogs and many Google Groups. A site named "Findians", or linked with it, even today, usually goes to the top of the search engines in a matter of hours simply because of the enormous number of links to that word and the previous 5000+ sites. That is because Jacob set up internet pages on all his diverse fields of interest— about forty of them. Each subject covered many internet pages, and his pages appeared at the top of almost every search engine. He was not cheating the robots but each was a genuine page. Keep in mind that there was no *Google* then but there were several hundreds of search engines.

This was also long before Search Engine Optimization and other such methods which are used nowadays to get to the top listing in search engines.

Though Jacob had remarkable sales of all the books he covered in his web pages, he had his comeuppance because of the fact that the media does not have freedom in Finland. Their Internet Service Provider warned Jacob and Annikki that their internet account was being jeopardized because "the authorities" were watching whether the Matthans were over-stepping the bounds of media freedom of Finland. Under that threat the Matthans moved their domain to an Internet Service Provider in Canada and registered their domain name in India in 1999. However, in the middle of 2003, spammers overran that domain name ("5000 spam mails in a day!"), and they were forced to close it, but the "Findians" concept continues to be active. Jacob and Annikki have stopped several who tried to usurp that name over the years.

The Findians Google Group is still in existence, the Findians current phone number is being used by Jacob, and many of the articles and web pages that started under the Findians domain name have been moved to the personal web servers of "jmatthan", "amatthan" as well as *http://koti.netplaza.fi/~findians/index.html*

The Retirement Season

Jacob decided to retire early so as to assist his wife to look after her aged mother and their youngest son who was ill. That was so demanding that Jacob chose to scale-down *Findian Briefings*. With his long-time interest in helping foreigners, he geared his activities to ethnic minority work.

Jacob joined the Oulu Sports Department to head a project called, "Will You Play With Me?" to enhance social integration of ethnic minorities in Oulu through sports. With hundreds of foreigners immigrating to Finland, he used a variety of sports – basketball, boxing, football, rowing, skiing, swimming – to help integrate foreigners, especially refugees from war-torn countries into Oulu and Finnish society. Despite winning many awards, the Oulu Administration unfortunately did not fund "Will You Play With Me?" So, when Jacob gave that up, there was no one to carry it on.

Jacob and Annikki are well known in the immigrant community of Finland. First, because of Jacob's two best seller books, Seven Years Hard Labour in Finland—A Finnish University (published in 1994) and Handbook for Survival in Finland (jointly authored with Annikki in 1994). Second, their fortnightly web Findians Briefings was being read by most foreigners. So, it is not surprising that Jacob was elected in 1998 by English speakers in Finland to represent them on ETNO, the Ethnic Minorities Advisory Board. He also represented the whole of Northern Finland on the Finnish Sports Federation Tolerance Board which was chaired by Tapio Korjaus, the Javelin Gold medallist at the 1996 Olympic Games in Atlanta. In order to try and fight racial discrimination, in 2000 Jacob organized an International ETHICS 2000 Conference with the theme, "Effective Tools for Harmonization and Integration using Culture and Sports".

What caused Jacob to withdraw from his high-profile social activities after the ETHICS 2000 Conference was a physical attack on him and a threat to his two grandchildren. The attack was organized by a group of people who were unhappy with the outcome of the Conference. He did not report any of this to the Police because he was convinced that the Finnish Police are often as racist as the attackers.

In 1998, Jacob was invited to join the Ethnic Minorities Advisory Group chaired by Finland's Secretary for Labour which influenced the Constitution of the country that came into force in 2000, and significantly shaped the European Union's 2003 Anti-Discrimination Conference. With a Zambian and a Chinese engineer, Jacob had formed an unofficial low-profile voluntary organization called CHAFF (Chamber for Assistance of Finns and Foreigners) in Oulu in 2004. Jacob feels that "It was a huge success as we strove to help people regardless of who they were Finns or foreigners. It was just a gathering of people with no chairperson, no membership fees, no managing committees and no funding. There were no positions or money to fight over!" When I asked Jacob why Finns needed help, he replied that "Finland is a strongly class-oriented society. So, poor Finns need the same assistance as the ethnic minorities". Many organizations have been spawned by CHAFF such as the O-India Google Group for Indians in Oulu, the Thai Association of Oulu, etc. The O-India Google Group with about 250 members in Oulu still helps each other regardless of their origin in India. About 50 percent of the members are Hindus and the rest are Muslims and Christians. They organize various festivals like *Divali, Id and* Christmas *in order to* promote our culture. Jacob enjoys the respect of being a gracious and generous grandfatherly figure among them. Jacob handed over the leadership of CHAFF to a younger group, but it folded because they lacked the dedication to serve others.

After handing over CHAFF, Jacob started to help Indian engineers who had been sent to work in Finland. They arrived in the sub-freezing temperatures of Northern Finland often with no bank accounts and no knowledge of how to go about opening one in Finland, inadequate shoes, no warm clothes and not even any housing! Jacob initially found himself managing a house for 18 Indians which he called L&T House because the first group he helped were from Larsen & Toubro in India. "Houses" for other companies followed and soonsnowballed in number. In 2011, Jacob ended up managing as many as sixty such Houses in locations as far away as Tampere and Helsinki. Now that he is in his seventies, Jacob is gradually downsizing. Furthermore, the economic downturn of Nokia and Nokia Siemens Networks has meant a fall in the number of Indian engineers attracted to Finland.

As one of Jacob's friends commented, Jacob's basic *modus operandi* has always been to cooperate, collaborate and co-opt: "I came to appreciate that *modus operandi* when I saw on one of Jacob's websites, an entry on the 'Art of Kamutaza Tembo'". Jacob wrote: "Kamu, who hails from Zambia, is an outstanding artist and a dear friend of mine. With his permission I am hosting pictures of his art creations on this page."[4] This sort of inclusive attitude and behavior is why Jacob served also on the Board of the "Same Law For All" Association, and was an advisor of the National Equal Opportunities Network (NEON).

Final Reflections

These are a few of Jacob's reflections on some pertinent questions.

Q: What are your reflections on why Malayalis do so well in foreign countries?

A: In Finland, non-Malayalis tend to give up, go back, or move out while Malayalis are diligent, active and persistent and therefore successful, especially if accompanied by a wife who is employable and/or helping with the family business. I am not saying that the others haven't done reasonably well, just that they have not succeeded as much as the Malayalis have."

Q: What about the children of Malayalis in Finland?

A: Of the 40 or 50 Malayalis in Finland, I find that the children, even when both parents are Malayalis, are more Finnish than Malayali. To the extent that the children have a Malayali culture, it is often due only to their formative years having been spent in India. The others, brought up in Finland may like Kerala cuisine, but probably donot know much about Kerala and its culture. It is worth noting that in earlier years, there was no alternative to the compulsory local Finnish education system, and that situation certainly did not help Malayalis to retain any identification with Malayali culture.

Q: What has driven you and Annikki in your lives?

A: As Findians, we have stood for justice, freedom of speech, fighting for the rights of minorities, good education, promoting the alma maters of school and college, spreading information regarding all facets of life, religious tolerance, secularism, and national pride.

Q: What do you feel about the future?

A: The forces of fascism loom large over us as the extreme right wing in politics gathers strength. I feel that Europe is a failed concept and it will degenerate in a couple of decades to something worse than what happened with the break-up of Yugoslavia. Many Finns do not want to belong to Europe. As was evident in the last election, the Fundamentalist Finns increased their support base from 3% to a high of 18%. This is harbinger of what is to come. Annikki and I held this view even before Finland joined the European Union because we know the thinking of people at the grassroots level. Today, the push is to take Finland into NATO so that the industrialists and politicians can benefit financially. Obviously, against the wishes of the majority of Finns!

Conclusions

As a result of the last few months of research for this chapter, I have come to the following conclusions: First, it does not make sense to separate the Malayali diaspora by country, as diaspora may mean settling in one country but perhaps for only one generation. It may mean onward migration for some, and still for others it may mean a sort of zigzag across countries. In my own case, I was a political exile from India who studied in Scotland for three years, then lived in England for sixteen years and moved to Switzerland seventeen years ago. But three of my four children are currently settled in England, so who knows where I will settle for the last period of my life – perhaps Kerala? In any case, countries are relatively new historical constructs and their boundaries have changed and will no doubt continue to change.

Second, from the 1960s onwards, many Malayalis settled in Continental Europe as a consequence of marrying Europeans perhaps as a result of studying with Europeans. Others settled here as a consequence of finding work as nurses, doctors, engineers, accountants and so on – though, since about 1999, most seem to have come for employment in the field of IT. Third, the children of Malayalis in Europe may or may not understand Malayalam but identify themselves more with the countries in which they are living than with India or with Kerala. Finally, unless there is an effort to document the lives of Indians in the West, everything about them disappears into the mists of time. The challenge to discover the life histories of Mr. Mathew Verghese and Mr. Jacob Matthan is proof of that unfortunate reality.

Notes

1. An older immigrant to Finland, Mathew Verghese, passed away earlier in 2012 of Parkinson's disease. He was married to a Swedish-speaking Finn. He worked for Outokumpu and Postipankki and in both enterprises he rose to Senior Executive positions. However, nothing more is known of him.

2. "My family in India was greatly opposed to my marrying outside of the Kerala roots. Besides my father, two of my mother's brothers were also sent to England to dissuade me. As that had no effect, they just hoped the situation would die down as an infatuation," says Jacob.

3. Most Malayalis in Finland seemed to have retained their Indian passports because the Finnish Language Test is a requirement for Finnish citizenship. Finnish is considered to be one of the most difficult languages on earth to learn. However, Jacob has mastered the language and has two published books to prove it.

4. Jacob's wife, Annikki is a creative artist. Among other things, she designs cakes. Her next book soon to be released is called Edible Art. This will be followed by a book about Snowmen and then a book on creating garden designs.

10

Blossoming of Indian Immigrants in America

ROY P. THOMAS

Introduction

It was the former late US President Ronald Reagan in his inimitable style who called the Indian immigrant community in America, "a model minority". [1] In a very unprecedented occurrence, the US Congress in 2005 unanimously passed Resolution 227 to honor the immigrant Indian community for its great achievements and contributions to American society. The Indian community in the US reached its present status through hard work and perseverance in spite of many adversities and obstacles along the way.

Early Immigrants

After immigrating to Chicago in the 1970s, I attended a meeting of the elders of the Indian community under the auspices of the India League of America. This organization predated most other Indian organizations in America and a few of the American Indian octogenarian members at the meeting had actively supported the Indian independence movement under Mahatma Gandhi. After meeting these venerable old members, I wrote in an Indian news weekly that a historical record of these first generation Indian Americans should be maintained for future generations. I soon received a call from a professor of history at the University of California. She asked me point blank, how I knew that the group I met in Chicago was the first generation of Asian Indians in America. She said that she was a fourth generation Indian in America, and the only other Indian that could possibly claim earlier roots in America than her may be someone from the Malabar coast in the late 17th century.

According to prevailing Hindu socio-religious strictures, the crossing of the "*kala pani*" (black waters) was considered extremely inauspicious and kept them landlocked. Migration out of the *punya bhûmi* ("virtuous, holy or sacred place") was believed to disrupt caste hierarchies and pollute the soul. Such relocation would mean that these aspirants will not be able to preserve their dietary restraints and personal devotion to local deities. Not surprisingly, nearly all of the early arrivals to America bore Christian names. The professor informed me that her research showed that the first sighting of an Asian Indian born on American soil is found in the diary[2] of a Reverend William Bentley of Salem, Massachusetts, recorded on December 29, 1790. His name is unknown but he came to America with Captain John Gibaut who was a frequent visitor to the Malabar Coast for trading in Indian spices. In all probability this unnamed man may have been a Malayali who came with Gibaut to the US by an East India Company ship. There is also a record of six young Indians participating in a July 4th Independence Day parade in 1851 in Salem, Massachusetts[3]. They also came on East India Company ships from the Malabar Coast. All these people disappeared into the darkness of history without a trace.

Many contemporary writers in the West then had erroneously considered the Malabar Coast as part of Madras. It is likely that these were indentured workers who first came to England and then migrated to America. In the course of time, it is possible that a few of these young men married local black women and settled in racially segregated areas in America. Only a genetic search of the African American community will reveal the contribution Kerala has made to their genome, if any. Tapan Mukerjee and John (Sunny) Wycliff who conducted research[4] on the immigrants from India of this period believe that as most of these indentured workers had Christian first names and as there was religious prohibition against orthodox Hindus crossing the oceans, these young men from the Malabar Coast were Christians. They also describe another interesting immigrant from India. This was not a human being but an elephant. In 1796, Captain Jacob Crownshield brought a two-year-old elephant from India and sold it at a substantial profit in New York.[5]

Another prominent early visitor from India to the United States was Swami Vivekananda along with Jain scholar Virchand Gandhi and a Buddhist monk H. Dharmapala from Ceylon came to Chicago on September 15, 1893 for the World Parliament of Religions. The next record of the arrival of Indians to the USA is found in a report in the *San Francisco Chronicle.*[6] The newspaper reported the arrival of four young Punjabis from India arriving by the Nippon Maru ship and landing on the San Francisco Pacific Mall. They were former soldiers in the British Indian army. Following this many peasants from Punjab came to work in the timber mills of California and agricultural lands of Washington State in the early part of the 20th century. A few Indian students and political activists against the British rule in India also arrived in America during the same period.

The hard working Indian peasants saved enough to acquire their own lands to farm and they began to prosper. The local Americans referred to them as Hindus though most of them were Sikhs by religion. They were discriminated against in the new land and were often victims of racial attacks. An organization called Asiatic Exclusion League was formed by the local population to prevent further immigration of Indians to America and to restrict those and their descendants who were already in the US from owning more property or gaining citizenship. Some among the new immigrants to the US formed a revolutionary movement called Ghadr Party to help liberate India from British rule. Soon World War I broke out and the US government very successfully prosecuted and eliminated this group.[7]

This small group of Indians in America had a further set back by the Immigration Act of 1917 which reserved the right of naturalized citizenship to only whites and barred the entrance of Indians to the USA. Few Indians had applied for US citizenship on the basis of a previous US Supreme Court ruling that said "white" means Caucasian. These Indians argued that on strict scientific grounds Indians are racially of the Aryan race and therefore were Caucasians and so were eligible for the US citizenship. On this basis, in 1913 A. K. Mazumdar[8] was given the US citizenship by the local immigration officials in California. He was the first South Asian to receive US citizenship. But all hopes were soon shattered as the Supreme Court clarified its ruling that what they meant by Caucasian was a person of European origin only. In a twisted logic the court argued that though Indians are Caucasians, they are not whites, though dark, they are not blacks, and so either way they are ineligible for US citizenship. Thus, ten years laterMazumdar's citizenship was thus revoked as a result of the Supreme Court decision that no person of East Indian origin can become a naturalized US citizen.

US Congress passed the Asiatic Barred Zone Act in 1917 which prevented legal resident Indians in the US the right to buy property and disallowed further immigration from the region of Asia and the Pacific Islands. President Woodrow Wilson vetoed this bill saying that it violated fairness and natural justice. Unfortunately, Wilson's veto was over ridden by a two-third majority in the US Congress and the law remained in effect until 1946. The racial prejudice of American society of that period is illustrated in a well-publicized incident. Rabindranath Tagore, the 1913 Nobel laureate in literature and the most world-renowned Indian poet of the 20th century was subjected to racial insults by immigration officials at the US-Canadian border in 1929.[9] Tagore protested and cancelled his American journey. Later, both his son and son-in-law studied at the University of Illinois at Urbana Champaign.

Post–1940 Immigrants

Indians in America continued their attempts to get fairness from the government. It is to be gratefully remembered that this small minority of only 1,476 (according to the 1940 Census), gained the support of great men like Pearl Beck, Louis Fischer and Albert Einstein. Finally, Republican Clara Luce and Democrat Emmanuel Celler successfully moved a bill in the US Congress giving the right of citizenship for people of Indian origin. It was signed into law by President Harry Truman in 1946. In 1956, Dalip Singh Saund, a leader of the small Indian community who led this struggle for justice was elected to the US Congress from California and was re-elected two more times with big majorities.[10]

Ironically, the 1946 Act allowed only 100 people from India to immigrate to the US each year and that limit remained until 1965. Some students, priests, and pastors also came to USA during this period. The prominent Indian visitors to Chicago included first Prime Minister Jawaharlal Nehru who addressed the faculty and students of the University of Chicago in 1949. After World War II, many students or academicians came to study or research at reputed universities in Illinois on government scholarships but they were required to return upon completion of their studies.[11] Astrophysicist Professor S. Chandrasekhar, had a distinguished career at the University of Chicago and was awarded Nobel Prize for physics in 1930. Professor K. S. Antony, Philip Kalayil, Mathew Chadrathil, George Eraly, and John Mathai were among the few early Malayali immigrants to Chicago prior to 1955.

Large numbers of Indians immigrated only after the Immigration Reform Act of 1965 which was signed into law by President Lyndon Johnson. This law took away the visa quotas for each country and made immigration permits available on the basis of US need for professionals and skilled workers. With the Vietnam War going on and with a great shortage of doctors and nurses in America, large numbers of Indian professionals were granted immigration visas to the US. Several received many incentives to immigrate. So when I immigrated to the US in 1971, I had not only my visa sponsored by the hospital that offered me residency training in medicine but they also paid for my airfare and accommodation.

Still much discrimination remained in the books and in the public attitude towards the new arrivals from India. Most of our doctors and nurses initially had to work in large cities or county hospitals which were not very attractive to local medical professionals. The best medical residency slots were always reserved for local American graduates. Even after completing residencies, many Indians doctors had to work in inner cities for several years before they could join thriving suburban practices.

In 1981, I went with a Bengali urologist friend to invite the Mayor of Chicago for a special function of Indian physicians. The Mayor's secretary very bluntly informed us that the Mayor will not find time to spend with us. She said our group did not have sufficient voting members and our political contributions were negligible. That was a very humiliating experience for both of us. That humiliation was partly relieved 14 years later when I watched the President of the Unites States, Bill Clinton who made a special trip to Chicago on Air Force One to address the annual convention of Indian physicians in America. By this time, about 42,000 Indian physicians had gained sufficient clout through nation-wide networking and organization. However, there were still many more obstacles in our way. Even as late as 1990, Medicare used to reduce payments to hospitals if there were more than a certain number of foreign physicians in their residency programs.

As Americans came to be aware of these highly skilled Indian physicians and began to relate to more and more of them, the public mood gradually changed to the positive. A Bengali physician was selected to operate on President Reagan for his colon cancer, and President George Bush Sr. was treated by a Malayali cardiologist when his heart went into atrial fibrillation. Indian nurses, especially the Malayali nurses, gained a reputation for their benevolent care and professionalism. Hundreds of Malayali scientists work in leading pharmaceutical and scientific organizations.

Post–1980 Immigrants

As to identity, there is still confusion for the local population as well as in our own minds as to what racial group the Indian immigrant belongs. *Indians* in America always refer to Native Americans. So in the numerous application forms one has to fill, one is unsure what should be written in the space after "race". Indian immigrants often fill the column differently – Asian, Aryan, Dravidian and Caucasian were sometimes used. After much deliberation, in 1980 the US Census Bureau categorized us as *Asian Indians* and we commonly called ourselves Indian Americans.

One must realize that 85% of all Indian immigrants to US came after 1980. Census reports show that in 1900 there were 2,050 Indians in USAbut that number rose to 815,447 in 1980 and to 1. 3 million by 1990. According to the 2000 US Census, Indian Americans are the richest ethnic community in the US and their average household income is 25% above the average American family income. 67% of Indians in the US have college degrees and 40% have postgraduate or professional degrees. According to University of California Berkley Study one-third of Silicon Valley engineers are of Indian origin and 7% of them are founders of successful high tech companies. In 2005, there were 2.3 million Indian immigrants but by 2008 there were about 3.2 million in the US. According to the latest Census in 2010, there are 3.18 million Asian Indians in the United States with the highest educational achievement and highest household income of all ethnic groups in the United States. Over 500,000 of these are from Kerala and Malayalam-speaking. Malayalam remains among the top five languages spoken in Indian American households of all ethnic groups in the United States.[12]

The Indian community in the last century produced two Nobel Prize winners, Dr. Subramanian Chandrasekar in Astrophysics (1930) and Dr. Har Gobind Khorana in Medicine (1968). Kerala-born George Sudarshan was passed over for the Physics Nobel Prize in 2005. The Indian rostrum includes world-class innovators like, Vinod Khosla, (founder of Sun Microsystems), Sabeer Bhatia (founder of hotmail. com), Vinod Dham founder of Intel Pentium chip). Amar Bose not only taught at the prestigious MIT, but also revolutionized audio engineering through Bose Corporation. Raj Chetty became the youngest tenured professor at the Harvard University at the age of 29 in 2009. Indian immigrants lead several large multi-national corporations like United Airlines, US Airways, and Citibank as CEOs or as presidents. When Indra Nooyi became the CEO of Pepsi Corporation, it was a proud moment not only for the Malayali community but for all the women across the world. An Indian American attorney Preet Bharara busted financial frauds on Wall Street and was named among the 100 most influential people in the world by *Time* magazine in 2012. Indians also have the notorious distinction of developing deadly concoction of energy drinks and insider trading scandal by Rajat Gupta.

Indians have also penetrated the Arts and the Media. Zubin Mehtha with his flamboyant and vigorous style is still among America's most favorite music conductors. Night Shyamalan is an Indian American who made his mark as a screen writer, film director and producer. Dr. Deepak Chopra, Dr. Abraham Varghese and Fareed Zakaria have excelled as writers. Indian American astronaut, Kalpana Chowla literally took the fame of this nation and that of her ancestral land to celestial heights before tragedy struck the space shuttle Columbia on February 1, 2003. Indian American astronaut Sunita William holds the record for the longest space flight by a woman. The children of Malayalis have earned their place in spelling bees and national science competitions in the United States. Kim Thayil is an American born lead guitarist of Kerala parents and Dan Nainan is among the leading American stand-up comedian.

Dalip Singh Saund was elected to the US Congress in 1956 when the Indian community was a very tiny minority in USA but later many others continued in political activity at various levels. Dr. Joy Cherian was appointed as Equal Opportunity Commissioner by President Reagan in 1987. Dr. Shashi Tharoor of Malayali heritage, born in London (UK) and educated in the US, rose to be the Under-Secretary General of United Nations and lost a close race to the highest office of Secretary General of UN in 2007. He later returned to India to contest in the Indian election to become Member of Parliament from Thiruvananthapuram and currently serves as Indian Minister of State for human resource development. It was a crowning achievement for the Indian community when a second generation Indian immigrant, Bobby Jindal was elected as the Governor of the State of Louisiana in 2007 and is purported to be a potential future President or Vice President of the United States of America. Nikki Haley is the latest of Indian Americans to achieve notoriety becoming the Governor of the State of South Carolina in 2010. Several others serve as elected officials on school boards to state senators and as advisors to the White House and other national and global agencies.

Conclusion

Indian immigrants can be proud that their children and grandchildren are also doing extremely well in colleges, universities, and in various professions in this country. Indians should be grateful to this great nation which gave them opportunities to blossom, fulfill their dreams and take pride in their achievements. United Sates of America is a rare nation which enables a new immigrant group like ours to achieve so much in one or two generations. America has shown the world how a free society can correct its past short-comings and welcome people of all races, religions and ethnic backgrounds together in the forward march of the human spirit.

Notes

1. Model minority refers to ethnic minorities who achieve a higher degree of success than the average population. This success is typically measured in education, income, and related factors such as low crime rate and high family stability. The term is believed to be used first by sociologist William Peterson in *New York Times Magazine* article titled "Success Story" in January 1966.

2. William Bentley. 1790. *The Diary of Rev. William Bentley D. D. (1759-1819)*, Volume 1, p 228. Available online: *http://archive. org/details/ diaryofwilliambe01bent* (accessed Dec 1, 2012).

3. S. Chandrasekhar, *From India to America,* (La Jolla, CA: Population Institute, 1982).

4. For history of early arrivals of Asian Indians in America, see *http://www. iafpe. org/php/showNewsDetails. php?linkid=5&newsid=5* (accessed Nov. 30, 2012).

5. See *http://naturalhistorymag. com/editors_pick/1928_05-06_pick. html* (accessed Dec 1, 2012).

6. *San Francisco Chronicle* dated April 6, 1899, p. 10.

7. For more on early Indian American experience, see Ronald Takaki, *Strangers from a Different Shores: History of Asian Americans* (Boston: Little, Brown and Co., 1998), 294-314. See more on Ghadar party archives at *http://www. sikhpioneers. org/gadar. html* (accessed Dec 1, 2012).

8. See his online biography at *www. mozumdar.org/* (accessed Dec 1, 2012).

9. See more on this incident, Rabindranath Tagore, *English Writings of Rabindranath Tagore: A Miscellany* (New Delhi: Sahitya Akademi, 1994), 784.

10. See more on Asian American Citizenship, *http://www. iafpe. org/php/ showNewsDetails. php?linkid=5&newsid=6* (accessed Dec 1, 2012). Dalip Singh Saund's autobiography *Congressman from India* (New York: EP Dutton and Co. , 1960). Also online *http://www. saund. org/dalipsaund/index. html* (accessed Dec 1, 2012).

11. See Indo American Center, *Asian Indians in Chicago* (Chicago: Arcadia Publishing, 2003).

12. For a detailed sociological analysis of Indian Americans, see Padma Rangasamy, *Namaste America: Indian Immigrants in an American Metropolis,* (University Park: University of Pennsylvania Press, 2000).

References

Bentley, William (1790), *The Diary of Rev. William Bentley D. D. (1759-1819),* Volume 1, p 228. Online: *http://archive. org/details/diaryofwilliambe01bent* (accessed Dec 1, 2012).

Chandrasekhar, S. (1982), *From India to America,* La Jolla, CA: Population Institute.

Indo American Center, *Asian Indians in Chicago* Chicago: Arcadia Publishing, 2003.

Mazumdar, A. K. Online Biography at *www. mozumdar.org/* (accessed Dec. 1, 2012).

Mukerjee ,Tapan and John (Sunny) Wycliff, "History of Early Arrivals of Asian Indians in America" online at *www. iafpe. org/php/showNewsDetails. php?linkid=5&newsid=5* (accessed Nov. 30, 2012).

Mukerjee, Tapan and John (Sunny) Wycliff, "Asian American Citizenship", online at *www. iafpe.org/php/showNewsDetails. php?linkid=5&newsid=6* (accessed Dec 1, 2012).

Rangasamy, Padma (2000), *Namaste America: Indian Immigrants in an American Metropolis,* University Park: University of Pennsylvania Press.

Saund, D. S. *Congressman from India,* New York: EP Dutton and Co., (1960), Online *www. saund.org/dalipsaund/index. html* (accessed Dec 1, 2012).

Tagore, Rabindranath (1994), *English Writings of Rabindranath Tagore: A Miscellany.* New Delhi: SahityaAkademi.

Takaki, Ronald (1998), *Strangers from a Different Shore: History of Asian Americans,* Boston: Little, Brown and Co.

Part C

MALAYALI LIFE IN THE DIASPORA

11

Malayali Educators in Diaspora:
Reflections of a College Professor in America

T. M. Thomas

Introduction

Malayalis are an enterprising lot. You can find them in every nook and corner of the world today. They move out of their familiar surroundings of home or village in scenic Kerala to live with relatives in rented apartments or houses in other cities and countries. They go on to explore opportunities overseas with their knowledge, skills, hard work and aspirations. Generally, they sought out jobs with higher wages or educational avenues with better earning potential. This spirit of adventure is on the rise in our age of communication and affordable travel. Some of the early pioneers who left the shores of Kerala to explore opportunities outside included traders, Christian workers and teachers. Teaching was considered a noble profession in Kerala and was highly regarded in the community. However, due to limited teaching positions in the state of Kerala, many educated Malayalis were forced to look for teaching prospects in English-based educational systems in the British Commonwealth nations and serve with their colonial masters with their knowledge in English and exceptional work ethic.

In this chapter, I present briefly my own journey as a teacher[1] that began in Kerala, India and nearly four decades later ended recently in the state of Connecticut in the United States of America. I wrote the story of my life after much reflection of my life achievements and failures, along with the priorities I made on the choices in life. I have always seen myself as a teacher both in India and America and hope these reflections would be an encouragement to you.

Early Education & Coming to America

The story of a person often begins with his or her early education. The first and best teachers for most of us were our parents and other adults in the family. The basic attitudes and values in life are formed in the first three and four years of life. I attended the neighborhood primary and middle schools at Kuriannoor belonging to the Mar Thoma Church. My high school at Kozhencherry was about two miles away which called for walking barefoot and crossing the wide Pampa River. All through school I worked hard and excelled in my studies.

I studied at two Colleges, one a Catholic College in Changanacherry, half a day distance from home by bus and the other in Trivandrum, a State University called University College which then took a whole day's travel by bus. Both were prestigious educational institutions. The state university had the highest percentage of professors holding Ph.D. degrees in the state of Kerala. Though not rich, my parents raised sufficient funds to send me to college by staying at hostels in both cities. Without failing in any class either in school or college, I became a graduate of Kerala University at the age of twenty in 1953. Graduating with a university degree was a rare achievement in those days. Upon graduation I went to teach in a high school. Though I enjoyed teaching high school, I had the inner conviction that there was a different or higher calling for my life. Hence I continued my pleasurable reading habit to become a scholar and to teach at the College level. I took leave of absence from high school teaching for one year to attain a Master's degree in Education from University of Madras.

The challenging task of moving out of one's own familiar surroundings in favor of a new and strange environment is usually undertaken in order to escape from the harsh realities of life in the home country while attracted by the promises and opportunities of the host country. While I was teaching in Kerala, I got a scholarship for higher education in America. I raised money for travel from family sources and reached America. I arrived at Putney Graduate School, Putney, Vermont in September 1963. Since my plan was to return after one year, I wanted to travel and see the country as much as possible. The longest chapter of my autobiographical reflections covers details of my extensive travel, called "An All-American Tour, 1963-64". That Fall, I started my doctoral program at Boston University and completed my doctorate in Education in 1968. While studying for my doctorate, I started my full time college teaching at Springfield College, Massachusetts.

Teaching Career

I had started teaching in 1953 at a famous school in Kerala, Asram High School in Perumbavoor. This school was known for its high percentage of students passing in state-level examinations, and excelling in co-curricular activities. Most teachers were dedicated and experienced in teaching with high achievements by their students in public examinations to prove it. An immediate vacancy rose soon after the school reopening. I was available to teach biology because the biology teacher was leaving to enhance his education in America. My first task was to establish myself as a good teacher of my students and I believe I was successful. Then I devoted time for co-curricular activities required for all at this residential school. My contributions to games, sports, drama and the school publications were recognized and appreciated. In short, I did my best to be an effective teacher. I continued teaching in that school until 1963. My full-time college teaching in America began in the fall semester of 1967 at Springfield College, one year before receiving my doctorate degree. Later, I joined University of Bridgeport in September 1969 and continued there until December 2004.

When I reflect on my life for the duration of thirty-five years at an American university, it can be divided into four chronological stages. First stage was the decade of growth and bearing fruit (1969-1978). The goal of this stage was to "be a good and smart teacher involved in scholarly or intellectual pursuits." I thoroughly prepared for each class and presented the ideas in the most interesting way possible. I encouraged class discussions based on questions and issues raised by students and teachers. My reading goals were heavy and demanding. I considered it remarkable to publish two books and five or six articles in academic journals The first book was a modified work of my doctoral thesis. The book was titled as *Indian Education Reform in Cultural Perspective* and the second book was *Images of Man: A Philosophical and Scientific Enquiry*. These two books gave me the incentive to write more.

The University of Bridgeport was regarded as a state institution with a private independent status. The proportion of international students attending was higher than most American institutions. It was true of the faculty ratio also. There were centenary celebrations of the birth of Mahatma Gandhi at the university. I was surprised to learn there was a 'Shastri Scholarship' named after a former Prime Minister of India already instituted by which one student was brought from India every year to pursue his/her academic career. In short, University of Bridgeport had established a prestigious name locally as well as globally.

The second stage was the declining decade of 1979 to 1988. In the 1980s educational institutions around the country were hit hard by low student enrollment. The institutions declined rapidly. The University of Bridgeport was badly affected. Since teachers could not find jobs in schools, many did not enroll to major in education. The depressive situation called for creative solutions. One was the creation of Intern Programs. It is a scheme to offer substitute teachers of school system around Bridgeport, the opportunity to earn a Master's degree in one year plus the summer. Graduates of colleges were selected for working as substitute teachers at one assigned school while attending courses in the evening at University of Bridgeport or satellite campuses. As the Education faculty we consulted with each other and designed a new program in the Education Department. The intern program which started in the early 1980s saved the department and other units at the university.

Another creative solution was to launch a doctoral program. When survival of an institution was at stake it may be foolish to begin a doctoral program. However, this is what the educational administration initiated. Attracted by such a fascinating idea, I joined its planning committee. We regularly met and worked out all the details for this unconventional program. I taught couple of core courses of the program – "School and Society" as well as "Comparative Education". The third creative solution was the Capstone Seminars. The undergraduate curriculum was revised at the university level with new courses and a different philosophy. These unique Capstone Seminars brought together senior students of various colleges and majors for inter-disciplinary studies. New courses were offered by an interdisciplinary team of professors. I developed a couple of them – *"Education for Peace"* and *"The Power of Non-Violence"*.

I was personally affected by the low student enrollment phase and I received a "termination of job" notice from the University Administration. Since I was a tenured faculty member, I discussed options with the Administration. It was agreed that I would receive two course credits of release time which enabled me to enroll at the University of Connecticut and start taking courses. Through this, I received my third Master's degree in Sociology in 1983. This was my sixth degree. It leveraged me to secure a joint appointment with the Sociology Department. I taught full-time courses for few years. Though I received termination notice, I continued at University of Bridgeport without being fired!

The third stage was the years of administrative duties at the University from 1985 to 1995. The declining years of 1980s resulted in an adversarial relationship between the faculty and the administration of the university. The faculty strike which began at the end of 1980s and into the early 1990s brought the university close to the brink of disaster. I became President of the Faculty Council when the strike was at its worst from 1990 to 1991. The responsibilities associated with this position were strenuous and very demanding. I worked day and night which meant moving our residence closer to our university. Later, I was appointed as the University Senate Secretary which was another demanding job with much responsibility. This brought the senate together with students, faculties and staff representatives to dialogue with each other. One thing I learned from the strike is that the various segments of the university should communicate with each other and work synergistically for the survival of an educational institution. I believe I played an active role in halting the demise of the University of Bridgeport and its continued existence. When the university finally came out of its precarious situation, I was recognized by both faculty and administration for my wise and timely service.

The final years at University of Bridgeport were from 1996 to 2004. The one-third salary cut for faculty and administration in existence for few years was finally restored to the former level. The relationship between faculty and administration had improved under my leadership. Inevitably, I became the enemy of a large number of faculty colleagues in all colleges of the University. I declined to take up any college or university responsibilities from the mid-1990s. My attention shifted from administrative roles to graduate teaching and research. I published journal articles and made paper presentations. I taught more courses at the Doctor of Education level and supervised a maximum number of students for writing their theses. I started my retired life in January 2005. As Professor Emeritus, I continue to maintain institutional ties in my retirement years.

Teacher of Teachers

Over the nearly four decades of my teaching career, I had the privilege to develop and teach variety of courses and train the next generation of teachers and leaders. Unlike in India, American higher education teaching required you to continually develop new courses and modify your classes on a regular basis with fresh research and reading materials. I was committed to studying the cultural context of schools. One of the unique courses I taught was *Education and Culture*. This helped the students to understand the impact of culture upon schools and the problems and issues which rise in response to the existing social-economic, political and moral needs of the culture. The process of education guarantees cultural continuity by stabilizing it. At the same time education tries to correct and improve the culture. On the one side, education maintains cultural heritage while on the other it changes and improves it by adding or creating new elements. Hence the role of formal education in relation to culture is both "transmissive" and "transformative."

Second was a course on *Crisis in Education*, which deals with the lament that we hear that our schools are in crisis. This is primarily based upon our inability to achieve the goals of education as formulated by each country. The solution is found in understanding schools in their cultural context as noted above. The term 'crisis' conveys two opposite meanings – threat as well as hope and optimism. The shift from a dangerous or pathetic situation to that of promise is by constructive social changes. This challenge and plan of action were placed before my students through my courses.

Third course I taught was Learning through Social Problems. It dealt with social problems and issues of the day to effectively teach the foundations of education courses. The systems or "schools of thought" would be included in the syllabus. This approach enabled student to relate to their learning with the world outside. The students are encouraged to take a stand on issues and seek necessary solutions to them. In this way, a person can make a difference in the society in which he or she lives. Other coursesI taught include – General Education in an Age of Specialization, Liberal vs. Conservative approach, Goals of Education etc. Altogether, I taught over thirty-five different courses during my teaching career.[2]

Being a Teacher

In the context of an American university, there are four duties of a college professor is to fulfill: (a) teaching, (b) research and publication, (c) administrative duties, (d) service to the community. Although I was part of the Education Department at the university, I taught courses in six different departments including Sociology, Psychology, Philosophy, Counseling and Capstone Seminars. I welcomed teaching many courses as I enjoyed the challenges of reading the latest books necessary to teach these courses. Reading has been a pleasurable activity for me and it came naturally. Reading and reflection makes one knowledgeable. Knowledge is to be shared with others when we enjoy life, the greatest gift teachers receive. All the books I bought to teach were sent to libraries in India where they were highly valued and appreciated by both students and faculties.

In America, teaching was not limited to classroom instructions, but one was expected to engage in ongoing research and publications in your field of discipline. 'Publish or perish' was the ethos of the American academia. I enjoyed reading within the area of education and beyond. All that reading fueled my writing which came under two categories: one related to professional life of a teacher and other related to my church. Over a period of thirty five years, I might have presented 70-80 papers in one hundred and fifty meetings or conferences. My publications include eight academic books, eighteen Church or Sunday school related books and dozens of chapters in books (of other authors) and Reviews.[3] My commitment to the profession of teaching and to church activities enabled me to formulate my personal values. Three of them are: knowledge and wisdom, service to others and eternal life.

Church and Community

My life at the University of Bridgeport was intertwined with involvements in my church and community. In the early 1970s there was an influx of Asian immigrants to the United States, including nurses and their families from Kerala.[4] Also the highly educated Indians and various professionals began migrating to the United States. There was a need for familiar styles of worship in Malayalam to be organized. I responded to the need to the formation of a parish to begin worship in New York City and other major cities of the United States. By the end of 1970s, the Mar Thoma Church was well established in all major cities of the United States. I cultivated relationships with several church members in various cities and with the leadership of our Church in India. This relationship enabled the growth of parishes which later resulted in the Diocese of the Mar Thoma Churches of North America and Europe.

One particular area that I spent enormous efforts was promoting Christian education in the Sunday school ministry of the parishes of the Mar Thoma Church. Here, I was able to significantly contribute because of the convergence of my early education, spiritual upbringing, academic training, and professional teaching career. I was the first headmaster of St. Thomas Mar Thoma Church Sunday School in Yonkers, New York. I helped organize the first Youth Conference in North America and a variety of regional and national children and youth events. Working closely with clergy and Church leadership in India, I helped develop the ministry for the children and youth of the churches in the Reformed Eastern traditions in the diaspora. I developed a revised curriculum and trained teachers for the diasporic context of North America.

The secularization of American academia has resulted in the dichotomy of spiritual values and the educational institutions. I believe this is a great loss of our times and hence we need the teaching of moral and spiritual values in both the East and the West. In most of history, education as an institution was entrusted to religion with its association to virtues. With the loss of the sacred, we are losing a sense of human worth and dignity. This is the modern predicament which educators should accept as a challenge.

Conclusion

Teaching is a noble profession. I had the awesome privilege in shaping the next generation of teachers who will continue to shape future generations in two countries – my native homeland of Kerala, India and my adopted home in the United States. We all are teachers, whether you hold an official teacher title or not. We influence those around with our lives, words actions and thoughts. I hope and pray you are having positive impact on the world around you. To teach one has to learn continually and have a love to knowledge. Keep learning and teaching to make the world a better place.

Notes

1. For a detailed autobiography, see T. M. Thomas, *Joyful Vocation of a Teacher: Autobiographical Reflections on Life and Teaching*, (2011).

2. On more on courses I taught, see my autobiography *Joyful Vocation of a Teacher* (2011).

3. See Appendix pp. 262-264 for the list of my publications in my autobiography *Joyful Vocation of a Teacher* (2011).

4.   Annamma Thomas & T. M. Thomas, *Kerala Immigrants in America: A Sociological Study of St. Thomas Christians*, (Cochin: Simons Printers, 1984).

References

Thomas, T. M. *Joyful Vocation of a Teacher: An Autobiographical Reflection on Life and Teaching*, (Tiruvalla: CSS, 2011).

Thomas, Annamma & T. M. Thomas, *Kerala Immigrants in America: A Sociological Study of St. Thomas Christians*, (Cochin: Simons Printers, 1984).

12

Malayali Nurses in America:
Caring for Others

SARA GABRIEL

Introduction

The growth of the Malayali community in the United States primarily can be traced to the emigration history of ONE nurse from a single family and the subsequent growth of that family over the years. Though there were other Malayalis who came over as students or as immigrants, no other group stands out as the major influential group as the nurses who were instrumental in the significant migration of Malayalis. History focuses not only on the details of the facts and events in a chronological order, but also shows the impact and outcome of these events that charted the course of the life of individuals, family, community and society in general. To understand and appreciate the present, we have to know the past, the cultural, social, economic and religious forces that had a direct or indirect influence on individuals and society. This chapter is written to highlight the struggles of these pioneers to establish a nursing career and a life for themselves and their families in the United States. Available information is primarily derived from the limited feedback obtained from the nurses as well as the author's own knowledge, personal experience and exposure.

Pioneering Challenges

Major migration of Indian nurses to the United States[1] started in the late 1960s and early 1970s. Prior to that time, nursing was not a sought after profession in India and young women were discouraged by others even if they had a calling for this service-oriented profession. Those who ventured out to be nurses endured many hardships, negative social stigma and a very low professional image. The unsatisfactory working and living conditions, poor wages and less than admirable social status of the nursing profession had a direct impact on the migration of nurses from India to other countries like US, UK or Canada. These developed countries provided better professional advancement, economic incentives, dignity of labor and social status for nurses and nursing as a profession.

The legislative changes of the United States immigration policy of 1965, removed the racial exclusion and the eligibility for immigration were allowed through the use of non discriminatory quota system for each country[2]. With this landmark change, the eligibility for US immigration was based on family reunification, personal qualification and the order of application. These changes in the immigration law, combined with the US nursing shortage opened the doorwide for many aspiring young professional nurses to seek immigration to the United States. A very high percentage of Indian nurses who emigrated hailed from Kerala and spoke the language Malayalam.

Like any other pioneers in history the first Indian nurses who came over to the United States experienced extreme challenges and had to struggle much to establish them selves in this country. Majority of the nurses were single women and if married they had to leave their husbands and children back in India. These brave ones left everything and everyone that were dear to them and embarked on a journey to the unknown expecting to find the land of their dreams and a promised land of opportunity. Many of them had a family member or friend as a contact in the US. Some of them might have heard the fascinating stories of the cowboys, or read about the adventures of the early settlers. Others may have been fascinated by the beautiful snowcapped mountain tops, or the evergreen trees beside country roads blanketed with hanging icicles, or a beautiful row of the spring flowers, or the vibrant flaming fall colors in a post card. But they knew very little about America or about the American lifestyle before landing in the United States. Upon arrival, many of them found themselves in dire straits with no money to spend, no job and no place of their own to stay. A few of the lucky ones who came on an "exchange visa" or "work visa" had the initial help and support of their hospital or employer. Very few could rely on others or their contacts to orient them to life in America. Nor could they receive help from them in any significant way because of a lack of time and resources.

Finding a nursing job as was next to impossible as they did not possess a Registered Nurse (RN) license. Even those migrant nurses who held managerial and tutorial positions in India had to start over from the beginning.[3] Many of them were forced to start their careers as nursing assistants or whatever small jobs they could get to support them. Many of them lived together in apartments sharing accommodation and food expenses to save money, reduce the loneliness, receive emotional support and ensure security. They shared their adventures, their stories, their struggles and helped each other to survive. Though they felt lonely and homesick they were determined to stay, struggle and pursue success.

Communication was the greatest road block for these Indian nurses. Though they all knew how to read, write and speak British-style Indian English most of them struggled to speak American English. With the difference in American and Indian accents and with the vast gap between Indian and American cultures and etiquette to engage in a conversation about the latest movies, fashion trends, sports, local politics, food etc., kept Indian nurses isolated even at the work place. The more they felt isolated, the more resilient the nurses became to connect with other Indian nurses or community to survive and succeed. They helped each other by sharing and teaching each other the cultural norms, the dos and don'ts of American society which they learned through trial and error or their own embarrassing encounters.

During this period the main goal of pioneering nurses was to make enough money to meet their own expenses and save whatever

they could to bring their families to the United States– the husbands
and children that they left behind and financially help their parents
and siblings as much as possible. Since these nurses were young and
healthy, they worked inone or two jobs andseized overtime
opportunities when possible. They struggled and sacrificed their own
wants and desires for others. The only vacation they took was to go
to Kerala with suitcases of gifts for their families and relatives.[4]Within
few years their family members started to immigrate. The married
women moved out and established their own homes and families.
Many of the single nurses returned to India and married men from
their own language and ethnic groups. The nurses became very
marketable at this time and well-placed men were eager to marry
them!

Many of these "nurse husbands" as they were called, left their
established careers to follow their wives to America. Most of them
did not realize the predicament they would be in. The nurses became
the primary breadwinners and resulted in their upward mobility
economically and socially, while their husbands fell into a downward
spiral owing to not finding jobs that commensurate with their
education or experience and some even become house-husbands.[5]
Most of them became deeply disappointed and some even depressed
when they were unable to find similar positions they were used to or
even find something within their field of expertise. Unable to find
the right jobs, the husbands experienced loneliness staying at home
while the wives worked extra hours to meet the added living expenses.
Many of the men went through this period with extreme anger and
resentment due to their inability to find a job in their profession as
many of them were highly educated, with excellent experience and
credentials. Slowly, the men began to accept the reality and adapt to
the contexts. One of the blessings at this time was the Indian
community helped each other. They appealed to their own supervisors
to consider their friends for vacancies and advocated for them with
their personal references. This made the greatest difference in men
getting hired during those early years.

The men started to work in whatever job that were available and
the family started to grow. A gender role reversal started to emerge in

the community.[6] With young children, both parents working, the husbands were forced to share the household chores including childcare. This was very difficult for some of the Malayali men as they were never exposed or expected to do any of these in India. Men who were able to accept or accommodate and helped their wives were able to manage the new family situation better. With both partners working, the economic aspects of family life greatly improved. However, the stress and strain heightened with issues and worries of child care. To avoid babysitting and daycare challenges many nurses strategized to work during the evening or night shifts and their husbands strove to find work during the daytime. So the parents took turns in taking care of their children and meeting their needs. With this arrangement, children also suffered to some extent without the presence of both parents together most of the week to assist them in their formative years of life.

Obtaining the Registered Nursing licensure was another major hurdle for these pioneer nurses. It took a long time to get credentials from India evaluated and accepted in the US. The majority of the Indian nurses were diploma nursing graduates. Since their diploma education from Indian nursing schools was not equal to the American education they were required to take additional hours of theory or clinical practicum to qualify to write the RN licensing exam. There were five different subjects and each one of them had a minimum passing score. Nurses had to pass these exams separately to obtain their license. Most of the nurses needed to make multiple appearances to write the exams they failed each time to attain the minimum passing grade for each subject at the same time. The factors contributing to their challenge were: the nurses were not used to the multiple-choice exam format; as slow readers of English most of them were not able to complete the whole written examination in the time allowed. Amazingly, they persevered in studying and reappearing for the exams. Eventually, a majority of the nurses passed the exam and became licensed professional nurses. This was a great accomplishment for each one of them, for their families and the community.

In the early 1980s, the nurses faced a new challenge with the arrival of siblings and their families. New immigration regulations[7] allowed nurses to bring their parents, siblings with their spouses and children all at the same time. Each new arrival needed some type of initial assistance with housing, food, finances and wise counsel to environmental adjustments, to get a job and start their life in the US. Some of the nurses had two and three families and their children with them at the same time. With no support system in place, and the added burdens of additional family, many nurses put their own professional goals and aspirations on hold to help with the new situation.

Socialization Challenges

Indian immigrants soon began to form their own social groups, cultural and religious activities to meet their social and spiritual needs. The majority of the Malayali nurses were from a Christian heritage and they missed their native worship and communal gatherings.[8] Therefore, Church was more than a place of worship; it was also a social gathering for fellowship, converse in Malayalam and the enjoyment of native food, music and arts. The parents tried hard to follow the traditional Malayali way of life and taught their children the norms and values of the heritage community. They worked hard to provide financial security and a good education for their children and expected full obedience at home and top grades at school. As the family became more financially secure, they moved from inner city apartments to suburban area houses to pursue a better school system for their children and a more comfortable and safer environment.

As the children got older, the first immigrant parents faced many issues and problems especially with their teenagers[9]. The parents were afraid of their children adapting the liberal American life style and controlled their social activities. The children of the first generation were caught in the middle with an orthodox Indian system at home and a liberal American system in school and society. Many children resented their parents' autocratic control over them or the lack of understanding of their need to participate in social activities like prom or group outings. The parents could not underst and the American teen lifestyle, or their preferred fashion choices, or other wild teen behaviors and therefore restricted their children from following them.

So parents formed their own religious, social and cultural organizations, and activities to keep their emerging generation together. The parents who tried to communicate patiently and sought to understand their children's social needs but set limits and sanctions for their behaviors maintained good family relationships.

Workplace Challenges

Every Indian nurse the author interviewed experienced some type of racial prejudice during the early years, mainly due to lack of understanding or the preconceived notions about Indians nurses. The initial euphoria of getting a job and the excitement of earning a living evaporated quickly for many nurses as they experienced the hard reality of perceptions and prejudices from their peers and superiors. They did not fully understand each other. Many Indian nurses were surprised that Americans knew very little about India or other parts of the world. In break and lunch-room conversations Malayali nurses wouldbe asked questions like," How come you don't wear a dot on your forehead?' Even the nurses with popular Biblical names would be asked if they are Hindus in their religious affiliation. Or, "How come your last name is different from your husbands?" (Many Malayalis take their husband's first name as their last name and Americans could not comprehend the logic of it.)

Some Americans found it very strange and unimaginable that most Malayalis nurses had an arranged marriage and they did not date their husbands before the wedding. They were also amused to learn that babies slept in the same bedroom even if they were ina crib. What most shocked andupset the Indian nurses was when these young American nurses freely talked about their casual sexual encounters and relationships.Indian nurses also found it ridiculous to hear that some Americans allowed their dogs to sleep in their bed. The Indian nurses patiently answered thequestions educating Americans of Indian culture, customs, and family values, and learning from them the norms of the American life and culture. Soon the Indian nurses were asking the Americans questions like, "Why do you talk so loud about your personal life in public?" or "How come unmarried girls have babies?" "How come you live common law without taking your marriage vows?" Or even worse," How come you take your teenage daughter to the doctor for birth control pills?" With time each group learned to accept, accommodate and tolerate each other's differences.

Generally, the Indian nurses were very diligent workers and they were kind, caring and always ready to help others. Initially, the Indian nurses were soft spoken, appeared timid, unassertive and avoided conflicts with others even when they were treated unfairly. As they learned and became more proficient in the American culture, system and patient care standards they became confident and excellent care givers. While most Americans reached out to Indian nurses with compassion and helped them to succeed there were unfortunate incidents of those who suffered from unfavorable perception and prejudice. Many well-deserving Indian nurses were denied promotions in their careers. The worst prejudice Indian nurses suffered from were not from white or Afro-American nurses but from Filipino nurses. When in large numbers, Filipino nurses tended to show their superiority to their Indian colleagues because of their nursing educational background being similar to the US and their mastery of Western culture.

By the end of 1980s, the Indian community put roots in many major Metropolitan cities, established themselves personally and professionally. Many nurses continued with upgrading their qualifications through further study and excelled in their work place. In recognition of their commitment, work ethic and quality of work many Indian nurses were promoted to supervisory or managerial positions in public or government institutions the nurses found it hard to get a break into those roles inmany private hospitals as the supervisors and superiors prefer American-born nurses for visible leadership roles.

The Malayali nurses continue to play a significant role in the Indian community in America. Thousands of more nurses from all over India migrated to US in the last two decades, primarily through direct recruitment by employers and through recruitment agencies. By the time these nurses arrived, standards for credential evaluation, English language proficiency tests and other measures were in place. There are now five centers of National Council Licensure Examination for Registered Nurses (NCLEX-RN) in India where the nurses can write their RN licensing exam and this author was part of the team that worked to establish these centers for nurses. Almost all of the nurses seem to have a support system and friends and/or families already settled in US who have the resources to help. Prior to arrival in the US they receive sufficient orientation to get acculturated and are able to be employed in their profession quickly. Though some Indian nurses have had negative experiences with some recruiters, majority of them wentthrough a much easier initial period than the pioneering nurses decades earlier.

The nurses make a substantial contribution to the Indian economy through their financial remittances to their families and personal investments. Nursing status and admissions in nursing schools increased significantly in India because of the opportunity to emigrate to the US and other countries, the status of the nursing profession has heightened among Indians. This has resulted in the increasing of nursing schools and their enrolments are growing.

Contemporary State and Scene

Over the years, Indian nurses have proven their professional abilities and succeeded in almost all arenas of nursing in this country. With higher education and commendable work record, they are competing and attaining key leadership roles in all most all fields of nursing. Many with their Masters and Doctoral degrees are drawing commendable salaries in key leadership positions. There are numerous Indians who are Directors of Nursing, Hospital Administrators, Deans, Professors, Educators, Advanced Nurse Practitioners, Researchers and Business owners to mention a few. The majority of the nurses can be proud of their highly educated and successful children as well.

Despite the four-decade history of Indian nurses in the US, they did not unite nationally to pay attention to the issues unique to them. Through the tireless efforts of few Indian nurse leaders from across the nation along with this author they were able to form in 2006, the National Association of Indian Nurses of America (NAINA) incorporated in the State of Illinois as a 501 (c) (3) chapter for all nurses of Indian origin and heritage in the USA. As the founding member and the first president of the organization the author can proudly say that NAINA is the first National Indian Nurses Association outside India. Since its inception, NAINA Board has endeavored to promote the cause of Indian nurses, and gain acceptance and recognition among the mainstream American nurses,nurses in India and other nursing organizations. Within a very short period of time, NAINA has become well known nationally and globally as a successful thriving nursing organization with biannual educational conferences and other community activities. NAINA provides scholarships and charitable contributions to support Indian nurses in America and in India. NAINA is also a member of other national ethnic organizations like National Coalition of Ethnic Minority Nurses in America (NCEMNA) and Association of Asian Pacific Islander Nurses in America (AAPINA). NAINA is a permanent board member of the Alliance for Ethical International Recruitment Practices for Foreign Educated Nurses, an organization formed to address the recruitment issues and abuse of foreign nurses who were recruited to work in the US. This author iscurrently working with leaders of this organization to connect with nurses from India through Trained Nurses Association (TNAI) and other agencies.

Conclusion

The story of pioneer nurses in America is an amazing one. Most of them have retired and are enjoying their life with their children and grandchildren. The statement from a young man summarizes the sentiment of all those people who migrated to America all because of ONE nurse. "Our family today is huge! We were a big family to start with, so many sisters and brothers for both of our parents. Now with children, spouses and their families we have over two hundred people here in America. We have an annual summer picnic in the park so we get together at least once a year. We are still close and we all owe it to ONE nurse, our mother who sacrificed so much for us and came to the US alone in 1970. We love her and will always remember her sacrifices." There are thousands of family members like this with similar sentiments and stories.

Notes

1. For a detailed sociological analysis of Kerala nurses in the United States, see Sheba M. George, *When Women Come First: Gender and Class in Transnational Migration,* (Berkley, CA: University of California Press, 2005).

2. Immigration and Nationality Act of 1965 (also known as the Hart-Celler Act of 1965) abolished the national origin formula that had been in place since the Immigration Act of 1924.

3. Elsie Baby Mathew,"Malayali Nurses in America", Unpublished paper, (2012), 2.

4. Elsie Baby Mathew, "Malayali Nurses in America", Unpublished paper, (2012), 2.

5. About this gender role reversal in the United States, seeSheba M. George. *When Women Come First.* 2005. For a similar phenomenon in Canada, see Lina Samuel's dissertation on Kerala Women Diaspora. 2008.

6. For an extended analysis on this, see Sheba M. George, "Dirty Nurse and Men who Play" 2008.

7. The immigration reform laws of 1980, 1986 and 1990 made new provisions for sponsoring family members of immigrants to the United States.

8. On social aspect of diasporic religious gatherings, see Raymond William, *Christian Pluralism in the United States,* (New York: Cambridge University Press, 1996) and Prema Kurien, *A Place in the Multicultural Table.* (New Brunswick, NJ: Rutgers University Press, 2007).

9. About the American born children and challenges of parenting a generation in the United States, see Sam George, *Understanding the Coconut Generation,* (Niles, IL: Mall Publishers, 2006).

References

George, Sam. (2006), *Understanding the Coconut Generation.* Niles, IL: Mall Publishers.

George, Sheba M. (2005), *When Women Come First: Gender and Class in Transnational Migration.*Berkley, CA: University of California Press.

George, Sheba M. (1998), "Caroling with the Keralites: the Negotiation of Gendered Space in an Indian Immigrant Church". In *Gatherings in Diaspora: Religious Communities and the New Immigration,* ed. R. Stephen Warner and Judith G. Wittner, pp. 265-94. Philadelphia: Temple University Press.

George, Sheba M. (2000), "Dirty Nurses and Men Who Play" In *Global Ethnographies: Forces, Connections and Imagination in a Postmodern World,* ed. Michael Buroway *et al.* California: University of California Press.

Kurien, Prema (2007), *A Place in the Multicultural Table*. New Brunswick, NJ: Rutgers University Press.

Mathew, Elsie Baby (2012), *Malayali Nurses in America*. Unpublished paper. Atlanta, GA.

Samuel, Lina (2008), "Disruption, Displacement, Ambivalence: the Making of Migrant Identities among Women in the Keralite Diaspora" Ph.D. Dissertation, York University, Toronto, Canada.

13

Religious Life of Malayali Diaspora:
Hindus and Christians in the United States

Prema Kurien

Once a month, in places around the United States such as Chicago, southern California, and Dallas, Malayali Hindu families gather at the home of one of their members, or in a rented hall, for *puja* and *bhajans* (worship and singing). And since 2001, when the Kerala Hindus of North America association was formed, Malayali Hindu Americans have also come together for a biennial conference in various cities. Similarly, large numbers of Malayali Christians attend church services organized by their denomination or group on Sundays; a number of these churches have been established for decades. Many Malayali Christians in the United States also attend regional and national denominational conferences.

As a sociologist of Malayali background, I decided to study some of these immigrant religious organizations early in my career, since I realized that religion played a central role in community life for Malayalis in the United States. This is not unusual, as research has shown that religion is the most common and most acceptable basis for community formation and expression for immigrants, particularly in the United States. Religious institutions come to define and sustain the cultural and ethnic life of immigrant groups, and even individuals who may not have been particularly religious before emigrating, participate in these institutions. Religion also becomes the means through which immigrants transmit their culture and values to their children.[1] However, immigrant religious institutions are not simply transplanted from the home country. They change to adapt to new conditions in the diaspora. Here, I focus on the religious life of Hindu and Christian Malayalis in the United States, drawing on research conducted in the 1990s on Hindu Malayalis, and in the first decade of 2000 on Christian Malayalis.[2] We will see how and why religion becomes important for immigrants, and the types of modifications they have made in their religious institutions to meet the challenges of being located in the American environment. As is the tradition in social science research, I have changed all names and identifying information of the organizations and members to protect confidentiality.

Religious Life among Hindu Malayalis

Early Hindu Malayali immigrants came to the United States in the 1960s and 1970s in search of an education or better economic prospects, and often planned only a temporary stay. They were able to continue their home-based religious practices and family rituals without much disruption, even after migration. Home shrines in the United States can consist of a whole room set aside for worship, an elaborate shrine cabinet with images of several deities and other sacred objects, or as is most likely, a few pictures or images in a closet or on the kitchen counter. In the 1960s and 1970s, before Hindu Indian temples were established and trained Brahmin priests were available to perform life cycle rituals at home, such rituals were either postponed and performed in India during a family visit or performed by lay Brahmin men who had some acquaintance with the required rituals and procedures.

Home-based religious gatherings were the first centers of group Hindu activity in the United States and provided the nucleus for the larger religious associations and temples that were subsequently established. As the children of the Hindu immigrants grew older and a return to India became less and less likely, it became important for parents to develop a more structured means of interacting with co-ethnics. Thus, in the 1980s *satsangs* (worship groups) and *bala vihars* (child development associations) based on region of origin in India began to proliferate among Hindu Indian community in the United States. The first largely targeted adults and celebrated and reenacted religious practice, the second was directed at teaching the children about the religion. Many immigrants who were involved in these organizations had not participated in such gatherings in India, but group religious activities became important in the diaspora. Since Indians are the most dispersed new immigrant group in the United States,[3] such gatherings were one of the few opportunities for individuals to get together with others from their home state in India.

A monthly satsang group for Hindu Malayalis, *Geethamandalam,* was formed in 1978 in the larger Chicago area.[4] The Kerala Hindu Society of North Texas began holding a monthly prayer meeting from 1985 and was eventually able to gather resources for a Sri Guruvayurappan Temple of Dallas, which started operations in 2011.[5] The Organization of Hindu Malayalees of Southern California was incorporated in 1992 and also holds monthly prayer meetings and annual cultural programs.[6]

One such satsang group formed by Hindu Malayalis held a monthly devotional meeting that I attended as a researcher in the mid-1990s. On a pleasant Saturday evening, a row of expensive cars was parked in front of an upper-middle-class house in a suburban locality. Shoes and sandals were arranged neatly outside on the porch. Inside, the furniture had been cleared away from the large living room and sheets spread over the carpet. In the center was a temporary shrine with pictures of several Hindu deities arranged against the wall. Several of the deities were adorned with fresh flower garlands. Tall brass oil lamps with flickering flames stood on either side of the shrine. Baskets containing fruit and flowers had been placed in front. A man dressed in a traditional South Indian *veshti* (lower garment) was seated on the floor before the shrine, his wife beside him in a silk sari. Around the couple were seated a group of about fifty people— the men and boys, in casual Western clothes, largely on one side of the room, and the women and girls, dressed in rich and colorful Indian clothes, on the other. The meeting started with the lay worship leader chanting an invocation (in Sanskrit) to the deities while gently throwing flowers before them, so that by the end of the invocation, there was a fragrant, multicolored mound in front of the shrine. The invocation was followed by the singing of bhajans. Different members of the group, including a teenage girl, took turns leading the singing: the leader of the bhajan sang a line and the rest of the group repeated it.

This was a meeting of a Kerala Hindu Organization (henceforth KHO), which had a membership of around fifty to seventy families, including Malayali Hindus and some Tamil Brahmin families who had lived in Kerala for generations. Members met on the second Saturday of the month in different locations (mostly people's houses) around the region for the puja and bhajans and a "Gita discussion" period toward the end of the puja. Around forty to sixty people attended each puja. The meeting was followed by a lavish, vegetarian potluck meal. Since the members were scattered over a wide area, except for the "regulars," it was a changing group that attended each meeting, depending on the locality. In addition to the monthly and cultural programs, the KHO also sponsored cultural programs several times during the year, when music and dance-dramas were performed by community members or by visiting artists from Kerala.

In one of the KHO publications, the secretary of the organization, Gopi Nair, offered a poetic explanation of its formation: "Before we established [KHO], many of the true lovers of Kerala heritage and culture were lost in the congested wilderness of [the region] without having any communication with other Kerala members who shared similar interests. Some of them felt lonely in the crowded streets of this faraway land, and hungry and thirsty, in this land of plenty, for company of people who recognized and understood them. They searched everywhere for some familiarity, to prove to their beloved children that the usual bedtime stories of their motherland and her heritage were not some fairy tales but existed in reality."

The founder president and chief initiator of KHO, Ravi Menon, talking about how the idea of forming an association occurred to him, said, "My idea was to develop a support group for Hindu Malayalis. Christians have the church as a support group, Hindus don't have anything." Hari Ramanan, an executive member of the group, mentioned during my first meeting with members of the committee, "Growing up as Hindus in a Judeo-Christian environment can be difficult. There are so many misconceptions here about Indians and Hindus. People ask us about the cows roaming the streets—they think we are all vegetarians, that India is full of snake charmers." Hari said that one of the reasons that the KHO was founded was to correct these misconceptions.

In addition to the needs of the immigrants, the teaching of Indian culture and values to children was an important reason for the formation of satsangs and the primary reason for the formation of the bala vihars. Indian parents were concerned about the environment within which their children were growing up, and the attitudes and values that the children were imbibing from school seemed completely alien to them and created a frightening feeling that the next generation was growing up to be total strangers with whom they could not even communicate. The children, in turn, had to deal with the difficult issue of negotiating their personal and cultural identity between the values and practices learned at home and those of the American society they faced outside. In the process, they raised questions about their own culture and religion, to which parents discovered they had no answers. As Sujatha Rajagopal, one of the KHO committee members, mentioned at my first meeting with them, "It is only when we got here that we realized how little we knew our culture. We wish our mothers and grandmothers were here to answer the questions. Our children and others keep asking us questions about yoga and rebirth, and I find I don't know the answers. This is another reason that we formed the KHO."

Since none of the KHO members had been part of a bhajan group in India, I was curious about how they had learned the bhajans that they sang at their monthly meetings. Most were in Sanskrit and a few were popular in Kerala, but from my conversations I gathered that many of the others were ones that "an average Hindu growing up in Kerala would not know." In fact, I was told that often it was only the person leading the bhajan who knew it. The rest of the group just repeated the bhajan, line by line. I talked to several of the bhajan leaders to ask them how they had learned the songs. Padma Iyer, wife of the lay priest and the primary bhajan leader of the group, said that she made it a point to pick up new bhajans from friends, relatives, and from cassette tapes. Kamala Devi told me that she learned them primarily from an older Tamilian woman. Latha, a teenager (who had led a few bhajans, including at least one in Hindi), and Ravi Menon, the president, had both learned them at their respective singing classes. Another woman sang two that she had just composed the previous day. It was only during the period of my research that copies of the bhajans (handwritten by Padma Iyer in English script) were handed out to members before the meeting. Later, using the south Indian practices with which she was familiar, Padma also tried to formalize the sequence of the bhajan singing according to the deities to which they are addressed.

Members of the KHO were able to develop a close-knit community, even though members were scattered over an area with a radius of around 125 miles. Gopi Nair told me:

> KHO is like an extended family. It helps to alleviate problems—it helps in crisis management, stress management. There are many problems here—job related, domestic. Before KHO I had around four or five people to turn to but now I have around twenty families that I can trust. I have several close friends and we call each other one or two times a week for personal conversation, quite apart from official KHO business. Just talking to others helps so much. The community is small enough to be close knit. The Kerala Association, on the other hand, is very large. Around four hundred people show up for each function so you won't know most of the people there.

Others talked about how beneficial the organization had been for their children. One of the women in the group told me, "Earlier they went through a period when they wanted to have nothing to do with anything Indian. My oldest child (who has a long, traditional name) had Anglicized and shortened his name earlier. Now he insists that his friends call him by his full name. And my other children ask me why I did not give them traditional names!" All of the teenagers that I spoke to indicated that it had helped them indirectly, by putting them in contact with adults and other children from the community. "It made me finally comfortable as an Indian. I realized that there were many other people out there who are like me, who talk like me and that I am not by myself" elaborated Mohan, one of the teenage boys in the group. My research showed that the children of Hindu Malayali immigrants, once they start attending college, are exposed to Hindu youth from other backgrounds in Hindu student organizations on campus. Through participating in such organizations, they get socialized into a pan-Indian, textual, intellectualized Hinduism, shorn of rituals and many of the distinctive regional practices.

In addition to attending the monthly KHO meetings, members also visited local temples periodically, particularly the large regional temple (which had a complex each for Vishnu and Shiva, and a range of deities) and also organized some of their annual celebrations there.[7] Hindu Malayalis in the United States also formed a national association, Kerala Hindus of North America, in 2001 to unite all Hindu Malayalis in the country. According to their website, they have "2500 plus" families at present.[8] The organization has been holding biennial national conferences in different cities to bring the community together for discussions (including special sessions for the youth), religious discourses, group prayers, and cultural and arts programs.

Religious Life among Christian Malayalis

The unique feature of the Christian Malayali migration pattern is that the primary migrants, particularly in the early period (early 1970s - early 1980s), were female nurses who were filling a nursing shortage in the United States. The nurses then sponsored their husbands and children, as well as other family members. Many Christian Malayali pastors arrived in the United States through the sponsorship of their spouses or siblings who were nurses. Since nurses in Kerala were mostly from Christian backgrounds, Kerala Christians immigrated to the United States in larger numbers than Kerala Hindus and Muslims. Raymond Williams, who has researched religious life among Indian immigrants in the United States, writes that "well over three-quarters of the immigrants from Kerala are Christian."[9] They came from a variety of backgrounds, from the traditional episcopal Orthodox, Catholic, and Protestant denominations to Pentecostal and Brethren. My research on Malayali Christians was focused on the Mar Thoma Church, a "Reformed Eastern" denomination, and I will draw from this research below to explore how religion shaped their community life.

The first U.S. Mar Thoma parish was established in 1976 in New York City, and the North American and European Diocese formed in 1988. In 2012, there were fifty-three Mar Thoma parishes and congregations in the United States serving 5,755 residentially scattered Mar Thoma families, or around 23,000 individuals. The Mar Thoma Church is unique among Malayali Christian Churches in the United States in that Mar Thoma *achens* (pastors) are not permanent residents but are sent on three-year terms to U.S. parishes and to parishes in other countries by the Synod of Bishops based in Kerala. As a result, there is a remarkable uniformity in the ritual and organizational practices of Mar Thoma parishes around the world. The congregations in India and overseas, maintain the long liturgical service in formal Malayalam, sung in a sonorous chant with congregational responses. As a concession to the children growing up outside Kerala who are often not fluent in Malayalam, parishes outside Kerala now offer services in English on alternate Sundays, with a translated liturgy.

The early wave of Mar Thoma immigrants, like other Christian Malayalis to the United States consisted primarily of female nurses and their families who had grown up in Kerala. Many of the husbands of the nurses worked in blue collar jobs at least initially, due to their lack of language skills and professional education. These families were able to do well financially, however, since the women worked long hours and nursing was lucrative in 1970s and 1980s, particularly with overtime opportunities. There was a smaller group of men who arrived in the United States for higher education and then stayed on. These individuals either came with their wives, or went back to India, got married, and returned with their wives. Some of these men came to study for advanced degrees in Christian universities that had affiliations with Bible colleges in south India. From around the late 1990s on, there was a new wave of Mar Thoma immigration, mainly individuals seeking employment in the information technology sector.

Immigrant members of the Mar Thoma parishes that I talked to emphasized that the Mar Thoma Church was part of their inheritance, and that they valued maintaining the language, liturgy, and traditions of the church for this reason, and also because they found them intrinsically beautiful and meaningful. In the diaspora, the Mar Thoma Church becomes more important in the lives of its members as the primary setting where members have contact with co-ethnics, and a refuge from the racism and cultural misunderstandings that members face in their work lives. Most of the immigrants indicated that their close friends were other Mar Thoma members and that the church in the United States was a "comfort zone" that provided emotional, social, and spiritual support during difficult periods. For instance, the Vergheses, one of the couples I interviewed in a Mar Thoma congregation, talked about how the church community in the United States was like their surrogate family, which was not the case in Kerala. "Since our families are around in India, we are not so close to friends or members of the church. The church community here substitutes for the family we had in India." Many parents also indicated that they drove the long distance to attend a Mar Thoma service with their families several times a month because they wanted their children to associate with other families from the same background. They hoped that this would help the children to imbibe their culture and language.

The American-born children of Mar Thoma immigrants also appreciated that their parish was like an "extended family." Since their parents often tended to be very restrictive, not allowing them to go over to the houses of their schoolmates, church was their one place of freedom where they could spend time with their friends. Anisha, a young woman in her late twenties echoed what a lot of other second-generation women and men said when she declared, "I *loved* going to church actually because it was fun. It was a place that my parents felt comfortable to go and be open with our friends because it was church and nothing could go wrong." And Viju, a young man also in his late twenties, said that his experience in the church when he was young had been good: "I met a lot of my, you know, really close friends . . . I learned a lot about the basics of Christianity and stuff . . . That was basically my community, my family . . . we spent most of our time outside of school, with those people." Comparing her life in the United States with that of her parents in India, nineteen-year-old Rekha disclosed, "We have a different life and different trials here so we have more questions than our parents." But she had found the answers to her questions in the Mar Thoma youth group. She concluded, "If not for youth, I wouldn't want to go to church. They are my second family."

However, as "ethnic" churches in a Christian environment, the Mar Thoma and other Kerala Christian churches have to confront the issue of how to retain the allegiance of the second and later generations in the face of intense competition from local American churches. During their three-year terms in the United States, Mar Thoma achens had to face the challenge of understanding and relating to children and youth who had grown up in a very different cultural and religious context. Reaching out to this group was particularly important, since many of the youth were attracted to American evangelicalism, largely through their involvement in evangelical churches and groups when they left home for college. Some American-born Mar Thomites left their parents' church to attend large, non denominational evangelical churches in the area. Even those who stayed had imbibed many evangelical ideas: for example, they were disapproving of the long liturgical services of the Mar Thoma Church and instead preferred non-liturgical praise and worship.

In response, the Mar Thoma Church modified some of its practices in the United States to meet the needs of its foreign-born generations. Besides offering two services a month in English (with a translated and shortened liturgy), many parishes had a praise and worship session led by the youth before the service, and also had a full praise and worship service for youth on the fifth Sunday of a month. The church developed booklets in English about the history of the Mar Thoma Church and its liturgy. They split the youth fellowship into two: one for the English-speaking group and another for the Malayalam speakers, and launched a young couples' fellowship. They organized annual national and regional youth conferences (in addition to family conferences and women's conferences) and, from the early 2000s, sent "youth achens" (immigrant Mar Thoma achens who had good English skills and showed a special expertise in working with youth) to regions of the United States that had a large number of Mar Thoma parishes to cater to the second generation. Finally, following complaints from the second generation and some of their parents that the church should support social service projects in North America, the Mar Thoma Church, with the active participation of lay leaders, started mission projects among a poor fishing community in Northern Mexico and among Native Americans in Oklahoma and Alabama in 2002; some parishes had also begun local outreach efforts.

Conclusion

Although Hindu and Christian Malayali immigrants in the United States have developed separate religious institutions, Malayalis of all backgrounds maintain cordial relationships through their common participation in the Kerala associations that are very active throughout the country. They also get together for Onam celebrations (the major Kerala festival) and to fund raise for humanitarian causes in Kerala - both Hindu and Christian Malayali groups channel substantial amounts of resources to support charitable, religious, and educational activities in Kerala and in other parts of India.

Malayalis in the United States have established a variety of religious institutions to maintain their ethnic and religious traditions and develop a support system in the diaspora. Whether the second and later generations will maintain these institutions remains to be seen. Since the Malayali immigration to the United States is still ongoing, this should not be a concern for some time, because new groups of immigrants are continuously arriving in the country. Consequently, Malayali culture and religious life will continue to thrive in the United States for several more decades to come!

Notes

1. Kurien 2007; Warner 1993; Williams 1988; Yang and Ebaugh 2001.
2. Kurien 2004; Kurien 2007; Kurien forthcoming.
3. Portes and Rumbaut 1996, 39.
4. *www.geethamandalam.org/* (accessed Jul 16, 2012).
5. *www.guruvayurappan.us/1/about-temple/* (accessed Jul 16 2012).
6. *www.ohmohmohm.org/index.php?option=com_content&task=view&id=12&Itemid =30* (accessed Jul 16 2012).

7. Because of the enormous expense involved in the construction, many Hindu temples in the United States tend to be "ecumenical," enshrining deities from several, sometimes opposing traditions. Rituals and worship in such temples are generally conducted in Sanskrit, and in the American context where the meaning of religious practice becomes important, frequently explained in Hindi or English for the benefit of the eclectic audience.

8. *www.namaha.org/seva.html*, (accessed Jul 16 2012).

9. Williams 1996, 39.

References

Kurien, Prema (2004), "Christian by Birth or Rebirth? Generation and Difference in an IndianAmericanChristian Church." In *Asian American Religions: Borders andBoundaries*,edited by Tony Carnes and Fenggang Yang, 160–181. New York: New YorkUniversity Press.

—— (2007), *A Place at the Multicultural Table: The Development of an American Hinduism*. New Brunswick: Rutgers University Press.

——Forthcoming. "Decoupling Religion and Ethnicity: Second-Generation Indian AmericanChristians." *Qualitative Sociology*.

Portes, Alejandro, and Rubén G. Rumbaut (1996), *Immigrant America: A Portrait*. Berkeley: University of California Press.

Warner, Stephen R. (1993), "Work in Progress toward a New Paradigm for the Sociological Study of Religion in the United States." *American Journal of Sociology* 98: 1044–1093.

Williams, Raymond B. (1988), *Religions of Immigrants from India and Pakistan: New Threads in the American Tapestry*. Cambridge: Cambridge University Press.

——(1996), *Christian Pluralism in the United States: The Indian Immigrant Experience*. Cambridge: Cambridge University Press.

Yang, Fenggang, and Helen Rose Ebaugh (2001), "Transformations in New Immigrant Religions and Their Global Implications." *American Sociological Review* 66: 269–288.

14

Malayali Family Life in the Diaspora

THOMAS KULANJIYIL

Introduction

The Kerala community is recognized as one of the most audacious, successful, and established Diaspora communities of Indian origin. In a recent estimate, there were over thirty million Indians living abroad in the status of 'NRIs' (Indian citizens not residing in India) and 'PIOs' (Persons of Indian Origin who have adopted the citizenship of some other country). This number continues to grow as more and more people migrate to foreign countries for the purpose of education, employment and business opportunities. With more relaxed rules of family migration, increasingly Kerala families are settling abroad. The global presence of Malayalis as medical professionals, engineers, lawyers, educators, computer engineers, business executives, and entrepreneurs has not only brought them world-wide acclaim but also much material prosperity. Even the so-called unskilled Kerala immigrants have been financially successful because of their industry. In countries like U.K, U.S, Canada, Australia and New Zealand, the Keralites live in the richest neighborhoods. Their children are educated in some of the prestigious educational institutions. Some are socially and politically prominent; some being elected even to political offices and positions of influence in their host countries. With all these material achievements, how are they doing with their families? How has immigration impacted the family life of people of Kerala origin? What is the tradeoff for these families for chasing after financial success? These are some of the questions I would like to explore in this paper.

When discussing about the Kerala diaspora community, we need to identify two types of community. The first can be described as the "Migrant Worker" community which emigrates to an overseas country, relatively for a certain period of time for employment purposes, and then eventually returns to Kerala. People who work and live in the Middle Eastern countries like Saudi Arabia, Bahrain, Kuwait, United Arab Emirates, Qatar and Oman belong to the first type. This group of emigrants is often branded as the "Going out and Coming in Community," because after being employed in the Middle East for a number of years many of them return home, and after a while they go back overseas to return again.[1] Some repeat this cycle multiple times during the active years of their life.

The second type of emigrant community can be described as the "Permanent Settler" community that emigrates to an overseas country to live there permanently. Living in the host countries with their families and adapting to the new cultural environment, it is most unlikely that these emigrants come back to Kerala to settle down there. Emigrants to the South East Asian countries (like Malaysia, and Singapore), the Western countries (like Canada, the U.S, U.K, Switzerland, Ireland and Germany), and African countries (like South Africa, and Kenya) are typically of this category. Because it is impossible to cover Malayali families worldwide, I will limit my scope to those in the Middle East and in the West as representative of the Malayali diaspora families.

Malayali Family Life in the Middle East

The Kerala Middle Eastern expatriate families are not so much displaced culturally from their native Malayalam as the common medium of communication at most homes, even though very few children are able to read and write in Malayalam. Regular contact with family members in Kerala and cultural similarities of the Middle

Eastern countries greatly help in maintaining many of the Indian customs and practices at home, including behavioral norms. Cultural influences such as arts, music, print media and cinema help to transmit the Indian social values and ideals to the younger generation.

Family structures and dynamics of the most Middle Eastern Malayalis are typically traditional. Households are predominantly patriarchal in structure, although matriarchy is practiced in few communities. The father is the apparent head of the family and the primary provider and protector. The father is the executor of discipline at home, and the mother is the enforcer. Traditional gender roles and expectations are basic to most marriages and family relationships, and this can sometimes contribute to conflict and tension between spouses and between parents and children. With increased exposure to a global culture and the values of personal autonomy and independence, cultural rigidity at home can escalate problems in marital and parental relationships. There are reported cases of spousal abuse and domestic violence within Middle Eastern expatriate Malayali families.

Predominantly, marriages are still arranged in these households, and marriage brings the immediate and the extended families together for a great time of celebration. The younger and the older generation are brought together and the family bond is renewed. This kind of family events helps to preserve the family customs and legacy. Relatively speaking, Middle Eastern expatriate Malayali families are more stable and culturally rooted to Kerala than the rest of the Kerala Diasporas. Part of the reason for this could be that the Middle Eastern expatriate families are actively in touch with their native land, coupled with frequent visits which ensure the preserving of their cultural, religious, and social values. They consider Kerala as their home country as they know that they cannot permanently settle in any of the Middle Eastern countries. For these various reasons migration-related stress is relatively low in this community.

Some Unique Problems Facing the Gulf Malayalis

Because of various immigration restrictions and income requirements, not all Gulf Malayali workforces are able to migrate with their families.

Among those that are qualified to have their families accompany them, there are individuals who prefer the family stay back in Kerala. For all these reasons, it is estimated that over 1.2 million married women are currently living in Kerala, whose husbands are employed overseas.[2] These women are generally labeled as "Gulf Wives." Similarly, there are relatively a small number of families, where women are employed abroad, and their husbands are caring for children at home. As we shall see, this has huge implications for the Gulf Malayali families.

Generally, families that live in the Gulf countries are forced to send away their children to India around the time they are ready for college or to look for secondary migration to countries like the U.S and Canada. Some are able to fund their children aboard for further studies. The destination countries for these families are frequently the U.S., Canada or Australia. Many of these children would never come back to Kerala to live or to work there, and like any other immigrant children in the Western countries, they are exposed to Western culture and education. At any event, often there is a foreseeable separation of family members for the Middle Eastern emigrants, and this can add to their anxiety and uncertainties about the future.

Migration to the Middle Eastern countries impacts the migrant families in some unique ways. As indicated earlier, there is a predictable family separation for these families and they might be short-term or long-term. In certain cases, men, as husbands and fathers, are removed from home for a number of years, only to come home on holidays. While some can afford to come every year for a few weeks, others cannot. This creates a vacuum at home which means all family responsibilities are left with the woman of the home. Many of these men miss out on several milestones of their children, like birthdays, and graduations. They rob themselves of the opportunity to be involved in the moral and spiritual formation of their children during the most formative years of their lives. When these men come home, their children have great difficulty to bond with them. When children are about to initiate meaningful relationship with fathers, it will be time for the latter to depart. This not only disappoints children, but makes them feel abandoned and uncared for. Although children might compensate for the absentee father in positive or negative ways, a number of them would find themselves having to deal with psychological, educational, and social problems that negatively impact their future. In the place of an absentee husband and father, it is upon the wife or the mother to singlehandedly take on meeting the physical needs, parenting responsibilities, and educational needs of the children. Some children take advantage of not having a father at home, and rebel against the mother's authority over them. A lot of time such children are hard to discipline, and they will exasperate the mother. These women are overwhelmed because of the enormous pressure put on them to do everything right for their children; and if anything goes wrong they know that they will be blamed for. Personal self-care is generally compromised in the midst of the various stressors that come over the course of time. Years of spousal separation makes these women physically weary and emotionally disgruntled. Lack of marital fulfillment leads to increased marital tension and conflicts.

Family separation impacts men as well, physically and psychologically. While living on your own, some men pay very little attention to their health, and they easily become subject to many types of illnesses that may include diabetes, hypertension, ulcer, and heart disorders. Depression takes on a number of these men in due course of time. The reality is that while these men are tirelessly working hard to make more money, they are deprived of a life together with their families. In spite of accumulating a lot of wealth, in a typical Gulf Malayali family, what is lacking is the joy of fully experiencing family life. Separated from their families, there are men who are given into gambling, drug and alcohol addiction, pornography, and extra marital affairs through internet dating. There are real reported incidences as well, where men upon returning home, have turned to violence, doubting the chastity of their spouses.

Another problem for the Gulf Malayali community is the impact of recent global recession on their job opportunities in the Middle East. Due to unemployment and under employment, many are forced to return to Kerala, or to send their families away temporarily or permanently. Whether they stay in the Middle East or come back to Kerala, there is a substantial financial stress put on these families.

Not being able to find suitable employment opportunities in India, especially in Kerala, some of these men recourse to family violence and other social crimes. Because of these outlandish behaviors, now-a-days, a lot of people look at the "Gulf Returns" with an attitude of mistrust and apprehension.

Malayali Family Life in the West

Proliferation of Kerala immigrants in the U.K, U.S and Canada have started since the 1950's. While a majority of the Kerala immigrants have become "naturalized citizens" of these countries, there are a small percentage of them that maintain the status of "resident alien", because they retain their Indian citizenship. In countries like the U.S. you can now maintain a dual citizenship, and become eligible for OCI (Oversees citizen of India) status. With legal provisions to bring family members to countries like the United States, and Canada, more and more Kerala families are migrating to these countries. This is a big difference in family migration from the Middle Eastern type.

The North American Malayali immigrant families are driven by the so-called "American Dream," and as hardworking they are, every Malayali seeks to provide a great and successful future to their children. They are conspicuous for their devotion to family. They are family-oriented, and are committed to the prosperity of the family. Although geographically removed from Kerala, they maintain regular contacts with friends and families back home. Extended family plays a huge role in the lives of these Malayalis, and in these days *Kudumba Yogam* or extended family celebrations are becoming quite common as a way to connect with immediate family members. Recognizing the likelihood of a total disconnect of the emerging generation with the extended families in the future , the first generation parents are now being intentional in creating opportunities for family networking.

The Indian cultural values shape the identity of the first generation immigrants, and they attempt to inculcate those priced values to their children. First generation parents largely speak Malayalam at home, although it gradually gives away to English with the younger generation. Very few in the younger generation seem to have an aptitude for learning Malayalam. Now-a-days, however, written and conversational Malayalam is taught in churches and communities. Characteristic of the Malayali diaspora community is the establishment of *Malayam Samacham* which becomes a forum for cultural expression through Indian arts, music and festivals, wherever they are. These cultural institutions help the Malayali diaspora to preserve cultural ties with Kerala.

Religion plays a central role in the lives of Malayali families throughout the globe. Malayalam is used as medium of worship in religious congregations of Kerala origin, but for the sake of the younger generation both Malayalam and English is simultaneously used. A very promising trend within the Christian diaspora community is the emergence of second generation leadership in the churches; some born and raised in the West are taking religious vocations within the Kerala churches.

Notwithstanding these great qualities and accomplishments, there are unique challenges and problems these families confront in the overseas. In many respects, these challenges and problems are representative of what the Malayali families are experiencing in other parts of the Western world. In the forgoing discussion we shall attempt to describe a few outstanding ones.

Immigration-related Stress

The life cycle phase at which one migrates to a new country makes a big difference in the adjustment process. It has been found that migration in later life is especially difficult, and with the exception of those who have arrived as students or as recent recruits of the international companies, most first generation Kerala immigrants are either middle aged or older adults. The skillset needed for this kind of a geographical relocation are quite different from that of the Middle Eastern type of immigrant. Having to relocate, to adjust, and to adapt to an alien cultural environment is quite challenging and demanding, and it is a long process that affects family members differently. Children may adjust faster than their parents as they begin to socialize with the outside world, but that can create increased strain between parents and children because of cultural conflicts. As Das & Kemp rightly point out immigration is a painful experience because people are being uprooted from a familiar world, leaving close relatives, friends behind. They explain this problem further:

> The typical Indian family, in its native setting, is embedded in a tight network of close relatives and friends. When a family immigrates, these networks are disturbed, and the family has to establish new societal contacts out of which new social support systems have to emerge. In the meantime, the capacity of family to provide emotional support to its members could be compromised. New stress may develop between husband and wife, and especially if the husband is trying to establish himself in a demanding career and the wife is home alone with little contact with the outside world.[3]

Characteristic of many Kerala immigrant families is that prior to immigrating to North America, they have had no exposure outside of Kerala, and they have lived their entire life in the confines of a small village or a town. Being uprooted straight from Kerala and being planted in an alien environment, they are overwhelmed by all the cues and demands of the new society where they have come to make their home. While they live with the hope that they will be able to return home once their children are relatively established, the realization that they might never go back worries them. In actuality, only a few are able to go back because very often families are tied up with numerous financial commitments and family obligations.

Another challenge for the immigrant families is that a large number of them, who have never been in a job before, are suddenly forced to find some kind of work to support the family. This can be too stressful for the individuals as well as the families. These new immigrants are to pick up a new trade or a skill, and the work environment is quite unfamiliar to them. Driving skills are a necessity for survival in most Western countries, and those without this ability have to depend on others for all transportation needs. Forced dependability on others may lead to feelings of lack of personal control, self-inadequacy and helplessness. Not being able to communicate adequately in English, force these individuals to confine themselves to the *"malayali"* enclave. There are other kinds of difficulties the new immigrants come across. Displaced from their familiar environment and social network, they experience loneliness and depression, often questioning their decision to migrate. In the initial stages of their adaptation to the Western society, most immigrant families find life very hard, but they overcome these difficulties over the course of time. In this transitional phase, family members demonstrate great support and care for one another and they draw strength from each other to become accustomedto their new world.

Intergenerational Tension and Value Conflicts

The children of the first generation Indian immigrants are often labeled as the "Coconut Generation" - brown on the outside, white on the inside.[4] Having to socialize in a dual cultural environment, the subculture of the Kerala family and the dominant culture of the mainstream American society, is a practical reality for the children of Kerala immigrants. This forces them to compartmentalize their lives; living at home as Indians, and at school, work, and other public places as Americans. Sam George writes:

> Most Indian American youth feel torn between being Indian and being American, a predicament shaped by their Indian upbringing and American socialization. Having grown up in a homogenized culture back in India, the first generation is often unaware and insensitive to the struggle of the second generation in discovering their identities in a new land.[5]

Conflicts frequently arise between parents and children along the lines of cultural norms and values because the typical first generation Malayali parents hold on to their traditional cultural values, family ideologies, religious beliefs, and customs and practices.[6] Cultural rigidity, lack of sympathetic understanding and rebuttal to conciliation, on the part of parents, augment the intergenerational friction. In the same token, apathy towards Indian culture, unrestrained adaptation of Western value system and life style, on the part of the younger generation, widen the communication gap between parents and children. Das Gupta points out that the fear of cultural obliteration by the trend of "Americanization" forces many Indian parents to be very protective of their children, and this is very true of typical Malayali families. By restricting socialization with Americans, by disapproving dating, by resisting marital integration with non-Indians (with non-Malayalis to be more accurate), and by imposing culturally approved behavior (Indian cultural norms), especially on females, they try to control their children's behavior.[7] Das Gupta further observes that the older their female children are, the more conservative their mothers become regarding women's role. It is speculated that as adolescents grow older, their mothers start experiencing the pressure of making their children socialize in the traditional gender roles. Das Gupta finds that children born and brought up in the U.S. hold more liberal views about men and women's roles in society than their counterparts in India, and they resent gender bias held by their parents.[8] Anitha Varghese, in her study on acculturation, parental control, and adjustment among Asian Indian women, has this to say about the effect of intergenerational conflict:

> Like other Asian Indian groups, intergenerational familial conflicts regarding cultural differences also appear to be salient for Malayalee families. Conflicts regarding independence and autonomy also are relevant for Malayalee families. Specifically, it appears maternal overprotection and control plays a prominent role in daughters' self-esteem.[9]

The subject of marriage is one of the most crucial issues of disagreement between children and the Kerala parents. Social status, caste, religious background, and in cases even dowry are important to Kerala parents, but the truth is that the general outlook of the younger generation to marriage is quite different from that of their parents. Generally, they have an aversion to traditional arranged marriage and parents cannot force children to marry someone they are not willing or ready to accept. The young people assert greater personal freedom to choose one's life partner. With some exception, they in general, prefer to marry someone that they have known for over a period of time, preferably in a dating-like relationship. Intellectual, psychological, and cultural compatibility is central to their choice of a life partner. They tend to be more flexible with caste, class, heredity, ethnicity, and religion. In many cases, the second generation themselves finance their marriage, plan and execute it. What they expect from parents is sheer approval and blessings for the partner of their choice, and some financial assistance to cover the marriage expenses. Although this way of approaching marriage is quite disturbing and unacceptable to most Malayali parents, often parents negotiate and compromise on many of these problem areas.

Marital Conflicts and Domestic Violence

The greater freedom for self-expression, autonomy, and economic independence the Kerala women find in the West can become a cause for marital conflict. Men who hold onto traditional gender roles and marital expectations find it extremely difficult to give up on their control over their spouses. The notion of an assertive, independent woman is loathing to traditional Kerala men who expect their spouses to be submissive and subservient to them. It is told that working Indian women in North America are forced to develop two different personalities, one that is assertive and appropriate for the American working culture, and the other that is subservient to the demands of a traditional Indian household. This kind of a split in thinking and functioning on a daily basis is detrimental to the psychological well-being and marital satisfaction of the Kerala women.[10]

Religious and cultural justifications of female subordination and submissiveness to men seem to perpetuate the abuse, and the Kerala community is no exception to this problem. Many families live under the constant threat of hostility and brutality, and yet they assume that domestic abuse is a normal part of life, something that is to be expected and tolerated. Leela Cherian, who has studied extensively the problem of domestic violence in the South Asian community, writes:

> Most South Asian women consider abuse in marital intimate relationships as normal. They tend to think that men are aggressive by nature and therefore it is their right to be aggressive to their spouses. Those who have been exposed to domestic abuse while growing up, do not consider it a problem. Some continue in an abusive marital relationship due to economic dependence on their husbands, lack of education, or lack of information on resources available to battered women and children in the community. Most victims often choose to continue in abusive relationships because they want their children to have a father figure in their lives. They genuinely hope that they can work things out with their partners and that one day the abuse will stop.[11]

For these various reasons, Malayali families cover up the perpetual abuses, and most cases go unreported. Nonetheless, reported cases of domestic violence in the Asian Indian households are in increase these days. The US has stricter laws on domestic violence than India, and with the kind of laws and provisions available to battered women today, women are refusing to be put up with the abuse. They are coming to a new awareness of their rights and choices, and some have mustered enough courage to report cases of abuse. In recent years, a few Asian Indian organizations have come forward to provide shelter, counseling, and legal services to battered women and children of South Asian origin and it is only indicative of how ominous is this problem among the Indian community.

Dysfunctionality marks the relational dynamics of a number of Kerala homes in the U.S, where marital disharmony makes home life miserable for everyone. In such homes, parental responsibilities are overlooked, and there are households where children control their parents because parents have lost their moral authority over them. There are families that are battling with the problem of addiction, and it includes both parents and children. Drug and alcoholic addictions are on the rise but practically none seeks the help of professional services.

Divorce among the Indo-Americans is fairly a recent a trend but it is escalating today, and unfortunately, this number is especially alarming for the Kerala families.[12] It appears that the attitude to marriage as a life-long commitment, informed by the religious and cultural traditions of India, is slowly vanishing among the new generation of Indian immigrants. What is alarming is that the divorce rate is going up even among the first generation immigrants. Taking advantage of the legal provisions of the Western countries, and the cultural tolerance for divorce, the Malayali immigrants find an easy way to get out of marriages that have been either abusive or less satisfying. Social anonymity also plays a part in it. It's not a big deal to be a divorcee in a Western society, whereas in India it still is, though attitudes are changing there as well. Numerous cases of divorce, marital separation, and re-marriages are reported within the community. Those who know the Kerala community closely are aware of this sad commentary of the Malayali families. With the knack to cover up personal and familial problems from the public, the typical Malayali acts as if everything is fine with him or her, but bleeds from the inside.

Broken Relationships

A lot of people in the Kerala diaspora community live their lives in the midst of broken relationships. People are at odds with each other in the process of trying to catch up with those who have come before them, or with those whom they perceive as better off than themselves. Relationships are often shallow and superficial. Even immediate family members are competing against each other to show that one set of the family is better than the other. Families are not able to appreciate the achievements of their own people, but rather, they are jealous, and angry. For many, family relationships are deteriorating to the extent of being permanently cut off from one another.[13]

Most families have come to North America through family- based immigration, and regrettably, it has been observed that within a short span of time, a limited number of these families experience a breakup in their relationship. One of the causal factors for this seems to be that after a few weeks or months, the host families expect the new arrivals to be of their own; however, generally the newly arrivals are not yet ready for such an immediate transition. They still need a lot of help and guidance from others to navigate the initiate adjustment. Asking them to be of their own in such a short span of time is, therefore, perceived as a kind of abandonment. This leads to rupture in relationships. In a personal interview, an immigrant from Kerala, stated, "My sister and her family brought us to this country, but sadly, today we don't even speak to each other. I wish I did not come to America. It hurts." Another responded, "We have every comfort here, but not any personal satisfaction. My families don't get along anymore." Material affluence in the midst of broken relationships makes the 'American dream' quite empty and meaningless.

The Older Adults

A significant number of Kerala households have elderly parents living with them. These aging parents are brought to the US primarily for baby-sitting needs or because there is none to take of them back in Kerala. Frequently relationship between these elderly parents and their children get strenuous on account of grandparents getting involved in the affairs of parenting. Intergenerational conflict escalates on account of values and norms, and as a result in some households grandchildren totally ignore the grandparents. Communication between grandparents and the rest of the household at times becomes so poor that it contributes to their loneliness. Taking care of the older parents adds to the stress level and financial commitments of these immigrant families, and there are times when the welfare of the elderly are compromised. In spite of these difficulties, it must be appreciated that the Kerala immigrant families are not giving up on their aging parents, as it is happening in many parts of India today.

In cases where the elderly are transitioned to an institutional care, most are dissatisfied, and the American elder care system is not adequately prepared to meet their needs. Language, food, life-style, cultural sensitivity, socialization and recreation opportunities are major problems for them. In a few instances of visiting Indian residents in nursing homes this author received the following responses: "I don't eat much; I drink a few cups of coffee daily. All that I need is little *kanjivellam*"; "I confine myself to this room. I seldom get out or talk to anybody." Thinking through a viable alternative to home-based elder care is still a matter of interest and practical necessity for the North American immigrants.[14]

The Aging Early Immigrants

A critical stage in the history of Kerala diaspora in the West is the aging of early immigrants that arrived in the 60's and the 70's. A large number of them are now senior citizens, and in the ensuing years this number is expected to rise. Will these elderly continue to stay in their adapted countries, or will they return to India? If they choose to stay back, could they expect the continued support of their families? Will the younger generation step up to their filial responsibilities to care for these aging parents? Will these seniors be open to the idea of elderly housing programs, popular in the West, or will they prefer independent living? If they return to Kerala, will they be able to adjust to the living conditions there? These are some of the practical questions that face Western immigrant Kerala families today.

Conclusion

In the forgoing discussion we have tried to look at the two major centers of the Kerala diaspora, countries in the Middle East and in the West. We have identified both the strengths and weaknesses of the Kerala families in these countries, along with some unique challenges they face. What is commendable in both of these diaspora communities is that even after decades of displacement from their native land; these expatriate Malayalis make every effort to preserve their cultural ties with India. They have not forgotten the fact that their cultural roots are in India.

As to the Gulf Malayali emigrants, amidst the many challenges and uncertainties they face with regard to continued employment opportunities in those countries, especially in the light of recent global recession, it must be appreciated that their families are relatively more stable than those in the West. The unique problem of family separation, especially, the father absenteeism detrimental to children, must be taken seriously and practicable solutions to reduce its impact on children must be explored.

With regard to the Malayali families in the West, families have the advantage of living together, and navigating through the many challenges of living in an alien cultural environment. While the first generation immigrants are selective in their cultural adaptation and slow in the acculturation process, the younger generation is quick in assimilating to the mainstream culture. Families in the West have less contact with Kerala, in comparison to families in the Middle East, and this contributes to the ever increasing disinterestedness of Malayali progenies in the West from the Indian culture. Unless parents are deliberate about maintaining cultural ties and family connections, it is possible that future generations will gradually lessen their links with India. This is especially possible in the context of increasing inter-racial marriages within the Kerala community. Intergenerational conflict over differing parental expectations, value systems and norms, makes relationship more complex and difficult in the Malayali families. There is a greater need for mutual dialogue to understand each other and to negotiate their differences to foster more lasting relationships. A significant problem area the Kerala diaspora families have to wrestle with is the institution of marriage, which is too unstable at present. Individualism and egotism largely dictate the Western notions of marriage, and these are the values that fundamentally shape the new generation's attitude to marriage. The inherited cultural values and spiritual tenets of the Indian immigrants can offer the needed corrective to this kind of an outlook on marriage.

The Malayali diaspora families will continue to thrive around the world; even as the migration trend continues. With a willingness to objectively assess the state of each individual family, together with a commitment to bring added health and wholeness in relationships, the global Malayali Diaspora can expect a brighter future.

Notes

1. Ali, Syed. "Going and Coming and Going Again: Second-Generation Migrants in Dubai," *Mobilites*, Vol. 6, No. 4, 2011, 553–568.

2. Zachariah, K.C. & Irudaya Rajan. "Impact of the global recession onmigration and remittances in Kerala: New evidences from the return migration survey" (RMS) 2009.

3. Das, A.K. & Kemp, S.F. Between two worlds: Counseling South Asian Americans. *Journal of Multicultural Counseling and Development*, 25, 1, 1997. 23-33.

4. Agarwal, Priya. *Passage from India: Post 1965 Indian Immigrants and Their Children.* CA: Yuvati Publications, 1991.

5. George, Sam. *Understanding the Coconut Generation: Ministry to the Americanized Indians.*Niles: Mall Publishers. 2006.

6. Kurien, G. "Intergenerational integration with special reference to Indian families." *Indian Journal of Social Work*, 47, 1986. 39-49.

7. Gupta, Das. "Marching to a different drummer? Sex roles of Asian Indian women in the United States." *Women and Therapy*, 5, 1986. 297-311.

8. *Ibid.*

9. Varghese, Anita "Acculturation, Parental Control, And Adjustment among Asian Indian Women," Unpublished Master's Thesis, University of North Texas, 2007.59.

10. Kar, S. B., Combell, K., Jimenez, A., & Gupta, S.R. "Invisible Americans: Indo-American quality of life." *American Journal,* 21, 1995/96. 25-52.

11. Cherian, Leela. "Hitting Out: Violent Behaviors in South Asian Indian Families," Ed. Thomas Kulanjiyil & Thomas T.V. *Caring for the South Asian*

Soul: Counseling South Asians in the Western World, Bangalore: Primalogue, 2010. 46.

12. George, Sam, *op cit.*

13. Kulanjiyil, Thomas. "Family Feud and Unhealthy Competitiveness." *India Tribune*, Vol. 36, No. 25, 2012.

14. Kulanjiyil, Thomas, "Mental health Needs of South Asian Indians." Ed. Thomas Kulanjiyil & Thomas T.V. *Caring for the South Asian Soul: Counseling South Asians in the Western World*, Bangalore: Primalogue, 2010, 46.

References

Agarwal, Priya. *Passage from India: Post 1965 Indian Immigrants and Their Children.* CA: Yuvati Publications, 1991.

Ali, Syed. "Going and Coming and Going Again: Second-Generation Migrants in Dubai," *Mobilites*, Vol. 6, No. 4, 2011, 553–568.

Cherian, Leela. "Hitting Out: Violent Behaviors in South Asian Indian Families," Eds. Thomas Kulanjiyil & T. V. Thomas. *Caring for the South Asian Soul: Counseling South Asians in the Western World*, Bangalore: Primalogue, 2010. 46.

Das, A.K. & Kemp, S.F. "Between two Worlds: Counseling South Asian Americans" in *Journal of Multicultural Counseling and Development*, 25, 1, 1997. 23-33.

George, Sam. *Understanding the Coconut Generation: Ministry to the Americanized Indians*, Niles, IL: Mall Publishers. 2006.

Gupta, Das. "Marching to a Different Drummer? Sex Roles of Asian Indian Women in the United States." *Women and Therapy*, 5, 1986. 297-311.

Kar, S. B., Combell, K., Jimenez, A., & Gupta, S. R. "Invisible Americans: Indo-American Quality of Life." *American Journal*, 21, 1995/96. 25-52.

Kulanjiyil, Thomas. "Family Feud and Unhealthy Competitiveness." *India Tribune*, Vol. 36, No. 25, 2012.

Kulanjiyil, Thomas, "Mental health Needs of South Asian Indians." Eds. Thomas Kulanjiyil & Thomas T.V. *Caring for the South Asian Soul: Counseling South Asians in the Western World*, Bangalore: Primalogue, 2010. 46.

Kurien, G. "Intergenerational Integration with Special Reference to Indian Families." *Indian Journal of Social Work*, 47, 1986.39-49.

Varghese, Anita "Acculturation, Parental Control, and Adjustment among Asian Indian Women," Unpublished Master's Thesis, University of North Texas, 2007, p. 59.

Zachariah, K. C. & Irudaya Rajan. "Impact of the Global Recession Onmigration and Remittances in Kerala: New Evidences from the Return Migration Survey" (RMS) 2009.

15

Malayalis Without Malayalam:
Language Proficiency of Children of Kerala Immigrants

Sam George

Introduction

Is it possible to be a Malayali without knowing Malayalam? Is a person more defined by ethnicity or linguistic competency? Can the primary or sole language a Malayali knows be English or German? Or what if children of Malayali immigrants get to learn only French, Mandarin or Spanish, instead of the language of God's own country? Or what about children who answer in English when you ask them a question in Malayalam? Will the emerging pan-Indian identity in diasporic contexts dissolve regional distinctions in subsequent generations? Will ethnicity be lost over many generations of life abroad? Will increasing inter cultural marriages diminish Malayali uniqueness or will they absorb the other race into Malayali culture?

Let me begin with myself. I grew up outside of Kerala in the Andaman Islands but I now live in the US. Malayalam is the heritage heart language of my parents. I learned Malayalam at home and in primary school, besides English and Hindi in a three-language educational system. But most of my schooling and particularly college education was all in English. Although I can understand Malayalam fairly well and can sustain meaningful conversations in Malayalam, I think in English. Most of my ideas and thoughts are generated in

English. I read, speak and write mostly in English. Some have translated a number of my speeches and writings into other Indian languages including Malayalam, but my dominant or heart language remains to be English.

This predicament is not limited to me. Mine is not an isolated case. Most children of Malayalis who have grown up in the West have lost linguistic proficiency in their mother tongue. The dilemmas of children of Malayalis in America go through are strange and sometimes painful. Their friends at school and neighborhood see them as Indian, as they cannot distinguish between regional and linguistic differences of India. On the other hand their parents are concerned that their children are becoming too American. A young Malayali woman feels the sting of being called a "coconut" (brown on the outside, white on the inside) by fellow Indian students in college 'just because she grew up in a white suburb" while her mother reminds her to "marry only a Malayali boy" preferably from the same church denomination! The tug of war between parental pressure to ethnic language competency and peer pressure to embrace Western culture and language accent goes on incessantly often swinging between extremities of ethnic and national loyalties and belongings.

Decline of Ethnic Language In The Diaspora

The ethnic language transmission, retention and loss are important concern for diasporic communities. Other key terms used for immigrant minority languages are mother tongue or heritage language. Language is inextricably interwoven with culture and teaching ethnic language is considered a high priority in migrant communities, yet remains an enormous challenge for immigrant parents for the lack of resources, training and support. Ethnic language is at the center of debates on assimilation, ethnic identity formation, integration, cohesion, citizenship and multiculturalism.

Many have explored language transmission across generations in the global Indian diaspora. Ebaugh and Chfetz called language in immigrant homes a cause of unity and conflict.[1] Dewan found that by the third generation Sindhis in Manila had replaced their ancestral language with English[2]. David analyzed the loss of language and its relationship to identity of Indians in Malaysia and found that primary language is shifting to Malay and English.[3] Helwegs noted that Asian Indian immigrants to the United States conducted Hindi language classes to the children but failed to generate enough interest.[4] Agarwal in her study of post-1965 Indian immigrants and their children learned that one of the least interested aspect of Indian cultural retention in the second generation were language and regional division.[5] Detarramani and Lock reported a marked reduction in multilingualism in Hong Kong.[6] Nair and Percot raised the concern of Malayali nurses in the Gulf countries that their children might become aliens not getting to learn Malayalam.[7] Barn studied the experience of the second generation Indian parents' views towards heritage language transmission in the United Kingdom (mostly north Indians) and found that majority of children spoke only English and the sole use of heritage language was very minimal.[8] Rangaswamy and George have dealt at length about the generational transmission of language among Indian Americans.[9]

People from Kerala have migrated out of India for centuries. However, a significant size of Malayali settlement outside of India occurred only in the twentieth century. In the 1930s, 40s and 50s hundreds left Kerala for Malaysia, Singapore and East Africa. The surge in emirgration of Keralites came in the1960s to the Gulf region, Europe and North America. The overseas Indians generally use three modes of self-identification: language, religion and originating region. The cultural, religious, professional and political associations have helped to sustain their communal and corporate identity. This is also true among Keralites. Malayalam newspapers have continually fed the insatiable need for news from their distant homelands and Malayalam television channels enthralled them with variety of entertainment programs and cine music. Malayalam movies and internet portals are popular in creating a transcontinental ethnic consciousness of the dispersed people.

Why the decline in ethnic language in the Diaspora? Many have attributed different reasons to this trend of generational discontinuity with respect to ethnic language competence. Malayalis generally ascribe lesser economic value to linguistic competence and send their children to English-medium schools. The socialistic ideology that prevailed in Kerala after the Indian Independence forced many well-educated Malayalis to look elsewhere for employment, beginning with major Indian cities and overseas destinations. Most Kerala migrants to the West were professionals and operated mostly in dominant languages in their host nations. Malayalis are adaptable and pragmatic people. To survive or thrive Malayalis are willing to adjust to local realities and to prosper in cross-cultural settings. Their global presence is both a testimony to that fact and a reminder of their loosing something of their own culture in the process.

However, the decline of Malayalam usage in the diaspora should not be seen as a failure of parents to pass on the linguistic skills to their foreign born offspring. Their host societies did not offer any value in the retention of ethnic languages, in fact they are often seen negatively as nurturing a ghetto mentality. The immigrant Malayali communities did not possess resources or vision to establish institutions that will sustain linguistic adeptness. Furthermore, the absence of a critical mass among the widely dispersed Malayali immigrants further caused the decline.

American Reality: One Language Nation

The immigrants to America face a strange reality – a rich linguistic diversity among immigrant generations which are often lost within a generation or two. The immigrants from around the world who arrive on the American shores value multilingual competency and were often schooled in two-or even three-language system or acquire minimal English proficiency soon after arriving in the United States. But their children fast become monolingual in America and start losing touch with their ancestral languages. American sociologist called the United States as "the language graveyard."[10]

Few immigrant groups have successfully maintained their ethnic languages as they become assimilated into the American life. Even in ethnic groups like Hispanic (largest in size) or Jews (strongest emphasis on cultural and linguistic preservation), there are clear signs of loss of language skills beyond second and definitely in the third generation. Though some can understand and learn to speak as needed, they think and operate mostly in English. This is more than an ideological shift but pragmatism driven. More opportunity exists for advancement in the West with English than any other language. The emergence of English as the world's lingua franca or default tongue enhanced its preference over provincial languages. McCrum in his recent book *Globish* is optimistic about English by declaring it as "the worldwide dialect of the third millennium."[11] Computers and the World Wide Web aggregated the hegemony of the English language further, making it as the dominant language for most children of immigrants in the West. The American reality is that it is a one language nation.

So, is the melting pot theory of cultures still valid? In spite of loss of language, emerging generations are preserving distinctive cultural aspects of their ethnicity. Even if Indian immigrants and/or their children can speak English perfectly with an American accent and style, they are still perceived as Indian by the majority culture. Consequently, a pan-Indian identity is becoming dominant as children of immigrants from the various regions of India face a similar dilemma. The loss of Indian regional language has become the uniting feature among American-born children of all immigrants from India.

Indian diasporic writers predominantly chose English as a language of their literature and went on to win coveted literary awards and recognition. Of course, writing in English appeals to a larger marketplace and makes more business sense, not to mention literature of cultural hybridity was highly sought after. The writings of Salman Rushdie to Arundhati Roy have interwoven character and landscape of Kerala in their award-winning works. The poetry of Meena Alexander, travelogues of Pico Iyer and news reports of Malayali origin journalists appear in newspapers and televisions daily around the world, all written and presented primarily in English and other languages.

Role of Language In Identity Development

Language is an important aspect in the formation of ethnic identity in the diaspora. Family, religious gatherings, cultural associations and ethnic media consumption determine language proficiency in the children of immigrants. The maintenance of language in the diaspora is an important issue among most of the diasporic groups, as it not only provides a forum to bind the community together, but also attaches them to their homeland and thereby their culture, tradition, and value system.

The diasporic Indians in this sense have retained much of their language through publishing newspapers, journals, novels, literary anthologies, and stage plays in their regional vernaculars literary. But the experience of racism and negative stereotyping makes children of immigrants to distance themselves from their ethnic selves, whether it is ethnic food, culture or language in a predominantly majority culture settings like the school cafeterias, hallways or college dorms. The derogatory name calling and labeling abound in multicultural societies. When children are forcefully enculturated and learn the heritage language at the cost of assimilation tend to possess negative views of mainstream culture and struggle to survive in meaningful vocational and relational commitments.

The loss of language is more than mere inability to acquire fluency in another language, it is also losing part of one's self that is related to self-conception, cultural heritage and religious traditions. The children of immigrants move in one direction of losing eloquence in their ancestral language and culture as they assimilate into dominant culture while their parents move in the opposite direction as they remain steeped in their own language and culture, leading to dissonant acculturation and generational discontinuity. Communication across generations breaks down, widening the generation gap and reduces parental authority and control. When immigrants attempt to maintain a ghetto mentality of cultural pride and superiority over the dominant culture, their children often polarize to the other extreme or become the conduit through which parents experience mainstream culture.

It is often difficult for the second generation Malayalis to answer the question 'who am I?' as they feel torn between two realities of their Malayaliness/Indianness and Americanness. They oscillate between their ethnic self and their American self, and their self-identification will change in different life stages. This is particularly most pronounced in their adolescence when their self-identity is being shaped. Their experiences of otherness and how they have been perceived by peer and majority culture will significantly shape their sense of self. Two major factors shape their self-conception of self-identity, namely assimilation and ethnic identity development. Children's ethnic self-identification varies from regional Indian (Malayali) to pan-ethnic (Indian) to hyphenated American (Indian-American) to all American to hybrid or mixed identity (Coconut).

Future of Ethnic Language Competency

Not everything is lost. Several Malayali immigrants in Malaysia and Singapore have successfully conducted Malayalam classes for their progenies. The vernacular education has been introduced in school curriculums in some countries wherever sizeable numbers of Malayalis have settled. A significant number of Indian schools in the Gulf countries offer such opportunities. A number of Malayali Christian churches and Hindu Temple *Bala Vihars* have promoted language classes in the UK and the US. Most Kerala cultural associations worldwide have fervently taken up the task of preserving and popularizing culture and heritage, including the Malayalam language as one of its chief objectives. Numerous web and video-based Malayalam learning tools have been developed and widely used today. Availability of more literature, popular media and ubiquitous Internet have definitely increased the appetite of global Malayalis in the usage of their mother tongue and help future generations acquire linguistic aptitude.

It is easy to introduce Malayalam as an option in societies which value and promote bilingualism, and thus children can grow up acquiring other language skills. This is particularly true of the Middle East, where immigrant parents do not see a long term future for their children. They tend to keep close contact with the ancestral home land and its culture and their children acquire more Malayalam proficiency along with English, Hindi and even with Arabic in some cases.

Hybridization of an Indian language with English is a common phenomenon in India and is more pronounced among children of immigrants. *Manglish*, as the hybrid of Malayalam and English as popularly known, is used extensively by celebrities, television show hosts and in popular culture. It is customary in immigrant households to regularly hear sentences containing both Malayalam and English, though it may be mostly English with few Malayalam words sprinkled here and there. Some Malayali Americans have acquired an uncanny ability to switch between languages and communicating their thoughts and feelings effectively in Manglish.

Diaspora scholars among widely dispersed people note the resurgence of ethnic language and culture in future generations. The search for ethnic roots intensifies in the third and fourth generations and thus the interest in the language might grow. The Christian mission have historically valued and encouraged development of language, such as the case of Scottish missionaries translating the Bible to Malayalam and the continued immigrant Christian engagement with Kerala will renew their interest in the language of their forefathers. The growing presence and profile of India as a global power and the positive perception of the New India might lead some foreign born Malayalis to return to pursue life and careers in Kerala or India, and that likely will renew interest in the language.

Conclusion

Language issues are more complicated for diasporic families than generally assumed. Let us return to the question we began with. Is it possible to be a Malayali without knowing Malayalam? Ethnicity is inherited and children of immigrants anywhere in the world have no choice in this matter. But language proficiency is an acquired skill and depends on available opportunity, value perception by parents and host nations. As regional ethnic identities get morphed into a pan-Indian identity and high out marriages have diluted Malayali self-conception. Also, people of other races are getting more interested in the Malayali culture and language. Who knows if the Malayali identity will survive beyond the first generation or at most, the second generation? Or if there would be a major resurgence of interest in learning Malayalam in the future generations!

Notes

1. Helen Ebaugh and Janet Chafetz. (2000), *Religion and the New Immigrants: Continuities and Adaptations in Immigrant Congregations,* (Walnut Creek, CA: AltaMira Press). 100.

2. R. Dewan (1987), Deethnicisation: A study of language and culture change in the Sindhi immigrant community of Metro Manila. Unpublished PhD thesis, De La Salle University.

3. Maya David (2008), "Does loss of language equate to loss of identity" Unpublished paper, Kuala Lumpur, Malaysia.

4. Arthur Helweg and Usha Helweg. (1990), *An Immigrant Success Story: East Indians in America.* (Philadelphia: University of Pennsylvania Press), 115.

5. Priya Agrawal (1990), *Passage from India: Post 1965 Indian Immigrants and Their Children.* (Palos Verdes, CA: Yuvati Publications). 41.

6. Champa Detaramani and Graham Lock (2003), "Multilingualism in Decline: Language Repertoire, Use and Shift in Two Hong Kong Indian Communities" in *Journal. of Multilingual and Multicultural Development* Vol. 24, No. 4.

7. Sreelekah Nair and Marie Percot (2007), "Transcending Boundaries: Indian Nurses in Internal and International Migration." Occasional Paper, Centre for Women's Development Studies.

8. Ravinder Barn. (2008), 'Indian Diaspora in the UK: Second Generation Parents Views and Experiences of Heritage Language Transmission' in *Tracing Indian Diaspora: Contexts, Memories, Representations.* Eds. Parvati Raghuram, Ajaya Sahoo and Brij Maharaj and Dave Sangha. (New Delhi: Sage Publications.).

9. Padma Rangaswamy (2000), *Namaste America: Indian Immigrants in an American Metropolis.* (University Park: Pennsylvania University Press) and Sam George (2005).*Understanding the Coconut Generation* (Niles, IL: Mall Publishers).

10. Reuben Rumabut. (2009), "A Language Graveyard?The Evolution of Language Competencies, Preferences and Use among Young Adult Children of Immigrants" in *The Education of language minority immigrants in the US.* Eds. Terrence G. Wiley, Jin Sook Lee, Russell W. Rumberger. (Buffalo, NY: Multilingual Matters).

11. Robert McCrum.(2010). *Globish: How the English Language Became the World's Language.* (New York: W. W. Norton & Company).

References

Agarwal, Priya. (1999), *Passage from India: Post 1965 Indian Immigrants and Their Children.* Palos Verdes, CA: Yuvati Publications.

Barn, Ravinder. (2008), 'Indian Diaspora in the United Kingdom: Second Generation Parents Views and Experiences of Heritage Language Transmission' in *Tracing Indian Diaspora: Contexts, Memories, Representations*, edited by.Parvati Raghuram, Ajaya Sahoo, Brij Maharaj and Dave Sangha, 191-209. New Delhi: Sage Publications.

David, Maya (2008), "Does Loss of Language Equate to Loss of Identity" Unpublished Paper, Kuala Lumpur, Malaysia.

Detaramani, Champa and Graham Lock (2003), "Multilingualism in Decline: Language Repertoire, Use and Shift in Two Hong Kong Indian Communities" in *Journal of Multilingual and Multicultural Development*, Vol. 24, No. 4.

Dewan, R. (1987), "Deethnicisation: A Study of Language and Culture Change in the Sindhi Immigrant Community of Metro Manila". Unpublished PhD thesis, De La Salle University.

Dosanjh, J. S. and P. A. S. Ghuman (1996), *Child Rearing in Ethnic Minorities*. Cleavedon: Multilingual Matters.

George, Sam (2006), *Understanding the Coconut Generation: Ministry to the Americanized Asian Indians*. Niles, IL: Mall Publishing Co.

Gibson, M. A. (1988), *Accommodation without Assimilation: Sikh Immigrants in an American High School*. Ithaca: Cornell University Press.

Ghuman, P. A. S. (2003), *Double Loyalties, South Asian Adolescents in the West*. Cardiff: University of Wales Press.

Helweg, Arthur and Usha Helweg (1990), *An Immigrant Success Story: East Indians in America*. Philadelphia: University of Pennsylvania Press.

Jayram, N. (2000), "The Dynamics of Language in Indian Diaspora: The Case of Bhojpuri/Hindi in Trinidad', *Sociological Bulletin*, 49 (1): 41-62.

McCrum, Robert (2010), *Globish: How the English Language Became the World's Language*. New York: W. W. Norton & Company.

Nair, S. and M. Percot (2007), Transcending Boundaries: Indian Nurses in Internal and International Migration Occasional Paper, Centre for Women's Development Studies. *www.cwds.ac.in/OCPaper/Transcending-sreelekha-ocpaper.pdf* (Accessed May31, 2012).

Rangaswamy, Padma (2000), *Namasteì America: Indian Immigrants in an American Metropolis*. University Park: Pennsylvania University Press.

Rumbaut, Reuben (2009), "A Language Graveyard? The Evolution of Language Competencies, Preferences and Use among Young Adult Children of Immigrants" in *The Education of Language Minority Immigrants in the US*. Eds. Terrence G. Wiley, Jin Sook Lee and Russell W. Rumberger. Buffalo, NY: Multilingual Matters.

16

Major Health Challenges of Malayali Diaspora

Enas A. Enas[1]

Introduction

Despite their rapid economic development, the Japanese have maintained the lowest rates of coronary heart disease (hereafter called heart disease) in the developed world for the past 50 years. This relative immunity from heart disease was lost among the Japanese who immigrated to the US. Compared to those who remained in Japan, the heart disease rates among the Japanese immigrants were two-fold higher in Hawaii and a 3-fold higher in San Francisco. This increase in heart disease was accompanied by a 60 per cent reduction in stroke, which is the dominant form of cardiovascular disease in Japan. These dramatic and opposing changes in heart disease and stroke rates were largely attributable to acculturation, whereby the immigrants modify and adopt the beliefs and behaviors of the host population. The increased risk of heart attack among the Japanese immigrants was attributed to an increase in blood cholesterol level resulting from greater consumption of saturated fat, whereas the reduced risk of stroke was attributed to lower blood pressure resulting from reduced consumption of salt as well greater use of modern medicine in lieu of traditional herbs.[2] These tantalizing observations generated great research interest on immigrant health, especially among the 30 million South Asians,[3] living outside the Indian subcontinent.

It is now firmly established that the health status and disease patterns of immigrants are intermediate between those of countries of their origin and the countries of emigration, ultimately blending with those of the host countries in 2 to 3 generations.[4] The South Asian Diaspora has been a singular exception to this rule. They have been documented to have a 2 to 3-fold higher rates of heart disease and diabetes, than their compatriots of other ethnic origins. Such high rates have been observed in countries as diverse as the United States (US), the UK, Canada, Singapore, South Africa, Uganda, Malaysia, Mauritius, Fiji, and the Middle East. Specific health information on Malayali emigrants is sparse but anecdotal evidence from Kerala as well as from the US strongly indicates that the rates of heart disease and diabetes are higher in Malayali Diasporas than in other Indian Diasporas. In light of limited data of the global Malayali Diaspora the article will primarily focus on the Malayali Diaspora in the US.

Indians comprise 75 per cent of the South Asians and they have the highest death rates of heart disease, despite the fact that nearly half of them are life-long vegetarians and smoking is uncommon among women, i.e. the *Indian Paradox*.[5] The risk of developing and dying from heart disease among Indians worldwide is double that of Americans and Europeans even after accounting for the differences in the prevalences of major risk factors (such as smoking, high blood pressure, high cholesterol, obesity, metabolic syndrome, and diabetes).[6] A tsunami of heart disease is now sweeping India, claiming 2.4 million lives every year (six times the number of American lives). Heart attacks kill 6,300 Indians every day – the equivalent to the crashing of twelve jumbo jets filled with Indians and four out of twelve with Indians 40 years or younger.[3] The risk of heart disease appears to be slightly higher among the Malayali Diasporas commensurate with the patterns observed in Kerala.

Factors and Patterns

During the past 40 years, heart disease death rates have decreased by 50 to 80 per cent in the general population of the US, Finland and several other countries, whereas these rates have dramatically increased by 300 per cent in India. Despite having the highest rates of literacy and other indicators of good health, Kerala has the highest rates of heart disease in India. It appears that language literacy does not translate into health literacy among Malayalis. Unhealthy diet, abnormal lipids, abdominal obesity, physical inactivity, high blood pressure, tobacco use, insulin resistance, metabolic syndrome, diabetes, and cardiovascular disease are highly interrelated. This article hopes to shine a bright light so that Malayalis can increase their health literacy and empower themselves against the rampant misinformation about diseases that affect them disproportionately.

Tobacco Use

Approximately 30 per cent of Malayali men in the US are smokers which is similar in proportion to the Kerala population. In contrast only 3 per cent of the Malayali physicians surveyed at the annual conventions of the Association of Kerala Medical Graduates (AKMG) are smokers. Malayali women do not smoke but ironically have as much heart disease and diabetes as Malayali men.

High Blood Pressure

High blood pressure is a leading cause of death and disability and is responsible for almost half of all heart attacks and strokes. In developing countries such as India, only half of the people with high blood pressure are aware of it; only half of those who are aware receive effective treatment; and only half of those treated have their blood pressure under control. This "rule of halves"is equally true for Malayalis.

Physical Inactivity and Poor Fitness

Physical activity is associated with several health benefits, especially increase in fitness and reduction in weight and cardiometabolic risk. Regular exercise such as brisk walking 30 minutes daily can reduce the triglyceride levels by 50 per cent. Any exercise is better than no exercise and a highlevel of physical activity is better than a low level of activity. Large volume of physical activity can also reduce abdominal obesity, even in the absence of weight loss. Poor cardiorespiratory fitness greatly increases cardiometabolic risk. Maintaining high levels of fitness mitigates most of the dangers associated with obesity – a phenomenon universally observed among the fat and fit American football players. Nonetheless, it is better to be fat and fit, rather than thin and unfit. However, it is best to be thin and fit.

Unhealthy Diet

A healthy diet is low in calories, saturated fats, trans fats, and simple carbohydrates but high in fruits, vegetables, whole grains, and low-fat dairy products; and moderate in nuts, legumes, and fish and possibly unprocessed lean meat. The consumption of foods with high glycemic index (i.e. withhigher capacity to raise blood sugar level) and low fiber content such as refined grains and calorie-rich soft drinks increase cardiometabolic risk, whereas the risk is reduced by modest intake of animal and vegetable proteins, as well as healthy carbohydrates from fruits and vegetables. Many Malayalis acquire 60 per cent of their energy from white rice, resulting in elevated triglycerides, lower HDL, (high-density lipoprotein or good cholesterol) and abdominal obesity leading to diabetes.

Excessive saturated fat intake is the principal determinant of elevated cholesterol – the foremost risk factor for heart disease.[7] Ghee, used liberally by affluent Indians worldwide is very high in saturated fat and is strongly correlated with high blood pressure and high cholesterol. The same is true for coconut products[8](coconut meat, coconut milk, and coconut oil) as well as full-fat dairy products (such as ice cream and curd) and palm oil, according to national and international literature. But most Malayalis are not aware of the health hazards of these foods and consume them with impunity.

Abnormal Lipids

Dyslipidemia is defined as abnormal quantity or proportion of HDL (good cholesterol) and LDL (low-density lipoprotein or bad cholesterol) and it accounts for half of all heart attacks worldwide. Indians have the worst dyslipidemia especially women, which is not reflected in the blood cholesterol level. Our penchant for fried foods results in high consumption of trans fat – the most dangerous of all dietary fats – leading to lower HDL and higher LDL and lipoprotein (a) levels. Lipoprotein (a) is the deadliest of all blood cholesterol and is generally believed to be genetic in origin. However, liberal consumption of trans fat may be an important dietary factor in Indians and Malayalis. Elevated lipoprotein (a) level is found in 35 to 40 per cent of Indians worldwide; this possibly explains why the risk of a heart attack in an Indian with a cholesterol level of 192 mg/dl is similar to a European with a cholesterol level of 300 mg/dl. The cholesterol level in Kerala is 40 mg/dl higher than the rest of India, indicating an important role of the unique dietary habits of the state's population. It may very well be true for the Malayali Diasporas also, who often maintain similar dietary preferences and cooking practices of Kerala.

General and Abdominal Obesity

Currently, body mass index or BMI (a ratio of body weight in kilograms and height in square meter) is the unit used to define obesity. At similar BMI, Indians have more body fat and less muscle mass resulting in higher risk of diabetes and heart disease than Americans or Europeans.[9] Several national and international guidelines have lowered the BMI cutoff points for obesity in Indians in recognition of this heightened risk. The optimum BMI is less than 23, BMI 23-24.9 is overweight, and BMI more than 25 is obesity for Indians. Using this definition, 50 per cent of Diaspora Indians and urban Indians are obese compared to only 35 per cent in the USgeneral population. Tragically only 10 per cent of the Indians are aware of their obesity and related risks.

Although women have more fat than men at similar BMI, the distribution of fat is more favorable in women than in men. Men generally have visceral fat accumulation resulting in *"apple-shaped"* abdominal obesity that increases cardiometabolic risk. Young women, on the other hand, accumulate fat in buttocks and thighs resulting in *"pear-shaped obesity"* that actually protects against cardiometabolic risk by providing a *"metabolic sink"* for storage and clearance of the extra energy derived from dietary excess.

Abdominal obesity is diagnosed by measuring the waist girth or waist circumference (WC). Given the higher cardiometabolic risk, the cut off points for waist girth are significantly lower among Indians – 90 cm or more in men (compared with 102 cm in American men) and 80 cm or more in womencompared with and 88 cm in American women). Abdominal obesity is found in 66 per cent of Diaspora Indians and urban Indians, but only in 24 per cent of rural Indians when these criteria are applied. Abdominal obesity is a powerful predictor of diabetes and heart disease, especially if triglycerides levels are also elevated creating the "*hypertriglyceridemic waist*". This pattern is unusually common among Malayali men. Recent studies indicate that a waist-to-height ratio of more than 0.5 is an even better index of abdominal obesity especially in children.

Most of the Indians, especially Malayalis, remain unaware of their risk from the "*paunch*" and erroneously ignore it as a sign of affluence and prosperity. The dangers of abdominal obesity can be markedly reduced by weight loss, which requires attention to both energy intake and expenditure. For example, a 500 calories reduction in energy intake and 500 calories increase in energy expenditure per day can produce a deficit of 7000 calories and a weight loss of one kilogram per week.

Insulin Resistance and Fatty Liver

Insulin resistance is a dangerous consequence of abdominal obesity and results in progressively higher levels of insulin to overcome the resistance. The pancreas compensates by pouring in more and more insulin to keep the blood sugar at bay. For example, in normal individuals, one unit of insulin lowers blood sugar by 40 mg/dl, which is reduced to 20, 10, 5 or 2 mg/dl, depending upon the degree of insulin resistance. Unchecked insulin resistance causes metabolic derangements leading to fatty liver, metabolic syndrome and diabetes. Some reports suggest that fat content of liver in Indians is twice that of whites with similar BMI.

Metabolic Syndrome

Metabolic syndrome appears to be the "*common soil*" for diabetes and cardiovascular disease – two inextricably intertwined epidemics raging in India today. Metabolic syndrome is found in more than eighty per cent of diabetics and accounts for the elevated cardiovascular risk (in diabetics) that begins to accrue 10 to 20 years before diabetes is formally diagnosed. Sedentary lifestyle and caloric excess lead to abdominal obesity which results in metabolic syndrome, when susceptible genes are turned on or unmasked. Thus, both nature (genes) and nurture (environment) are involved in metabolic syndrome. People with metabolic syndrome have a 2 to 3-fold risk of cardiovascular disease; the risk may be as high as 5-fold in young women. In some studies, metabolic syndrome was associated with a cardiovascular risk comparable to that of an LDL level of 200 mg/dl. The risk of diabetes is as high as 5 to 24-fold, depending upon the number of components or severity of metabolic syndrome.

In 2009, various international organizations jointly developed a "harmonized" definition of metabolic syndrome,[10] reconciling the differences between them. Abdominal obesity is no longer required for the diagnosis of metabolic syndrome. Unlike BMI, thecut off points for waist girth are not only gender specific but also ethnic specific. In Indians, metabolic syndrome is diagnosed when any three of the following five specific components are identified: abdominal obesity as measured by waist girth of 90 cm or more (35.4 inches) in men or 80 cm or more (31.5 inches) in women; HDL less than 40 mg/dl in men or less than 50 mg/dl in women; blood sugar 100 mg/dl or more; and blood pressure 130/85 mm Hg or more.

When compared with Americans, metabolic syndrome develops 10 years earlier in Indian men and 20 years earlier in Indian women. The prevalence of metabolic syndrome increases with increasing obesity. At any given BMI, compared to Americans, Indians have double the prevalence of metabolic syndrome (see Table) and further underscores the rationale for lower cut points for obesity among Indians.

Metabolic syndrome is found in one in two women and one in three men in urban India, but the rates are half in rural India. The high prevalence of metabolic syndrome may partly explain the high rates of heart disease among young Indian women who seldom smoke tobacco. It is worth highlighting that failure to use the lower waist

**Differences in the Prevalence of Metabolic syndromebetween
Americans and Indians at Similar BMI**

BMI *category*	18-22.9	23-24.9	25-29.9	>30-34.9	>35
Indian in India	18%	40%	53%	NA	NA
Indians in the US	NA	38%	50%	45%	58%
Whites in the US	NA	10%	25%	65%	80%

Sources: 1. Enas EA, Mohan V, Deepa M, Farooq S, Pazhoor S, Chennikkara H. The metabolic syndrome and dyslipidemia among Asian Indians: a population with high rates of diabetes and premature coronary artery disease. *J Cardiometab Syndr.* Fall 2007; 2(4): 267-275.

2. Kanaya AM, Wassel CL, Mathur D, *et al.* Prevalence and correlates of diabetes in South asian indians in the United States: findings from the metabolic syndrome and atherosclerosis in South asians living in america study and the multi-ethnic study of atherosclerosis. *Metab Syndr Relat Disord.* Apr 2010; 8(2): 157-164.

girth criteria among Indian men (90 cm in Indians versus 102 cm in American men) and Indian women (80 cm in Indians versus 88 cm in American women) can result in the under estimation of metabolic syndrome by 50 per cent.

The principal goal of identifying and treating metabolic syndrome is to prevent the progression to diabetes as well as heart attacks and strokes. An estimated 42 to 59 per cent of the burden of stroke, heart attack, and diabetes can be reduced by eliminating metabolic syndrome in the US. This figure is likely to be much higher (70 to 80 per cent) in India, where prevalences of heart disease and diabetes are 3 to 4-fold higher than in the US.

Pre-diabetes and Diabetes

Pre-diabetes is defined as fasting glucose levels between 101 to 125 mg/dl or now HbA1C of 5.7 – to 6.4 per cent. Metabolic syndrome and pre-diabetes each increases the risk of diabetes 5-fold and the risk is as high as 25-fold when both conditions are present. At similar age and BMI, risk of developing diabetes is three times higher in Indians[11] than whites although the contribution of genetics to diabetes is only15 per cent. Rates of diabetes are highest in Kerala (18 to 20 per cent) than other states (5 to 15 per cent) in India. However, data on Malayali diaspora are currently lacking.

The major risk factors for diabetes include abdominal obesity, physical inactivity, unhealthy diet, especially one high in saturated fat and trans fat and glycemic load (such as a plateful of overcooked white rice, idly, appam etc). Increasing physical activity, maintaining weight control, reduction in saturated fatintake, and carbohydrate moderation form the mainstay of prevention and management of diabetes. Intensive lifestyle modification with reduction of glycemic load and increased physical activity (60–200 minutes/day depending on waist reduction needed) can prevent and/or delay the development of diabetes, heart attack and stroke by 60 per cent among people with pre-diabetes or metabolic syndrome.

Heart attacks and strokes account for nearly 80 per cent of deaths in people with diabetes. It is often not appreciated that treatment of dyslipidemia and high blood pressure is more effective in reducing cardiovascular risk and deaths than lowering glucose levels in people with diabetes. Statins are highly effective in tackling the lipid abnormalities in both metabolic syndrome and diabetes.

Toward A Healthy Future

Control of Modifiable Risk Factors

The good news is that heart disease has now become highly predictable, preventable, and treatable. According to World Health Organization, 80 per cent of premature heart disease, stroke and diabetes are preventable. The 70 to 80 per cent decrease in heart disease death rates documented in the US, Finland and many other countries was no accident. It was achieved through nationwide reduction of risk factors by changes in lifestyle and appropriate use of life-saving medications. Indian and Malayali doctors in the US have significantly reduced the levels of most of the modifiable risk factors. Ironically, most modifiable risk factors remain higher among doctors in India than in their patients - a strong impediment for the fight against the tsunami of heart disease in India.

Health Literacy, **Karma** *and* **Dharma**

Health literacy is the ability to understand health information and to use it to make good decisions about one's health and medical care.

Many Malayalis believe that *"what is dotted cannot be blotted"* and blame most heart attacks to *Karma,* totally ignoring their *dharma* to apply the enormous knowledge gleaned over the past 40 years that produced the dramatic reduction in heart disease death rates in many countries. Many Malayalis often fail to recognize the difference between alternate medicine and evidence-based modern medicine, which has come a long way from the "Galenic concepts" which attributed most diseases to an imbalance of four basic humors: *blood, phlem, black bile and yellow bile.* The so-called *"depletory regimen"* consisting of bleeding, blistering, purging, vomiting and sweating has long been abandoned and replaced by evidence-based medicine. Spectacular progress has been made in understanding the genetic, biochemical, and molecular basis of many chronic diseases. The discovery and use of evidence-based medicines such as statins, aspirin, ACE inhibitors, and beta-blockers have made it possible to reduce the risk of a heart attack by 75 per cent. Control of infections with antibiotics, diabetes with insulin, elevated cholesterol with statins and elevated blood pressure with several safe and effective medications along with advances in hygiene and sanitation have contributed to the doubling of human lifespan in the twentieth century despite a doubling of obesity and diabetes.

Many Malayalis have a special fondness of alternative medicines, especially *Ayurveda* which still invokes an imbalance of three *doshas: Vata, Pitha and Kapha,* for most diseases. We will leave it up to the imagination of the readers as to what would happen if a person with elevated blood pressure, elevated cholesterol, diabetes, heart attack, stroke, cancer, or tuberculosis is treated with massage, herbal supplement and/or stress reduction with yoga. The extremely high rates of strokes in rural China are attributed to uncontrolled hypertension due to a reluctance to use modern blood pressure-lowering medicines in favor of traditional Chinese herbs. This may be equally true for Malayalis.

Although *Ayurvedic medicines* are widely perceived to be safe, two large US studies have reported toxic levels of heavy metals such as lead, mercury, and arsenic in about twenty per cent of Indian-manufactured Ayurvedic medicines sold in the US. Other serious concerns include the use of herbs containing toxic compounds that can damage the liver and kidney or markedly alter the efficacy and safety of modern medicines (especially blood thinners), as well as the lack of quality control in manufacturing. As former President Kalam has repeatedly admonished – the time is past due to demonstrate and accept what is scientifically valid in the alternative medicine and abandon those that are not. Nonetheless, Ayurvedic massage may be of some benefit in non-life threatening muscle and joint disorders. Yoga enables you to develop flexibility, strength, and balance, but one must proceed cautiously to avoid injuries and strain from overstretching of muscles. Some yoga classes include meditation and provide great relaxation.

Kerala Paradox and Kerala Health Initiative

Kerala has high literacy, high life expectancy, and other indicators of socio-economic progress including access to state of the art medical care for those who can afford it. Naturally, one would expect lower rates of heart disease and diabetes. Kerala Paradox refers to the paradoxically high prevalence of lifestyle diseases – heart disease, diabetes, high blood pressure, and obesity, resulting in very high mortality and morbidity. Indians in Canada and UK have reduced the death rates from heart disease by 30 to 40 per cent. There is every reason to believe that the dramatic decrease in deaths from premature heart disease achieved in many countries can be duplicated in Malayalis worldwide. This will require garnering of all scientific knowledge and concerted action by the government, the medical community, the general public, and the media at large to improve health literacy and expand the use of evidenced-based medicine. The Kerala Health Initiative (soon to be launched) is an ambitious and multifaceted public-private project to address and remedy the heightened burden of cardiovascular disease and other chronic non-communicable diseases and transform the landscape of health in Kerala.

Conclusion

Compared with Americans and Europeans, Indians have higher risk of diabetes and heart disease both accruing at younger ages and at lower body weight and waist girth. The risk is even higher in Kerala than other states in India, despite greater literacy and other indicators of good health. The health status and disease pattern of Malayali Diasporas appears to be similar or worse than the Indian Diasporas from other Indian states, given that the disease pattern of the Diaspora is intermediate between their land of origin and the land of living. According to World Health Organization, 80 per cent of premature heart disease, stroke and diabetes are preventable and the US has decreased the death toll from heart disease and stroke by 70 per cent in the past 30 years. This was achieved through nationwide reduction of risk factors by changes in lifestyle. Malayalis could and should do achieve the same by increasing the health literacy and adapting and adopting the strategies outlined in this chapter.

Notes

1. I want to thank the able assistance of Arun T Kuruvila, MD., Janeesh Sekkath Veedu, MD., Paul Cherian MD., and Roy P. Thomas MD for their valuable input to this chapter.

2. Reed DM. The paradox of high risk of stroke in populations with low risk of coronary heart disease. *Am J Epidemiol.* 1990; 131(4): 579-588.

3. South Asians are people who originate from the Indian subcontinent (India, Pakistan, Bangladesh, Sri Lanka, and Nepal, Bhutan and Maldives) and represent one-fifth of the world's population.

4. *www.cadiresearch.org* (accessed Nov 5, 2012).

5. Enas EA. Coronary artery disease epidemic in Indians: a cause for alarm and call for action. *J Indian Med Assoc.* Nov 2000; 98(11): 694-695, 697-702.

6. Forouhi NG, Sattar N, Tillin T, McKeigue PM, Chaturvedi N. Do known risk factors explain the higher coronary heart disease mortality in South Asian compared with European men? Prospective follow-up of the Southall and Brent studies, UK. *Diabetologia.* Nov 2006; 49(11): 2580-2588.

7. Waqar AB, Koike T, Yu Y, *et al.* High-fat diet without excess calories induces metabolic disorders and enhances atherosclerosis in rabbits. *Atherosclerosis.* Nov. 2010; 213(1): 148-155.

8. Enas EA, Senthilkumar A, Chennikkara H, Bjurlin MA. Prudent diet and preventive nutrition from pediatrics to geriatrics: current knowledge and practical recommendations. *Indian Heart J.* Jul-Aug 2003; 55(4): 310-338.

9. *www.cadiresearch.org* (accessed Nov 5, 2012).

10. Alberti KG, Eckel RH, Grundy SM, *et al.* Harmonizing the metabolic syndrome: a joint interim statement of the International Diabetes Federation Task Force on Epidemiology and Prevention; National Heart, Lung, and Blood Institute; American Heart Association; World Heart Federation; International Atherosclerosis Society; and International Association for the Study of Obesity. *Circulation.* Oct. 20 2009; 120(16): 1640-1645.

11. Lee JW, Brancati FL, Yeh HC. Trends in the Prevalence of Type 2 Diabetes in Asians Versus Whites: Results from the United States National Health Interview Survey, 1997-2008. *Diabetes Care.* Feb 2011; 34(2): 353-357.

17

Aging Malyali Diaspora in America:
Triumphs and Struggles

P. T. Thomas

Introduction

The largest influx of Malayalis immigrating to the US began in the early 1970s. That pioneering generation of Malayalis like the American "boomer generation" are aging. They are part of the "grey power" generation of 56 million Americans who are over the age of 60.[1] They are expected to live longer and will do so with lower rates of disability and poverty than previous generations.[2]

The Migrant Dreams

Malayali immigrants who left Kerala as young persons for higher education or for a much needed job hardly gave thought of getting old in America. It was not even entertained as a remote possibility. Their dream of emigrating from Kerala was to also return to Kerala and grow old there.

The goals of the pioneer Malayali immigrants were more immediate – get a job, support parents and siblings, get married, have a family, ensure financial security and then return to Kerala before retirement age.[3] So going back to the ancestral home, family and community was their constant dream and longing. They readily identified with the longings of exiles in a foreign land as the writer records in Psalm 137.

In most cases, both parents plunged themselves into their jobs and careers (some with two jobs), raised their children and provided for a better future for them. A high percentage of immigrant Malayalis have achieved an admirable level of economic independence and enjoy a lifestyle that their forefathers could never dream of. Coming from Kerala homes where they grew up without running water and toilet facilities, they studied with kerosene oil lamps, walked to school barefooted and considered having two shirts to wear a bonus; they are now enjoying the beautiful and convenient amenities of life that the American dream promises.

At the same time many struggle with some haunting thoughts. Many of them left their home, community and land in India in their late teens or early twenties and were not able to live a full life with their parents and siblings. Over the years the crucial relationships with members of their extended families and friends have not been nurtured. Connections with their *alma mater,* church or temple and other places of importance are now superficial. They have lost touch with much of the past without meaning to. They have not kept up with the evolving Kerala society and culture. They could feel they are somewhat like strangers in their own land of birth.

The Fading Dream

Most Malayalis have slowly realized that their original dream to return and settle in Kerala has gradually faded over the years. The reasons are many but the following are the primary ones. First, their children after completing their education have found good jobs; many are married and have their families. Their second generation offspring are well-adjusted and are happily settled in America. Sarah Lamb in her book, *Aging and the Indian Diaspora: Cosmopolitan Families in India and Abroad* addresses the plight of the senior citizens of Indian origin who live in the United States as well as in India. She concludes that such parents who come and live with or near their children in the US enjoy a much homier lifestyle.[4]

Therefore, two questions facing the aging generation are (1) If they return to India, how can they afford to be so far away from their children and grandchildren? They will be robbing them of the immediate physical and emotional relationships which they could not enjoy a generation earlier with their parents and siblings. (2) If they stay, how can they be involved meaningfully and offer help to their children and families without interfering in their own priorities and plans?

Secondly, the Kerala the pioneering immigrants left is not the same Kerala that they visit now. Kerala society has undergone drastic changes over the last four decades in values, morals, fashions, lifestyles, etc. The fusion of huge foreign remittances especially from the Gulf region has raised expectations and high standards of living. Wages and prices have soared high. Income of the Middle-class has swelled and they have disposable income like never before. Thoughts of living less expensively in Kerala than in the US are becoming a wishful dream.

Thirdly, the lack of genuine warmth and cooperation among members of the heritage community in Kerala is most surprising. It is not uncommon to observe siblings and relatives displaying such disappointing attitudes. Many immigrants have realized that Keralites are happy to receive benefits from them but not equally happy to share much; they are appreciated as visitors but not as long-term residents!

Fourthly, the immigrant Malayalis live in homes that have been fully paid off, enjoy a comfortable lifestyle and have adequate health insurance. Moreover, they have a network of friends and families built up over three decades. Malayalis returning to Kerala means giving up all these benefits and once again starting from scratch. A few have attempted to return and live permanently with mixed success. Most of them have abandoned that plan and have returned to re-settle in the US.

The Way Forward

One undeniable fact is that the pioneering immigrant Malayali generation did not realize that they were advancing into their senior years. Their priority was meeting the needs of others – their own children's development and the needs of parents and siblings back in Kerala. They did not plan for their own senior years. Neither has the Malayali community at large.

Psychoanalyst Erik H. Erikson offers help to understand the state of senior Malayali immigrants. Erikson categorized human development into eight psychosocial stages:[5] (1) Trust vs. Mistrust (2) Autonomy vs. Shame (3) Initiative vs. Guilt (4) Industry vs. Inferiority (5) Identity vs. Role Confusion (6) Intimacy vs. Isolation (7) Generativity vs. Stagnation (8) Ego Integrity vs. Despair.

These stages are developed as a pillar with Trust vs. Mistrust at the base. The successful completion of an earlier stage is necessary to move on effectively into the next stage. By reason of supporting their families, raising their children, investing for their future, and also by being productive members of the society, a large number of aging Malayalis would find themselves having moved on to the stage of *Generativity*. They have the satisfaction that their lives have been well lived. Some aging Malayalis would end up at the stage of *Stagnation*, and they would experience very little connection with others, and would have little to offer to society. They have lived most of their lives being self-absorbed. At their last stage of life span, these people would pass through the stage of *Despair* and experience a sense of desolation and disappointment. On the other hand, people who have achieved *Generativity* would move on effectively to the stage of *Ego integrity*, where they would live their senior years with a sense of wisdom, serenity, and optimism. The table in the following page provides a helpful summary of Erikson's psychosocial stages.

With good financial planning, adequate health care, and a reasonable degree of health, the aging Malayalis could live their lives quite comfortably, wherever they choose to spent their retirement years. It is important that they have opportunity for socialization and meaningful connections with family and friends, without which they will experience periods of solitude that can contribute to depression. Solitude becomes much more difficult when seniors themselves or their spouses are hit with debilitating diseases such as Cancer, Alzheimer's, Parkinson's and Aphasia. Under such circumstances,

Table 1
Erikson's Eight Stages of Human Development

Stage	Basic Conflict	Important Events	Outcome
Infancy (birth to 18 months)	Trust vs. Mistrust	Feeding	Children develop a sense of trust when caregivers provide reliability, care, and affection. A lack of this will lead to mistrust.
Early Childhood (2 to 3 years)	Autonomy vs. Shame and Doubt	Toilet Training	Children need to develop a sense of personal control over physical skills and a sense of independence. Success leads to feelings of autonomy, failure results in feelings of shame and doubt.
Preschool (3 to 5 years)	Initiative vs. Guilt	Exploration	Children need to begin asserting control and power over the environment. Success in this stage leads to a sense of purpose. Children who try to exert too much power experience disapproval, resulting in a sense of guilt.
School Age (6 to 11 years)	Industry vs. Inferiority	School	Children need to cope with new social and academic demands. Success leads to a sense of competence, while failure results in feelings of inferiority.
Adolescence (12 to 18 years)	Identity vs. Role Confusion	Social Relationships	Teens need to develop a sense of self and personal identity. Success leads to an ability to stay true to yourself, while failure leads to role confusion and a weak sense of self.
Young Adulthood (19 to 40 years)	Intimacy vs. Isolation	Relationships	Young adults need to form intimate, loving relationships with other people. Success leads to strong relationships, while failure results in loneliness and isolation.
Middle Adulthood (40 to 65 years)	Generativity vs. Stagnation	Work and Parenthood	Adults need to create or nurture things that will outlast them, often by having children or creating a positive change that benefits other people. Success leads to feelings of usefulness and accomplishment, while failure results in shallow involvement in the world.
Maturity (65 to death)	Ego Integrity vs. Despair	Reflection on Life	Older adults need to look back on life and feel a sense of fulfillment. Success at this stage leads to feelings of wisdom, while failure results in regret, bitterness, and despair.

Source: www.About.com.Psychology

some seniors will be forced to accept the role of caretaker. Gail Sheehy in her book, *Passage in Caregiving: Turning Chaos into Confidence*[6] speaks about her experiences as a caregiver when her husband suddenly was diagnosed with cancer. Sheehy identifies eight crucial stages of caregiving and offers insight for successfully navigating each one. Even with her great care, her husband succumbed to the horrible disease of cancer.

Death is an inevitable part of life that needs to be prepared for. A person can meet death with courage and grace. Our job is to prepare our seniors for such a courageous moment. The aging Malayalis have some critical needs. Churches, temples, cultural associations, senior citizens centers, ashrams, organizations and government agencies should formulate policies and programs to help our seniors to cope and thrive in their twilight years. Each person's faith and hope also plays a vital role in this preparation for the next stage of life. But until that stage comes, they can be productive members of the community with a lot of people to love and to be loved.

Notes

1. World Population Aging 2009: A United Nations Study. See report *www.un.org/esa/population/publications/WPA2009/WPA2009_WorkingPaper.pdf* (accessed Dec 1, 2012).

2. Barry Rand, *AARP Bulletin*, December 1, 2010.

3. Similar patterns of thinking can be identified among the vast majority of Malayalis of that generation in the global Malayali diaspora.

4. Sarah Lamb (2009). *Aging and the Indian Diaspora: Cosmopolitan Families in India and Abroad.* Bloomington, IN: Indiana University Press.

5. Erik Erikson (1950). *Childhood and Society.* New York: W. W. Norton & Company.

6. Gail Sheehy (2010). *Passages in Caregiving: Turning Chaos into Confidence.* New York: Harper Collins.

References

Erikson, Erik. H. (1950). *Childhood and Society.* New York: W. W. Norton & Company.

Lamb, Sarah (2009). *Aging and the Indian Diaspora: Cosmopolitan Families in India and Abroad.* Bloomington IN: Indiana University Press.

Sheehy, Gail (2010). *Passages in Caregiving: Turning Chaos into Confidence*. New York: Harper Collins.

Rand, Barry A. (2010). *AARP Bulletin*, December 1.

United Nations, *World Population Ageing 2009*. New York: United Nations Publications. *www.un.org/esa/population/publications/WPA2009/WPA2009_WorkingPaper.pdf* (accessed Dec 1, 2012).

18

Malayalam Media in the Diaspora

JESUDAS M. ATHYAL

Introduction

Media, the organized means of dissemination of news, opinion, entertainment, and other information such as newspapers, magazines, films, radio, television, world wide web, books, CDs, DVDs, videocassettes, video games and other forms of broadcasting, has long been a central part of the life of Malayalis. The history of media in Kerala can be traced back to 1578 when *"Doctrina Christam"* written by Father Henrique, a Portuguese Jesuit priest, was printed in Kollam. In 1821, Benjamin Bailey, a British missionary who served in Kerala for 34 years, established the first printing press from where the first book in Malayalam was published.[1] The establishment of printing technology was a major milestone that made available to the lay public the Biblical Scriptures and the other literature in religions, followed by the wider publication of literature and mundane day-to day activities such as news and entertainment. In 1847, German missionary, Hermann Gundert brought out eight cyclostyled sheets in demy octavo size from a press at Illikkunnu near Thalassery. Historical developments such as these paved the way for a strong media culture in Kerala.

In Kerala, the development of the media and radical social transformation went hand-in-hand complementing each other. The struggles against caste-based discrimination, the movement for the equality of women in all spheres of life, harmony among various religious groups and a conscious attempt to bridge the gulf between the "haves" and the "have-nots" were all notable developments in the nineteenth and early twentieth centuries when social reformers made effective use of the media. Distinguished among the social reformers were V. T. Bhatadiripad who, with the aid of publications such as *Yogakshemam* and the *Unni Namboodiri*, wielded his powerful pen to break the conservatism and "lofty isolation" of the Namboodiri community[2] and K. C. Mammen Mapillai who was imprisoned for campaigning for the merger of Travancore with the Indian Union and whose newspaper *Malayala Manorama* was confiscated. The credit for the radical social changes in Kerala largely goes to the social awareness spearheaded by a media revolution in the state.

From the early decades of the twentieth century, theatre and cinema too entered the scene and became major arenas forculture and creativity in Kerala. The role of the theatre in creating a climate conducive for social reform – especially in the struggles for women's equal rights, status, and thefight against caste prejudices and religious bigotry – is significant.[3] Theatre also played a crucial role in the growth of the Communist movement in Kerala. However, by the middle of the twentieth century, the cinema had overtaken theatre as the major source for mass entertainment in the state. While cinema elsewhere in India was often "show biz" that focused largely on glamour and glitter, Malayalam cinema took a wide variety of themes and was "far ahead of Hindi or Tamil cinema in terms of its artistic value, because of the reflection of social consciousness attributed to the literary connection it had from 1960s."[4]

The status of Kerala as a state with a high literacy rate meant accessibility to social and political trends around the world. Analysis was everyday business for the Malayalis. For long decades, the state-owned All India Radio was the sole means to quench the insatiable thirst for instant news and developments from around the world. By the 1980s, however, television had captured the news and entertainment scene. Initially, television was state-controlled and confined to Doordarshan but soon an array of private television channels emerged. In Kerala today, there is a wide variety of cable television channels that broadcast 24x7 with a mix of Malayalam, English and international channels. While theatre and cinema carefully choreographed programs on one theme, radio and television emerged for breaking news and voicing opinions. Radio and television (especially the latter) further enhanced their position by establishing a long-term place for entertainment versatility in the Malayalam media.

The twenty first century is the era of the internet. The internet was a radical breakthrough to the world of media on the corporate as well as personal level. The advancement of digital media in recent years has opened a totally new world before Keralites. "With increasing concentration of software professionals, the state has seen the launching of a plethora of Malayalam websites. With the advance of technology, most of the telecom operators like Hutch, Airtel and Escotel have tied up with the websites and news channels. The news headlines, sport news, stock quotes, breaking news and political news are now available with a single click of the mouse button."[5]

Regardless of the telecommunication and digital advancement in media, the Keralites maintain a highvolume of newspaper and magazine subscriptions. The traditional image of the Malayali as a man (Yes, culturally, Kerala is essentially a patriarchal society!) settling down in the morning with a cup of black coffee and the day's newspaper while the radio blares news from around the world, lingers. But the Malayalis have also been open to the potential of the wide array of media outlets that have emerged since the 1980s. The traditional print media, telecommunications, broadcasting and cable services have all added to the media revolution that has contributed richly to transforming Kerala into "God's own country".

Media in the Diaspora

Uprooted from their traditional moorings and separated from each other by great geographical distances, the people and communities in the diaspora underwent momentous changes and struggled to keep in touch with each other and with their homeland. From the early decades of the twentieth century, the Malayalis had migrated from their homeland, to Ceylon (now Sri Lanka), Burma (now Myanmar), Malaysia, Singapore and Africa. As Malayalis moved out of their state in large numbers, they took with them all that they cherished – culture, religion, food. Their deep concerns to keep in touch with their homeland and to pass on their heritage, values and cultures to the coming generations prompted them to adapt the Malayalam media. However, it was following the Malayali migration from the 1970s onwards that the Malayalam media assumed genuine diaspora characteristics – initially in the Middle East, and then in North America and Europe. The Middle East has a significant Malayali population but due to the inability of most migrants to permanently settle down there and to fully adapt to the local cultures, most Malayalis eventually return to Kerala or to one of the urban Indian centers. So, a strong diaspora media culture is yet to evolve there locally and consequently, a large part of the Malayalam media in the Middle East originates in Kerala.

The situation in North America is different. Several factors – the large scale migration of the Malayalis, the inclination of the majority of the migrants to take root in their new surroundings, their deep desire to "preserve" their traditional values and culture and to pass them on to the younger generations – have facilitated in the development of a strong diaspora Malayalam media in North America. The Malayalam media in North America is assuming distinct characteristics, especially in recent years.

As migration across national borders became a major human activity from the middle of the twentieth century onwards and as the Malayalis carried their religions, traditions and cultures along with them, the question arose: How important a factor would media be in the evolution of the diaspora society? Recent studies reveal that the Kerala organizations in the diaspora are at the forefront in introducing the media as a tool for communication with each other and with their homeland. By the beginning of the twenty first century, most Kerala organizations in the diaspora had well-established websites that primarily serve their own members but also provided a window for others to gain an insight into the culture and practices of the Malayalis.

The Malayalam media in the diaspora also serve the vital sociological function of consolidating the various Keralites together under one umbrella and in facilitating the emergence of a pan-Malayali solidarity that cuts across the religious and cultural divide.

The Malayalam media in the North American diaspora can broadly be divided into three categories: (1) Social & Cultural (2) News & Entertainment (3) Religious. These are briefly discussed below:

Social & Cultural Media

The global migration is often the result of political unrest, tyranny or famine. The overseas migration of the Malayalis, however, was largely to seek better fortunes, and to explore avenues for higher education and jobs. Soon after their existential needs were met, the attention of the Malayali migrants turned to establishing vital links with their homeland and fellow Keralites in the diaspora. The Malayalis have a natural instinct to be abreast of the various social and political developments around the globe. In the earlier days, newspapers from Kerala used to be sent to the United States by regular mail but in recent years the Malayalis in the diaspora have begun to publish their own newspapers. A concentration of software professionals among the migrants has facilitated a digital revolution that has overtaken the conventional media in a major way. Most publications and organizations in the diaspora now maintain elaborate websites dedicated solely for the purpose of discussing social and political developments - in the diaspora, in Kerala, India and around the world. The Kerala Express, "the leading Malayalam Newspaper in the USA" published from Chicago has a website (*www.keralaexpress.com/*) while "Malayalam Pathram" (*www.malayalampathram.com/*), published from New York, maintains both a website and a print edition.

The various social and cultural organizations of the overseas Malayalis also serve as forums for media and communication. The Federation of Kerala Associations in North America (FOKANA), "the biggest socio-cultural organization of the Malayalis outside Kerala", has a website (*www.fokanaonline.com/*) that updates its members and the general public on all the major developments, especially those that pertain to the Malayalis. The Federation of Malayali Associations of Americas (FOMAA), founded in 2006 and, "representing more than 110,000 Malayalis in the United States and Canada" maintains a website (*www.fomaa.com/*) that provides information to its vast constituency. The various regions in North America have Kerala Associations that have a wide network of avenues for the dissemination of news and information.

As the Malayalis in the diaspora settle down and second and subsequent generations come to leadership positions, the Malayalam media is undergoing changes by providing more specialized and focused information. "Malayali" (*www.MalayaliMag.com*), a free monthly magazine, "keeps parents up-to-date on family events, current trends in education and useful info to help ease the transition from one stage of parenting to the next". These various media outlets serve the vital purpose of sharing and discussing views, information and news of common interests to the overseas Malayalis. They also provide avenues for the publication of the creative work of the diaspora community.

News & Entertainment Media

A major part of the Malayalam media in the diaspora is the entertainment industry with television playing an important role in news and entertainment. The well-known Malayalam TV channels, "Asianet Plus", "Surya" and, "Yes Indiavision" are available in most parts of the United States and they meet the need of the diaspora Malayalis for entertainment. "Best of Malayalam TV" (BoMTV), a Broadband TV service in Malayalam, currently offers twenty-one Malayalam channels and delivers service throughout USA, Canada, UK, Europe and rest of the world. BoMTV focuses on entertainment by bringing to the Keralites "the latest Malayalam movies and other entertainment events on offer pay-per-view basis". DISH Network, another avenue, focuses on music, dramas, sports, movies and children's programs. The reporting and analysis of news pertaining to the political and social realms is an important area and channels such as "Asianet", "Jaihind TV" and the "24 hour news channel Kairali People" meet this need. While TV programs produced in India were earlier relayed directly to North America, in recent years, local channels that are more sensitive to the challenges of the diaspora Malayali community have emerged in the United States. "Malayalam Television USA" (*www.malayalamiptv.net/usa/channels-list.php*), the "first Malayalam Channel outside of Kerala, India started by Pravasi Malayalees" is one such.

Religious Media

Perhaps the most significant institution that ties the Malayalis in the diaspora to their roots is the various religious institutions. For most Malayalis – even for those who were not religiously affiliated in India –religious institutions are the center of their social and cultural life in the diaspora. With the aid of members who are software professionals, the religious institutions maintain media links for the dissemination of news and information. "The Organization of Hindu Malayalees" has an elaborate website (*www.ohmohmohm.org/*) that provides information on spiritual matters including pooja, instructions to the faithful and news from Kerala. Several other overseas Malayali Hindu organizations also have their own publications including magazines and journals, though email and websites are increasingly replacing the traditional print media. The effective use of online technology has helped the faithful in the diaspora to transform and adapt their spiritual life to suit their current needs. Accordingly, new forms of religious practices - such as long-distance rituals, virtual pilgrimage and other religiously motivated undertakings - are increasingly becoming popular. The internet is the latest milestone in the long evolution of the media to suit human needs and conditions.

Perhaps the most organized Malayali religious group in the diaspora is the Christians. Most mainline churches have central offices and an elaborate network of parishes all over North America. Through the traditional print media as well as with the aid of electronic resources, a variety of news, reflections, devotions and other publications are made available to their members and to the general public. The Malayali Christians in the diaspora also make use of radio and television as means of communication. The various churches use a variety of radio channels all across America. "Shalom Vision" and "Powervision" are two of the TV channels that address the religious needs of the Malayalis in the diaspora. Among Muslims of Kerala origin, several of them in the United States are affiliated with "The Association of Indian Muslims of America" which maintains a website (*www.aimamerica.org/*) that carries information pertaining to Indian Muslims, particularly in the area of Education.

Conclusion

The internet undoubtedly is the emerging avenue for media, especially in the diaspora. In a study titled, "Diaspora on the Electronic Frontier: Developing Virtual Connections with Sacred Homelands,"[6] Christopher Helland explores the manner in which diaspora groups use the Internet to make network connections "not only among each other but also with the homeland they left behind". His study demonstrates that while the people who moved far away from their homelands took their religions, traditions and cultures along with them, they adapted their beliefs to suit their new surroundings instead of transplanting their original institutions in the new location.

With over four million Keralites now living outside Kerala and maintaining strong family and social ties with their home state, the Malayalam media in the Diaspora has emerged as a major industry. Traditional forms of media such as the newspaper and television continue to be popular with the Malayalis but the digital challenge has opened up a new vista in media. The proliferation of Malayali software professionals in strategic locations around the world has undoubtedly accelerated the building up of a robust digital culture for people to be in touch with each other and with their homeland. However, the challenges before the Malayalam media in the diaspora are enormous. The hegemony of various forms of media originating directly from Kerala continue to dominate the scene in North America and raising questions about credibility, relevance and cultural sensitivity.

The Kerala society is a highly pluralistic one, with diverse cultures, religions and political parties existing within a small geographical territory. These diversities are represented in the diaspora as well. The media, however, often tend to portray a culture that is homogenous and which has little resemblance to the realities of the outside world. The persistent reluctance of the mainline media to recognize the "little traditions" represented by caste, gender and economic inequalities have led to the creation of a sanitized and stereotypical media that lacks genuine credibility. An authentic and representative diaspora media culture is yet to evolve.

Notes

1. Indfy.com India For You, "Media in Kerala," *http://www.indfy.com/kerala/media.html* (accessed November 2, 2012).

2. Kerala Press Academy, "History of Media in Kerala," *http://pressacademy.org/content/history-media-kerala.* (accessed November 2, 2012).

3. "Kerala Theater Contemporary blogspot," *http://keralatheatre.blogspot.com/.* (accessed November 2, 2012).

4. Datta, Amaresh, *Encyclopaedia of Indian Literature* (New Delhi: SahityaAkademi, 1987), 751–753.

5. India for You, "Media in Kerala," See online: *www.indfy.com/kerala/media.html* (accessed November 2, 2012).

6. Christopher Helland, "Diaspora on the Electronic Frontier: Developing Virtual Connections with Sacred Homelands" *Journal of Computer-Mediated Communication, 12*(3), article 10. *http://jcmc.indiana.edu/vol12/issue3/helland.html* (accessed November 2, 012)

References

Alonso, Andoni, and Pedro Oiarzabal. *Diasporas in the New Media Age: Identity, Politics, and Community.* Reno & Las Vegas: University of Nevada Press, 2010.

Cunningham, Stuart and John Sinclair. *Floating Lives: The Media and Asian Diasporas.* New York: Rowman& Littlefield Publishers, 2001.

Gillespie, Marie and Tom Cheesman. "Media Cultures in India and the South Asia Diaspora." *Contemporary South Asia* 11, no. 2 (2002): 127-133.

Samuel, John, "Migration from Kerala: The end of an era?" (2011), *http://base.d-p-h.info/es/fiches/dph/fiche-dph-8773.html.* (accessed November 2, 2012).

Zachariah, K. C. and Irudaya Rajan (2007), "Kerala Migration Survey 2007" *http://www.cds.edu/admin/homeFiles/Kerala%20Migration%20Survey%202007.pdf.* (accessed November 2, 2012).

Conclusion

T. V. THOMAS

August 27, 2011 was a very special day for me. It marked the fifth
Golden Anniversary of the *Kumbanattu Kudubam* (Kumbanattu Family)
in Kerala. Some 250 years ago, John Sanyashi, a Christian evangelist
brought a young man, my forefather, Kochu Easaw Pannikker to this
elephant-infested forest to establish a home for him and his family.
We have since been there for generations. I belong to the sixth
generation. This special *kudumbayogam* (family gathering) labelled as
the 'Global Meet' brought together extended family members
representing over sixty countries! This jubilant crowd included
accountants, contractors, clergy, dentists, doctors, educators, engineers,
entrepreneurs, lawyers, nurses, technicians, IT professionals and
others. Fifth through eighth generations were all well represented at
the all-day-long celebration. Some had not seen each other for decades
while others met for the very first time. Loving hugs and spurts of
laughter along with introductions and explanations of relationships
happened creating a noisy throng.

The Kumbanattu family had gathered from all five continents.
They spoke Arabic, Bengali, French, German, Hindi, Kannada, Malay,
Marathi, Oriya, Punjabi, Tamil, Telegu, Singahalese, Swahili and
Swedish besides Malayalam, English and *Manglish*. Though most were

Christians, they were affiliated to different denominations and attended churches with different languages and styles of worship. As a result of interethnic marriages, this clan now comprises of people from Asia, America, Australia, Britain, Europe and Latin America; Most of them have minimal connection with Kerala or with Malayalis. This rich diversity is the consequence of some members of the fifth generation leaving Kerala for gainful employment some seven decades ago. Some of the pioneers travelled to the major urban centers in India while others spread out to Ceylon (Sri Lanka), Malaya, Singapore, Ethiopia, Nigeria, Kenya, Tanzania and Arabia. It was amazing to realize that the Kumbanattu family that gathered there with roots in a rural village in Kerala had become a transnational, trans cultural, trans-generational, intercontinental and a global family in less than a century!

My own extensive global travel over the last three decades has both convinced and baffled me about the Malayali diaspora. I know of a Malayali pharmacist in Iqaluit, the capital of Nunavut (Canada) close to the Arctic Circle and of a teacher in Port Vila in the Republic of Vanuatu in the South Pacific. I have met daily wage earners in the Arabian deserts and wealthy businessmen of Malayali heritage in South East Asian cities. Some work in echelons of power while others do simple entry-level jobs in obscurity. I regularly meet newly arrived students from Kerala in North American universities and elderly pioneers who are languishing in nursing homes all alone. Malayalis are really everywhere! They are in every region of the globe. Every rung of the ladder. Every life stage. Every walk of life. The more I realized about its global spread and its astonishing diversity the more humbled and curious I became.

A leading sociologist defines globalization as 'intensification of consciousness and compression of the world'.[1] In recent decades, the Malayali migration has soared in volume, velocity, direction and complexity. A historically migration-averse Malayali community has turned the tide from being a parochial and provincial community to be a global force to be reckoned with. With the shrinking of distances and escalating experiences of inter connection, Malayalis are weaving together a world wide network and a global consciousness. This shared cultural space of the global Malayali diaspora is continually being made and remade through flows of ideas, information, material, money and people.

The linkages established and enhanced by modern telecommunication and transportation have created a trans nationalism which sustains this global community of Malayalis. These transnational connections result in the exchange of all kinds of information (employment opportunities, housing costs, children's education options, family counselling, investment possibilities, political news, religious perspectives, entertainment news, fashions, recipes etc.), movements of people (migrants, visitors, family, friends) and trade of merchandise.

The early pioneers who ventured beyond the shores of Kerala explored new horizons while maintaining close ties with their ancestral lands. Facing many challenges the pioneering migrants set blazing trails in foreign lands that many other Malayalis followed. Initially, just to survive, many of them were working in jobs below their vocational and professional qualifications and skills. They persevered, worked extremely hard and sacrificed much to establish themselves in their host nations. In the process they sustained their kith and kind back home with resources to survive, sponsored many of them to emigrate and supported them upon arrival. Such efforts were both a gesture of benevolence to aid their loved ones as well as to recreate a community of like-minded people in a foreign land. It helped ease the struggle with displacement in a strange environment, the nostalgia of home and the quest for new identity. In each nation the Malayali diaspora consciousness is maintained with the proliferation of religious groups, Kerala associations and other cultural programs. Through this collective identity they express solidarity with each other, loyalty to the host land and carve out a place in adopted land of settlement. However, the global Malayali diaspora is far from being homogenous.

Migration out of Kerala and its global spread will continue to rise. In spite of the fact that, in the beginning of twenty-first century, migration is more regulated than ever before, migration scholars are buoyant about the prospect of future of global migration.[2] In a world more interconnected than ever before, people with the motivation and the means to migrate will only escalate. Migrants are catalytic for chain reaction for more migration. Both the global economy and the Kerala economy will significantly influence the rate of migration. The trend may shift toward a new set of skills and professions. It may flow towards newer destinations. It might come from different pockets of Kerala than the ones who have dominated Kerala migration in the past. Other states in India may accelerate faster in migratory trends. Though the rapid surge in large scale migration has caused disruption of families and a brain-drain in Kerala, it is not going to dissuade Malayali from seeking their fortunes elsewhere. Whatever be the case, the Malayali diaspora will remain a significant share of global Indian diaspora.

This book project is an attempt to capture the breadth and intricacies of the global Malayali diaspora in the early twenty-first century. In the preceding chapters, Sam George and I presented voices of Malayali diaspora from around the world, chosen carefully to bring out their distinct perspectives. The audacious Keralite emigrants who left the comforts of their parental homes and have settled in diverse ecologies, resulting in adaptation, innovation and learning. Malayalis have acquired new linguistic skills while their own children and grandchildren lose touch with their ancestral land and language. The migrant Malayalis were forced to gain new knowledge and developed cross-cultural competencies. Through these voices one can observe the uncanny ability of Malayalis to adapt and survive; their devotion to their chosen professions; their appetite for achievements and advancement; their spirit of adventure, eye for opportunities, perseverance through challenges and yet never losing touch with the land of their forefathers. We see the critical nature of socio cultural and historical context plays in the emigration from Kerala and global economic and political forces that shaped where they settled. It is important to give heed to divergent voices from different parts of the world to understand the complexities of global diaspora. This book contributors include all major regions of the world; both men and women scholars; different professional backgrounds; those who were born in Kerala, elsewhere in India and in foreign lands.

Education, work and marriage remain the major causes of global dispersion of Malayalis. Faith and family life have played crucial role in the life in overseas destinations. Though they lose linguistic competencies in a generation or two, yet they maintain their Kerala identity in foreign lands. The contemporary media and technology marshals the global network to stereotypical homogenous Malayali culture. This is far from being authentic and does not expose or engage adequately with life and issues in the diaspora. The lifestyle changes and food habits of diasporic Malayalis have created new health challenges and senior years are of grave concern that most established diasporic institutions tend to overlook.

The completion of the *Malayali Diaspora* publishing project has been an amazing feat in itself. We had only eight months to complete the volume because we wanted published copies available for the book launch during the *Pravasi Bharatiya Divas* at Cochin in January 2013. Identifying, inviting and confirming a global slate of Malayali diaspora contributors who could share the diverse facets of Malayali migratory journeys was our initial challenge. We are indebted to this team of scholars and practitioners who were willing to work within our stiff submission timelines and provide repeated revisions of their drafts. We must confess that the gathering and editing of information from around the world amidst our regular work, travel and family life has been extremely challenging. We are also grateful to the publisher and cover designer who expedited the release of the book. Without the collaborative spirit of my diligent Co-Editor, Sam George and the blessing of the internet this project would have been impossible!

This volume is no way exhaustive or prescriptive. Limitations of this work are obvious and many. First of all it is written in English (not Malayalam) to serve a global audience. Secondly, a few chapters did not make the deadline of the publisher. Some could not undertake such an assignment amidst their busy schedules; others who were assigned to write a chapter had unforeseen health challenges. Thirdly, perspectives of other fields like arts, economics, political science etc. are lacking. We wish we had more Hindu and Muslim scholars writing from their perspectives. The diasporic stories of Malayalis in the United Arab Emirates, Saudi Arabia, Britain and Latin America are absent. We wish we could have included the many more voices out there of diasporic Malayalis. Our hope and prayer is that many other Malayalis, Indians and others will undertake to record living histories and reflections of migrant journeys from around the world. This needs to be done not only for the sake of their descendants but to honor those who went before us and in the process make our lives meaningful in the present.

We hope this book has invoked your curiosity, stimulated your minds and stirred your hearts to explore further the unique nature of diasporic communities and their strategic impact on adopted host nations as well as their ancestral homeland. If you are of Malayali heritage, we hope you will dig deeper to uncover your own roots and explore the wider dispersion of people in your own extended family network. We believe your exploration will bridge chasms of generations, cultures, languages and disconnectedness arising out of global scattering and develop a richer appreciation of the great heritage of the past, a fuller understanding of the realities of the present and be propelled with hope of a brighter future. Remember, 'the sun never sets on the Malayali diaspora!'

Notes

1. Roland Robertson, *Globalization, 1992, 2.*
2. See Ian Goldin *et al.*, *Exceptional People,* 2011 and Castles and Miller, *Age of Migration,* 2009.

References

Castles, Stephen and Mark Miller (2009), *The Age of Migration: International Population Movements in the Modern World.* 4th Edition. (New York: Palgrave Macmillan).

Goldin, Ian, Geffory Carmeroon and Meera Balarajan (2011), *Exceptional People: How Migration shaped our World and will define our Future,* (Princeton, NJ: Princeton University Press).

Robertson, Roland (1992), *Globalization : Social Theory and Global Culture.* (London: Sage Publications).

Author Profiles

George Oommen, *Ph.D.* is an ordained presbyter of the Madhya Kerala Diocese of the Church of South India. He received his doctorate at the University of Sydney, Australia.He was a Professor and Chairperson of the Department of History of Christianity at the United Theological College, Bangalore, where he taught the history of Indian, Asian and World Christianity. His publications include *It Began In Copenhagen: Junctions in 300 Years of Indian-Danish Relations in Christian Mission* (2005). *Local Dalit Christian History* (2002); *Paths of Dalit Liberation in Kerala: Pulayas' Interaction with Christianity and Communism* (forthcoming) and several articles in journals. He currently lives with his wife in Phoenix, AZ (USA).

Dr. O.M. Panicker was born in Singapore, lived in Malaysia and studied in India before moving to Kenya to begin his teaching career in 1981. Eleven years later with his wife Mercy, he pioneered a non-governmental organization engaging in relief, development and charitable work among refugees and internally displaced people in East Africa. Currently they live in Lancaster, Pennsylvania (USA) and are proud parents of two adult children. He spends several months each year in Kenya and in India.

Stanley John is a member of the Malayali diaspora, who was born and raised in Kuwait. He is currently enrolled in a Ph.D. program in the United States and specifically researching on Kerala diaspora in the Middle East. Stanley is an emerging scholar and teaches with passion and creativity. He is an adjunct faculty member at the Institute for Diaspora Studies in Manila, Philippines and Eurasian Diaspora Study Center in Kyiv, Ukraine.

Roshan Varughese, *M.Com. M.S., CPA.* was born in Kerala and grew up in Zambia, United Arab Emirates and India. He earned his Masters in Commerce from Mahatma Gandhi University and worked as an accountant in a multinational chemical company based in Dubai. He moved to Australia in 2007 to pursue his Masters in Accounting at the University of Melbourne. Since then he has completed his CPA. Roshan is an accountant at Grace Villa Aged Care in Melbourne where he lives with his wife and their son.

Lina Samuel, *Ph.D.* is a lecturer in the Sociology Department at the University of Toronto, Canada. She is of Malayali heritage and grew up in Canada. Her current research examines intergenerational cultural retention and the construction of diasporic identities among South Asians in Canada. She teaches in the areas of Work and Occupations, Family, Immigration, Transnationalism, Diaspora and Ethnicity. She is the author of the forthcoming book *South Asian Women in the Diaspora: Reflections on Arranged Marriage and Dowry Among the Syrian Orthodox Community in Canada.*

Mathew T. Thomas, *M.D.* is a physician who immigrated to the USA in 1983. He works for the US Food and Drug Administration. Since coming to the USA, he has been active within his church, ecumenical circles and in the Malayali community in Philadelphia and in the Greater Washington D.C. areas. Dr. Thomas has had the distinct honor of serving as the President of the Kerala Cultural Society of Metropolitan Washington (KCSMW) and as the Vice-President of the Kerala Association of Greater Washington. He continues to be an active member of both these Malayali Associations and currently serves as a Council Member of the Mar Thoma Church Diocese of North America and Europe.

Ipe Mavunkal, *Ph.D.* completed his BSc in Kerala, his MSc at Aligarh Muslim University and received his PhD from Indian Institute of Technology, Mumbai. He did postdoctoral research in various universities including the University of California at Los Angeles (USA), National Tsin Hua University (Taiwan) and the University of Cape Town (South Africa). He worked as senior lecturer at the University of Botswana and was a research scientist at the University of Notre Dame (USA). He is currently employed at a pharmaceutical research organization in Edmonton, Canada.

Prof. Prabhu Guptara's mother hails from Kerala and he grew up in New Delhi. He has lived in UK and Switzerland during most of his professional life. He retired recently as the head of a division of the Swiss bank UBS. He is a sought-after speaker and consultant to wide range of issues. Prabhu is a Distinguished Professor of Global Business, Management and Public Policy, William Carey University, India; Member of the Board, Institute of

Management, University of St Galen, Switzerland; Member of the Board, King's Kurry AG, Switzerland; Publisher, *The International Indian* magazine, Dubai, UAE; Honorary Chairman, Career Innovation, Oxford, U.K.; Advisor to *Forward Press* magazine, New Delhi, India, and to New Global Markets, U.K. He is working on his next book, *"Indian Philanthropy: A Portrait from Earliest Times to the Present"*.

Roy P. Thomas, *M.D.* has practiced General Medicine in Chicago for over three decades. He graduated from Kottayam Medical College as its first batch in 1961 and migrated to the US in 1972. He is one of the founders and past president of the Association of Kerala Medical Graduates (AKMG) in North America. Roy is also one of the founders of Federation of Kerala Associations in America (FOKANA), the Indo- American Democratic Organization (IADO), and Federation India Association in America (FIA). His weekly Malayalam medical program on health issues can be seen on Kairali TV and Youtube.

T. M. Thomas, *Ed.D.* is a Professor Emeritus at University of Bridgeport, Connecticut (USA). He was born, brought up and educated in his native state of Kerala. He came to the US for his doctoral research and then joined the Faculty of Education and taught undergraduate and graduate students. He and his wife, Annamma now live in New York and they have two adult children and four grandchildren. His publications include eight academic books, eighteen Church related books and dozens of articles in books and journals.

Sara Gabriel, *RN, MSN, MBA.* was born and brought up in Kerala and did her B.Sc. Nursing from Christian Medical College, Vellore, India. After graduation and marriage, she migrated to the United States on a spousal immigrant visa. She started her career as a staff nurse in 1974 and steadily advanced to higher leadership positions including Director of Nursing and retired from a County Hospital as a Senior Hospital Administrator. She was the Founder President of National Association of Indian Nurses in America (NAINA). Currently she lives with her family in the suburbs of Chicago and serves as an educator and private consultant.

Prema Kurien, *Ph.D.* is Professor of Sociology and Director of Asian/ Asian American Program at Syracuse University (USA). She is the author of many publications including *Kaleidoscopic Ethnicity: International Migration and the Reconstruction of Community Identities in India* (2002) and *A Place at the Table: Multiculturalism and the Development of an American Hinduism* (2007), which received Honorable Mention in 2009 from the Sociology of Religion section of the American Sociological Association. She serves on the editorial boards of *Journal for the Scientific Study of Religion* and other publications.

Thomas Kulanjiyil, *Psy.D., Ph.D.* grew up in Chennai, lived and worked in Calcutta before coming to the US for his doctoral studies. Presently he teaches Psychology and Philosophy at the College of Dupage and Wheaton College in the western suburbs of Chicago. He is a seasoned family counselor, educator and researcher in culturally appropriate care to the Indian American community. He has authored multiple articles and recently co-edited *Caring for the South Asian Soul*. He has composed many devotional songs in Malayalam. He and his wife Omana are parents of two adult children.

Enas A. Enas, *MD, FACC* is the Founder President and CEO of CADI Research Foundation, a nonprofit organization dedicated to reducing the ravages of heart disease among Indians worldwide. His pioneering research has produced more than sixty scientific publications in American, British, and Indian medical journals. He is the author of the widely-acclaimed book *How to Beat the Heart Disease Epidemic Among South Asians: A Prevention and Management Guide for Asian Indians and their Doctors*. He is a former President of the Association of Kerala Medical Graduate (AKMG) and a former Chairman of the Board of the American Association of Physicians of Indian Origin (AAPI).

P.T. Thomas, *M.A. M.Div., LMSW* is from Kerala and migrated to the United States in 1983 from New Delhi. He has several degrees including Bachelor of Arts (Kerala University), Master of Arts (Meerut University), Master of Divinity (Drew University) and Master of Social Work (Fordham University). He is a Licensed Master Social Worker in the State of New York and works for Rockland County. He has served with numerous civic, community and religious organizations. He lives with his family in New York.

Jesudas Athyal, *Ph.D.* is a visiting researcher at Boston University, Boston (USA). Earlier he served as Associate Professor of Social Analysis at the Gurukul Lutheran Theological College in Chennai, India. He was the Associate Editor of the two-volume *Oxford Encyclopedia of South Asian Christianity* (2011) and is now the Editor of the forthcoming *Religion in Southeast Asia: An Encyclopedia* (ABC-CLIO Publication, 2014). He is also the Editor of an Indian American magazine, *The Meeting Point*. He lives with his wife and son near Boston.

Sam George is of Malayali parentage, born in the Andaman Islands and now lives with his wife and two sons in the suburbs of Chicago (USA). He holds an undergraduate degree in Engineering, two masters degrees in Business Management and Theology, and recently completed his PhD research on Indian diaspora. He worked in software industry and consulting, and now serves as the Executive Director of Parivar International. He is a speaker and trainer; author of *Understanding the Coconut Generation;* He and his wife Mary are authors of *Before the Wedding Bells*.

Dr. T.V. Thomas, was born in Malacca, Malaysia of Malayali parents and now lives with his wife, Mary and three adult children in Regina, Canada. He studied in Malaysia, India, Canada and United States. He holds a doctorate and for over three decades has enjoyed transcontinental speaking, teaching and networking. He serves on numerous national and international boards including being Chair of Ethnic America Network (EAN) and Co-Chair of International Network of South Asian Diaspora Leaders (INSADL). He has authored numerous publications and most recently co-edited *Caring for the South Asian Soul.*